Paul Golden

LITIGATING ADVERSE POSSESSION CASES

PIRATES v. ZOMBIES

AMERICAN BAR ASSOCIATION
Real Property, Trust and Estate Law Section

Cover design by Andrew Alcala

Printed in the United States of America.

28 27 26   5 4 3 2

ISBN 978-1-63905-438-1

Once again, to my beautiful, perfect wife Keiko who inspired me to keep writing; our sons Benkei and Kenji; my parents Dick and Beth; and my "new" parents Kazue, Toyoo, Teri, and the late Harry.

義理の息子が不法占有に関する本を書いてくれるのが夢だと言った、私の義理の両親にこの本を贈ります。

Contents

Acknowledgments

I would like to thank everyone at my law office, Coffey Modica, LLP, including Joseph D'Avanzo, Sara Tomanio, Mike Mezzacappa, Mike Coffey, and Rob Modica. I would also like to thank my sister Tammy (MST3K) Golden and my friend Justin Kidd.

About the Author

Paul Golden is a partner at Coffey Modica LLP, in New York, and concentrates on appellate practice. Since entering law school, Mr. Golden's goal was to become New York's premier appellate attorney. His previous book, *Litigating Constructive Trusts,* was published by the ABA in 2022, and his other legal writings have been published numerous times, including his articles on appellate law. His articles have been cited by a federal case, legal articles, and *McKinney's Consolidated Laws of New York Annotated.* He has been cited for comments on current legal issues by *Newsweek, USA Today,* the *New York Law Journal,* and other publications. He has also given two lectures on constructive trusts and one lecture on depositions, for attorneys' continuing legal education requirements. He has also lectured in two Japanese law schools.

Mr. Golden received his law degree from the University of Illinois Law School and his undergraduate degree from New York University. At the University of Illinois, he received awards and honors, including being first in his class in tort law.

He has successfully argued two cases before the Court of Appeals, New York's high court. In one case, the court agreed with Mr. Golden's argument, and curtailed the powers of one of New York City's administrative agencies. In the other, he convinced the court to change New York law on a crucial issue of insurance coverage period. Since then, that case has been cited more than 1,500 times by courts, secondary sources, expert opinion reports, and other appellate briefs. It was also cited by Mealey's Litigation Reports as one of the nation's ten most significant insurance coverage decisions of the year. He has argued numerous cases before New York's other appellate courts as well. In one of those successful cases, the appellate court affirmed an award declaring that his clients had acquired eight properties by adverse possession. Another one of his successful appellate cases from 2013 was the subject of a front page article in New York's legal newspaper.

Mr. Golden also has litigated a variety of commercial and real estate cases at the trial court level. Some of Mr. Golden's past accomplishments include successfully moving to dismiss a $10 million cause of action filed by a major telecommunications provider, and successfully moving to dismiss a $1 million sister state judgment on constitutional grounds. He has won a trial and appeal in which the court awarded his client with title to a residential building, even though his client had no recorded deed for the premises. He has also successfully moved to dismiss personal injury cases, one involving a party's death through his clients' alleged negligence. Mr. Golden's hobbies include card tricks, chess, studying Japanese, riding bicycles, and writing books about obscure legal topics.

Mr. Golden can be reached by email at pgolden@coffeemodica.com or prgolden@aol.com.

Introduction

When is a door not a door? When it is ajar. When is theft of land not theft of land? When it is adversely possessed.

In the middle of writing this book, a lawsuit was filed concerning adverse possession in Manhattan, of all places—the most densely populated space in the United States. One would have thought all space on the island would be fully accounted for, but that is apparently not true. There is now a battle between two luxury high-rises on Fifth Avenue, at Seventy-ninth Street, across from Central Park.[1] They are fighting over a 350-square-foot ditch, which is known as "the Pit." One co-op claims to have been using it for 30 years for storage, even if it apparently does not have written title for such space. The attorney for the claimants, Adam Leitman Bailey, was reported as being confident in success. He also stated, "This is euphoria for a real-estate attorney." One of his adversaries is Eliot Spitzer, the former governor of New York, who seeks to use the Pit when replacing one building with a new potential construction. Spitzer reportedly called the lawsuit "an embarrassment." As he sees it, it is outrageous that he let his neighbor store bricks in the Pit, as an accommodation, and now the property could be lost. As he sees it, it is the ultimate case of no good deed goes unpunished.

If that were not enough about adverse possession in Manhattan, a few months later the Appellate Division, First Department upheld a decision that, at least temporarily, prevented a developer from building the first luxury hotel in the midtown Diamond District. The developer's adversary, an adjoining property owner, claimed that cinderblock and an extension wall gave it potential adverse possession of a strip of land. And without the right to that strip, the developer could not do the work as planned.[2] The appellate court held that the developer had not yet proved that the adjoining property owner lacked a legitimate adverse possession claim. The Wall Street Journal pointed out emotionally that

1 Micah Hauser, *The Pits*, New Yorker, Feb. 27, 2023.
2 N47 Assoc. LLC v. Jemsco Realty LLC, 218 A.D.3d 413 (N.Y. App. Div. 2023).

now the "site was quiet, although work had begun on the foundation of the building. A 'Work in Progress' sign affixed to the site showed a rendering of a thin, gleaming tower."[3]

One famous Talmud story is about a Roman who indicated he would only convert to Judaism if a rabbi would teach him the entire Torah while he, the gentile, stood on one foot. The Jewish religious leader Hillel then told him, "That which is hateful to you, do not do unto your neighbor. That is the whole Torah. The rest is explanation. Now go and learn it."

If one wanted to explain adverse possession while standing on one foot, he could cite case law and say: "The doctrine could be encapsulated in one understandable sentence: possession is adverse when the claimant possesses the property for [the statutory time period] as the true owner would and asking no permission for such use."[4] Another way would be to paraphrase the line "Tragedy plus time equals comedy";[5] one would change it to "Trespassing plus time equals adverse possession."

Now that we have had those brief descriptions, we can collectively put our other foot[6] down. The rest of this book is a beginning to the explanation that can be studied.

Typically, a nonlawyer will have a knee-jerk negative reaction to the idea of adverse possession (once he learns what the term means). Such a person is likely thinking of one end of the scale. He imagines going on vacation for a week and returning to find a *Deliverance* hillbilly in his home with a shotgun who says, "It's mine now." But there's another extreme. Mr. Z purchases property for a million dollars from Mr. X, who explains that he inherited it from his great-great grandmother. Mr. Z clears the land, builds a house there, puts up a picket fence around his lawn, and pays real estate taxes every year. Fifty years later, he has grown old and feeble, and is enjoying his last days on earth before he can transfer the land, which is now worth $10 million, to his own family. But then one fine morning, Mr. Z, without having done anything wrong,[7] is approached by a Brit who looks like the Monopoly man. The visitor says, "Cheerio, old chap. My brother, Mr. X, just died. I looked through his papers, and realized my great-great grandmother's will was not properly notarized, and therefore he did not have the right to sell this land to you. It still belongs to the estate. So how long will it take for

3 Corinne Ramey, *A Mogul's 33-Story Luxury Hotel Faces Battle Over 18 Inches*, WALL ST. J., Aug. 14, 2023.

4 LeBleu v. Aalgaard, 193 Wash. App. 66, 83 (Wash. Ct. App. 2016).

5 See Woody Allen's *Crimes and Misdemeanors*.

6 Feet?

7 Easter egg for Kafka fans.

you to pack your bags?" Both cases concern potential adverse possession claims, but one will work, and one will fail. A good litigator has to make his side sound more like the side deserving sympathy.

A few final notes. Non-attorneys are more familiar with the term "squatters' rights" than with the term "adverse possession." So, if one needs to explain the concept quickly to a client, that may be the best way of going about it. I do not normally use that term, because it reminds me of someone in a *Little House on the Prairie* style outhouse.[8] Also I assume readers will understand that not only are there exceptions to rules, but there are also changes to rules all the time. There are also some simplifications in this book here and there. This book is not intended as a final word on anything; at best this is meant to spur thought for a litigator handling an adverse possession case. Also, this book addresses real property, and not personal property.[9]

8 "Words that are horrible to one writer may not be horrible to another, but if you are a writer for whom no words are horrible, you would do well to take up some other activity."—The Economist Style Guide.

9 There is some law that might support an adverse possession case based on personal property, but this book does not delve into such issues.

Part 1

Basics and Preliminaries

Chapter 1
Rationale and History of Adverse Possession

Just as a soldier does not need to know the physics of firearm propellants, or why squeezing a trigger will lead to the release of a bullet from a gun, an attorney taking on an adverse possession case may not need to understand the history of adverse possession, or even understand its rationale. All one needs to do, theoretically, is understand one's state law, and understand the facts. That can be difficult enough.

But even if the history or rationale of the law does not wind up explicitly in one's arguments, it may be helpful to have these issues in the back of one's mind. Understanding the roots may be useful to explain why the alleged adverse possessor should win or lose. One always needs to find a way to make it appear that history and logic are on the side of one's client, if that is at all possible. With this in mind, one can paint one's client in the most sympathetic way, regardless of the technicalities of the state's law.

HISTORY

It is not just the United States—the entire world has a long history of handling adverse possession claims. As one Utah court put it, "From Attila, the Hun, down through the colonial expansions of the Seventeenth and Eighteenth centuries to the present, the right of one with sufficient nerve and courage to extend his dominions by the simple process of taking possession has been recognized, subject only to growing and more definite and refined methods and requirements of manifesting the possession and the intention to take and hold."[1]

Probably every society past the hunting/gathering stage would agree that if a person holds onto property long enough, it should be presumed that it belongs to that person. It's such a natural human attitude that laws covering the topic have probably developed independently in many societies, similarly to the idea behind convergent evolution, the

1 Hammond v. Johnson, 94 Utah 20, 32 (1937).

independent evolution of similar features in various species at different periods of time.

As one court indicated, the law's roots go at least as far back as the Code of Hammurabi.[2] This is a Babylonian legal text that seems to have been composed in 1755–1750 BC, and is one of the oldest well-preserved legal texts. It was proclaimed by the Babylonian king Hammurabi. The Code was carved onto a black stone pillar, which was rediscovered in 1901. Law 30 states: "If a chieftain or a man leave his house, garden, and field and hires it out, and some one [sic] else takes possession of his house, garden, or field and uses it for three years: if the first owner return and claims his house, garden, and field, it shall not be given to him, but he who has taken possession of it and used it shall continue to use it."[3] Even that portion of the Code seems to have exceptions, just like in modern times. For example, a soldier who had been captured in battle and then returned years later apparently would not lose his land.

In understanding our country's legal history on this issue, we first have to turn to England. Our English predecessors first used an amalgamation of Roman and Germanic doctrine in common law. They later settled upon statutes of limitation to bring about adverse possession.[4] Those statutes prevented a rightful owner's ability from regaining possession after a certain number of years had elapsed. This effectively gave title to the adverse possessor.[5] One example was a 1623 statute of King James I, which restricted the title owner's right of entry to recover possession of land to a period of 20 years.[6] In other words, he would have to seek that potential right within 20 years of the date someone else had taken the land.

In the United States, that 1623 statute was considered part of our common law.[7] Many states used that 20-year time period as the limitation period. As time elapsed, each state had not just common law, but some statutory form of adverse possession, typically requiring proof that "possession was actual, hostile, open and notorious, exclusive, and continuous for the period of the statute of limitations. Color of title

2 Fraley v. Minger, 829 N.E.2d 476, 483–84 (Ind. 2005).

3 As translated by L.W. King.

4 Cahill v. Morrow, 11 A.3d 82, 86 (R.I. 2011), citing Axel Teisen, *Contributions of the Comparative Law Bureau*, 3 A.B.A. J. 97, 126, 127, 134 (1917).

5 *Id.*, citing RESTATEMENT (THIRD) PROPERTY: SERVITUDES § 2.17 cmt. b at 263–64 (2000).

6 *Id.*, citing 10 THOMPSON ON REAL PROPERTY § 87.01, at 74–75 (2d Thomas ed. 1998) (citing An Act for Limitation of Actions, and Avoiding of Suit in Law, 1623, 21 Jas. I. c. 16).

7 *Id.*, citing 10 THOMPSON ON REAL PROPERTY § 87.01, at 75.

and payment of taxes can also be elements in some cases."[8] Some laws change very little; in Connecticut, its statute, which establishes 15 years of repose on an action to oust an adverse possessor, "appears to have remained largely unchanged since its original enactment in 1684. The 1684 statute, in turn, was derived from a 1624 English statute."[9]

RATIONALE

Money for nothing and the chicks for free.

—Dire Straits

For someone who believes that, in the right case, a person should be able to make a viable adverse claim, explaining why can become frustrating. Sometimes, for even the most basic things about human behavior, it can be difficult to explain why people have the right to do what they do. In this context, adverse possession has its own particular challenges. This is especially true because there are many ways of looking at what it is, and what it does for society—both the good and the bad. Explaining the rationale behind it is somewhat like the old story of the blind men describing the elephant they have encountered.

Some people might simply believe the concept of adverse possession is natural and expected on a gut level. Justice Oliver Wendell Holmes, Jr. indicated that the rationale of adverse possession is based on the idea that "[a] thing which you have enjoyed and used as your own for a long time, whether property or an opinion, takes root in your being and cannot be torn away without your resenting the act and trying to defend yourself, however you came by it."[10]

Judge Richard Posner, the most cited legal scholar on record, who focuses on economic theories and how they tie into the law, further explained Justice Holmes's ideas on the topic. Judge Posner indicated that Holmes's theory was that if a person grew to believe he actually owned the property, but then lost it, the effect would be "wrenching." But over the same period of time, the title owner whose property was being occupied by an outsider would start to believe he no longer owned it. So the potential restoration of the property back to the title owner "would cause only moderate pleasure." If an adverse possession claim failed, "[t]he adverse possessor would experience the deprivation

8 *Id.* at 87, citing Jeffrey Evans Stake, *The Uneasy Case for Adverse Possession*, 89 Geo. L.J. 2419, 2423 (2001); William G. Ackerman & Shane T. Johnson, Comment, *Outlaws of the Past: A Western Perspective on Prescription and Adverse Possession*, 31 Land Water L. Rev. 79, 84 n.42, 111 (1996) (collecting adverse possession statutes for the 50 states).

9 O'Connor v. Larocque, 302 Conn. 562, 579 (2011).

10 Oliver Wendell Holmes Jr., *The Path of the Law*, 10 Harv. L. Rev. 457, 477 (1897).

of the property as a diminution in his wealth; the original owner would experience the restoration of property as an increase in *his* wealth." To put it another way, the negative effect of a "loss" of property in this context is greater against an adverse possession claimant, than the positive effect of a "restoration" of property to the title owner. Therefore, from an economic theory, assuming those two parties had the same wealth, "their combined utility will be greater if the adverse possessor is allowed to keep his property."[11] (In this context, "utility" means the total sum of satisfaction a consumer receives from using a piece of property.) This combined utility approach is part of the reason, according to Judge Posner, that society should keep adverse possession as a part of our law.

A similar, but more cynical, way of describing why adverse possession laws exist, is that we live in a J.G. Ballard world—our civilization is nothing more than a veneer. The natural tendency of human beings, like many animals, is to grab apparently discarded things and claim them as their own. If someone has held onto property long enough, there's an instinct to believe it "belongs" to him, and no flimsy piece of paper from decades in the past is going to convince him otherwise. The adverse possession law just codifies that which is already part of human nature. The more legislators draft laws that are counter to human nature, the more chance of societal disquiet, if not outright flouting of laws. To provide a further explanation of the matter might be just a rationalization.[12]

But there are those who try to provide logical explanations for why the laws exist. One commentator indicated that there are "four traditional justifications or clusters of justifications which support transferring the entitlement to the [adverse possessor] after the statute of limitations runs: the problem of lost evidence, the desirability of quieting titles, the interest in discouraging sleeping owners, and the reliance interests of [adverse possessors] and interested third persons."[13]

Other policy reasons used to justify adverse possession include "(1) the stabilization of uncertain boundaries through the passage of time; (2) a respect for the apparent ownership of the adverse possessor

11 Richard Posner, Economic Analysis of Law 79 (6th ed. 2003).

12 Michael: "I don't know anyone who could get through the day without two or three juicy rationalizations. They're more important than sex."
Sam Weber: "Ah, come on. Nothing's more important than sex."
Michael: "Oh yeah? Ever gone a week without a rationalization?"
The Big Chill.

13 Cahill v. Morrow, 11 A.3d 82, 87 (R.I. 2011), citing Thomas W. Merrill, *Property Rules, Liability Rules, and Adverse Possession*, 79 Nw. U. L. Rev. 1122, 1133 (1984); Finley v. Yuba Cnty. Water Dist., 99 Cal. App. 3d 691, 160 Cal. Rptr. 423, 427 (1979) (summarizing the rationales supporting adverse possession).

who transfers his interest; and (3) assurance of the long-term productivity of the land."[14]

One commentator noted that the law is based on the idea that "all things should be used according to their nature and purpose" and when an individual uses and preserves property "for a certain length of time, [he] has done a work beneficial to the community."[15] That person's "reward is the conferring upon him of the title to the thing used."[16] If we are thinking in terms of rewards versus punishments, and good versus evil, then one can consider the abandoning owner as the "quintessential villain in the adverse possession drama."[17] The villainous action he is guilty of is to leave his land untouched, without using it to serve man.[18]

The adverse possession doctrine may be a part of our history, and may even be in our DNA, but that does not mean courts are in love with it. One court indicated that it is based on an "arcane rationale."[19] Some courts have questioned "whether the concept of adverse possession is as viable as it once was, or whether the concept always squares with modern ideals in a sophisticated, congested, peaceful society."[20] Some commentators have also criticized the effect of adverse possession laws because of the "infringement of a landowner's rights, a decrease in value of the servient estate, and the encouraged exploitation and development of land. In addition, they represent the generation of animosity between neighbors, a source of damages to land or loss of land ownership, and the creation of uncertainty for the landowner."[21]

An extreme view would indicate that adverse possession "is nothing more than a person taking someone else's private property for his own private use. It is hard to imagine a notion more in contravention of the ideals set forth in the U.S. Constitution protecting life, liberty and *property*."[22] Another judge complained that "[t]he law of adverse possession can be arcane, at times inconsistent, and many times has to be extracted from old cases that do not fully explain their reasoning."[23]

---

14 Cumulus Broad., Inc. v. Shim, 226 S.W.3d 366, 376 (Tenn. 2007).

15 11 A.3d at 87, citing Axel Teisen, *Contributions of the Comparative Law Bureau*, 3 A.B.A. J. 97, 127 (1917).

16 *Id.*

17 Stump v. Whibco, 314 N.J. Super. 560, 576 (App. Div. 1998), citing John G. Sprankling, *An Environmental Critique of Adverse Possession*, 79 Cornell L. Rev. 816, 872 (1994).

18 It's a cookbook.

19 11 A.3d at 88.

20 Finley v. Yuba Cnty. Water Dist., 99 Cal. App. 691, 697 (Ct. App. 1979).

21 11 A.3d at 86–88, citing Ackerman & Johnson, *supra* note 8, at 92.

22 *Id.*, citing Ackerman & Johnson, *supra* note 8, at 94–95 (brackets and internal quotation marks omitted).

23 Gan v. Van Buren St. Methodist Church, 224 A.3d 1205, 1214 (D.C. 2020) (dissenting opinion).

Certain modern commentators also criticize the concept of adverse possession: "A good work ethic forms the American foundation and a person gaining title via adverse possession or the use of another's land without paying for it rewards the wrongdoer and is contrary to the American way of life."[24] One court noted that "[a]dverse possession has been looked upon as being a form of legalized theft."[25]

Other commentators indicate that adverse possession made sense in the past, but not in the present. In the past, one effect of adverse possession was to make sure land was used as much as possible. Presumably this was in part because so much land was used for farming. That is not necessarily a proper goal, especially in the context of the fear of global warming and related issues. In modern times, the brakes are sometimes put on land development. In some cases, the government even pays farmers not to use their land to plant crops.[26]

Sometimes it is critical to understand the history and rationale of adverse possession, because it may influence what issues a court will consider. For example, in Washington, a court held that:

> The doctrine of adverse possession was formulated at law for the purpose of, among others, assuring maximum utilization of land, encouraging the rejection of stale claims and, most importantly, quieting titles. Because the doctrine was formulated at law and not at equity, it was originally intended to protect both those who knowingly appropriated the land of others and those who honestly entered and held possession in full belief that the land was their own. Thus, when the original purpose of the adverse possession doctrine is considered, it becomes apparent that the claimant's motive in possessing the land is irrelevant and no inquiry should be made into his guilt or innocence.[27]

Perhaps another way of looking at adverse possession is in terms of capitalism versus communism. Is taking property that no one is using and no one is claiming a form of pulling oneself up by the bootstraps, and therefore a form of capitalism? Or is it a form of communism, where society approves of sharing assets, and of taking assets away from the rich who have so much property they do not even notice when it is missing? If one knows the judge's politics, one may decide how to approach the topic; a potential argument from the left is just as possible as an argument from the right.

---

24 Ackerman & Johnson, *supra* note 8, at 94 (footnotes omitted).

25 *In re* Haynes, 283 B.R. 147, 151 (Bankr. S.D.N.Y. 2002) (citation omitted).

26 *See* Jeffrey Evans Stake, *The Uneasy Case for Adverse Possession*, 89 Geo. L.J. 2419, 2435 (2001).

27 Chaplin v. Sanders, 100 Wn.2d 853, 859–60 (Wash. 1984) (citations omitted).

Chapter 2
Basic Pleading Issues

> *Learning magic . . . turned out to be about as tedious as it was possible for the study of powerful and mysterious supernatural forces to be. The same way a verb has to agree with its subject, it turned out, even the simplest spell had to be modified and tweaked and inflected to agree with the time of day, the phase of the moon, the intention and purpose and precise circumstances of its casting, and a hundred other factors, all of which were tabulated in volumes of tables and charts and diagrams printed in microscopic jewel type on huge yellowing elephant-folio pages. And half of each page was taken up with footnotes listing the exceptions and irregularities and special cases . . . .*
>
> —*The Magicians*, Lev Grossman

An adverse possession claimant can handle a case proactively or defensively. In fact, some adverse possession claimants do not even realize that they have overstepped the title owners' boundaries, and may not find that out except after being sued for ejectment, at which time they will have to raise counterclaims, or at least an affirmative defense, based on adverse possession.[1] If one's client has a valid defense for a trespass case, based on adverse possession, that defense may be deemed waived if not pleaded.[2] It is another question entirely whether an affirmative defense is enough, or whether a counterclaim is necessary, for a defendant to prove an adverse possession case; at the very least the defense should be raised.[3] If an adverse possession claimant is going to simply raise the defense, without a formal counterclaim, then he should also

1 "Adverse possession may be asserted as an affirmative defense to bar the owner of record title from asserting title by reason of the running of a 21-year statute of limitations." Wagoner v. Obert, 180 Ohio App. 3d 387, 402 (5th Dist. 2008).

2 *See* Falco v. Pollitts, 298 A.D.2d 838, 839 (N.Y. App. Div. 2002).

3 *See* Lambert v. WAHA, 375 P.3d 202, 214 n.12 (Haw. 2016); Brown v. Akin, 790 So. 2d 893, 895 (Miss. Ct. App. 2001).

include a general prayer for relief, which may trigger the court into deciding which of the parties has a superior title.[4]

On the non-defensive side, no judicial action is necessary to establish title for an adverse possession claimant, or at least that is how certain courts see it.[5] So long as a party has met the elements for the necessary time period, title automatically vests to an adverse possessor.[6] Taking no action might work, theoretically, if one intends to keep the property in the family for generations. It also might make sense if an adverse possessor is afraid to wake the sleeping giant.

But if an adverse possession claimant does not have an explicit court order indicating what land the claimant owns, title to some or all of the property in question would likely be unmarketable. "A title acquired by adverse possession is not a marketable title until the title is established by judicial proceedings against the record owner."[7] No one would be likely to pay for the full value of property if there is no formal court order, in recordable form, indicating what the adverse possession claimant owns. But of course, filing a formal complaint, from the point of view of a claimant, has its own risks. For some people, it may be better to leave well enough alone, remain on the property for as long as possible, and during that time period take whatever steps are necessary to even further solidify an adverse possession claim.

If one's client wants to bite the bullet, and seeks to formalize his adverse possession claim, then obviously pleadings will be needed. An attorney drafting pleadings for an adverse possession case will need to review the state law concerning what requirements are necessary to quiet title; in New York, as one example, Real Property Actions and Proceedings Law (RPAPL) 1515 indicates what allegations should be included in the complaint, including such issues as describing the property at issue. One needs to pay attention to the language, even though some language is no longer considered politically correct. RPAPL 1515(1)(c) requires the plaintiff to plead "[w]hether any defendant is known or unknown, and whether any defendant is or might be an infant, mentally retarded, mentally ill or an alcohol abuser."

Rhode Island also requires certain parties to be given notice in a case concerning adverse possession and quieting title. In that state, chapter 16 of title 34 sets forth a mechanism whereby "[a]ny person or persons claiming title to real estate" may bring an action to quiet title. One

4 Ogden v. Beverly, No. 2011-CA-001227-MR, at *8–9 (Ky. Ct. App. Oct. 4, 2013).

5 *See* Graybill v. Lampman, 332 P.3d 511, 522 & n.15 (Wyo. 2014); Q-2 L.L.C. v. Hughes, 368 P.3d 86, 91–92 (Utah 2016).

6 Ofuasia v. Smurr, 198 Wash. App. 133, 148 (Wash. Ct. App. 2017).

7 Howard v. Schaniel, 113 Cal. App. 3d 256, 264 (Cal. Ct. App. 1980).

Rhode Island court held that an adverse possession claimant "did not provide notice to and join as necessary parties the record owners of the [lot] pursuant to chapter 16 of title 34. Therefore, it is our judgment that the trial justice properly declined to reach the merits of [the] adverse possession claim."[8]

One must also consider standing issues. One Wisconsin court held that "[i]n an adverse possession, the only parties who generally have standing are the property's titleholder and the party claiming adverse possession."[9]

Another issue for an attorney pursuing an adverse possession claim is whether to file a notice of pendency, also known as a lis pendens. This document would put the world on constructive notice of the lawsuit, and anyone purchasing the property at issue would take it subject to the potential adverse possessor's rights, with little question. However, in certain states, a lis pendens could open up one's client to a slander of title claim. The latter issue is addressed further in Chapter 38.

The attorney representing the adverse possession claimant should also name the elements of such a claim. Reviewing one's state law on the matter is crucial. The elements of a successful adverse possession case depend on both common law and statutes, so one must be careful to review both. Although this book describes many of the general elements, it cannot describe them all.

The elements are relatively (but not completely) standard, but how they are divided is not. Just as the Ten Commandments (which actually have more than ten different imperative statements) are divided differently depending on the religious sect, the states do not universally agree on explaining the elements. Although states generally use the same basic elements of adverse possession, it sometimes seems as if nearly every state has its own method of numbering them or classifying them. To make it even more confusing, some states do indeed have elements that other states do not have. The following are some examples of how states classify or categorize the elements.

Maryland categorizes the elements in only three groups: "[P]ossession must be (1) actual, open and notorious, and exclusive; (2) continuous or uninterrupted for the requisite period; and (3) hostile, under claim of title or ownership."[10] Many states list four elements. For example, in Wisconsin, "The claimant's possession of the land must be (1) exclusive,

---

8 Costa v. Silva, 996 A.2d 607, 611–12 (R.I. 2010).

9 Auer Park Corp. v. Derynda, 230 Wis.2d 317, 321–22 (Wis. Ct. App. 1999); *see also* Donnelly v. Cowsill, 716 A.2d 742, 749 (R.I. 1998).

10 Senez v. Collins, 182 Md. App. 300, 334 (2008).

(2) actual and uninterrupted, (3) open and notorious, and (4) hostile."[11] In Minnesota, to succeed on an adverse possession claim, a plaintiff must prove five elements: "an actual, open, hostile, continuous, and exclusive possession for the requisite period of time."[12] Six elements are required to prove an adverse possession claim in Mississippi: it must be "(1) under claim of ownership; (2) actual or hostile; (3) open, notorious, and visible; (4) continuous and uninterrupted for a period of ten years; (5) exclusive; and (6) peaceful."[13] Rhode Island courts list seven elements: the claimant must show that possession of the property was "actual, open, notorious, hostile, under claim of right, continuous, and exclusive" for the duration of the statutory period.[14] In Maine, a court named eight elements, which seems to be a record: one must prove the "use of the property was: (1) actual, (2) open, (3) visible, (4) notorious, (5) hostile, (6) under a claim of right, (7) continuous, and (8) exclusive for over twenty years."[15]

The state of Washington seems to be one of a handful that recognizes that its traditionally described list of elements—"(1) open and notorious, (2) actual and uninterrupted, (3) exclusive, and (4) hostile"—is artificial. One of its courts noted that it "results from the compulsion of scholars and judges to make lists of elements and to unnecessarily organize the law. Excessive organization leads to disorder, since human activity does not lend itself to compartmentalization." It also noted that "at least two of the elements, (1) open and notorious and (2) actual and uninterrupted, have two components with the result that the doctrine actually comprises six factors. When one adds the requirement of ten years, the doctrine adopts a seventh element."[16] If a claimant can convince the court in a state like this that the breakdown of elements is artificial and stilted, then the claimant may be able to avoid the pressure of being forced to focus in on a particular element, especially the weakest link element.

The chapters in Part 2 address most of the critical elements for a valid adverse possession case, but one must first explain the facts in a manner to meet the elements as described by one's state's law. If one can include in the pleadings at least one separate paragraph for each particular element, that would be best. Moreover, even within the same state, some courts classify the elements differently from others. Therefore, an

---

11 ITT Rayonier, Inc. v. Bell, 112 Wn.2d 754, 757 (1989).

12 Ehle v. Prosser, 293 Minn. 183, 189 (1972).

13 Thornhill v. Caroline Hunt Tr. Est., 594 So. 2d 1150, 1152–53 (Miss. 1992) (citation omitted).

14 Tavares v. Beck, 814 A.2d 346, 350 (R.I. 2003).

15 Harvey v. Furrow, 2014 ME 149, ¶ 11, 107 A.3d 604, 611.

16 LeBleu v. Aalgaard, 193 Wash. App. 66, 78–79 (Wash. Ct. App. 2016).

attorney representing the adverse possession claimant should attempt to find case law making it appear there are only a handful of elements, and the attorney representing the title holder of record will find case law indicating the opposite.

Although a long list of elements may seem impossible to overcome, the Virginia Supreme Court held that "[a] single act or piece of evidence may tend to prove more than one element of adverse possession." In that case, the court noted that, "[f]or example, occupation, use and improvement of the property can prove a claim of right, occupation, use and improvement may also prove actual possession. Similarly, occupation, use, and improvement may also be used to establish exclusivity and visibility."[17]

In Appendix A of this book there are some sample pleadings, all from New York, simply because it was relatively easy for a New Yorker to obtain access to copies of New York adverse possession complaints. Note that the sample pleadings contain some direct quotes and some cutting and pasting. For the parties' privacy, I did not indicate which cases the language was "borrowed" from.

17 Quatannens v. Tyrrell, 268 Va. 360 (2004) (citations, internal quotation marks, and internal ellipses omitted).

Part 2

The Traditional Elements

Chapter 3
Hostility and Claim of Right

It's easier to ask forgiveness than to get permission.[1]

In order to have a successful adverse possession claim, then unless one has "color of title" (discussed further in Chapter 4), one must possess the property in a "hostile" manner, and/or under a "claim of right." (In some states, even if one does have color of title, these elements may still be necessary.) Deciding whether a claimant meets these tests can be extremely difficult, especially due to the lack of universal law on the subject.

The concepts of hostility and a claim of right cut to the bone of the philosophy behind adverse possession cases. Why should someone who believes he has a claim of right be entitled to something that does not really belong to him in the first place? And what kind of claim of right from an interloper would conceivably be sufficient to take away property from its original rightful owner? Nonlawyers always seem dumbfounded by these issues. Even lawyers have trouble with these issues, which may explain why it is such a complicated topic, lending itself to a rather lengthy chapter.

In any event, there is a little good news for a claimant. Some case law from certain states indicates that one or both elements are not even necessary to prove, in certain contexts. For example, a Wisconsin court held that "[i]f the elements of open, notorious, continuous and exclusive possession are satisfied, the law presumes the element of hostile intent."[2] A Pennsylvania court put it this way: "[H]ostility is implied when all other elements of adverse possession are established."[3] Hawaii has an identical rule.[4] An Idaho court held that "[u]ninterrupted and

1 Never teach your children this phrase until they have left home for good.
2 Burkhardt v. Smith, 17 Wis. 2d 132, 139 (1962).
3 Tioga Coal v. Supermarkets Gen. Corp., 519 Pa. 66, 76 (1988) (concurrence).
4 Hartley v. Marsh, 309 P.3d 971 (Haw. Ct. App. 2013) (citation omitted).

continuous use for the prescriptive period raises the presumption that such use was adverse and under claim of right."[5]

However, any implication of hostility may be rebutted, or may not exist at all, in certain contexts. For example, it can be rebutted by proof that the party claiming title by adverse possession "s[ought] permission for use [of the property] from the record owner" or had "a close and cooperative relationship [with] the record owner."[6] Presumably, a claim of right implication may also be rebutted. Issues about presumptions are further described in Chapter 16 and Chapter 33.

Although the issue of burdens is crucial, the remainder of this chapter focuses on what is traditionally required for hostility and a claim of right.

HOSTILITY

One critical issue is not to be confused by the word "hostile." This is just jargon, and its definition in this context has nothing to do with how a normal English speaker uses the word. It is not Will Smith confronting Chris Rock. In fact, one can be perfectly neighborly, but "hostile." "[O]ne may smile, and smile, and be a villain."[7] In an extreme example, if one just makes an innocent mistake about where his boundary line lies, in at least one state he could be acting in a "hostile" manner when he occupies the space beyond the actual line.[8]

The definition of "hostile" is mushy, and not all courts or states define it identically. But it is easier to understand what it means by describing the polar opposite of hostility—permission. "To say that possession is hostile should mean nothing more than that it is without permission of the one legally empowered to give possession, usually the owner."[9] Notably, "permissive use" is different from "acquiescence," at least according to one case. In that case, the court held that "[w]hile permissive use defeats an adverse possession claim, acquiescence is simply another form of adverse possession."[10] In other words, if a neighbor does not "permit" the possessor to occupy space, but "acquiesces" to

5 Hogan v. Blakney, 73 Idaho 274, 281 (1952).

6 Est. of Becker v. Murtagh, 19 N.Y.3d 75, 82 (2012) (internal quotation marks and citation omitted).

7 Shakespeare, *Hamlet*, act I, scene v, line 108.

8 *See, e.g.*, Katona v. Low, 226 A.D.2d 433, 434 (N.Y. App. Div. 1996).

9 Henninger v. Brewster, 357 S.W.3d 920, 926–27 (Ky. Ct. App. 2012), citing 3 Robert W. Keats, et al., Kentucky Practice: Methods of Practice § 5.3 (3d ed. 1989).

10 Fabry v. Jagiello, 386 Wis. 2d 630 (Wis. Ct. App. 2019) (citation and internal quotation marks omitted).

the occupation, then the neighbor may not be able to defeat an adverse possession case. How to tell the difference is a challenge, of course.

There are other ways to define the term "hostility." One state indicates it means "an assertion of ownership adverse to that of the record owner."[11] Another state indicated it is not an attitude; it is action adverse to the interest of the true owner.[12] And another court indicated that hostile possession means that "the possession constitutes an actual invasion of or infringement upon the owner's rights."[13] Yet another definition is "a possession antagonistic to claims of all others, with an intent to occupy as one's own." In that state there is no requirement that the claimant even intended to take away title from the true owner.[14]

In Oregon, adverse possession claimants have two ways of proving hostility. "They may rely on the 'pure mistake' doctrine, which, if established, obviates the need to prove an actual or subjective intent to possess the property as its true owner. If they cannot bring themselves within the pure mistake doctrine, then they must establish hostility by demonstrating a subjective intent to possess the property as its true owner."[15]

One potentially critical issue for hostility is that not only must the occupant be occupying the premises in a hostile manner for the limitation period, but either (1) the initial entry must be hostile, or (2) if it was not initially hostile, there must be a clean demarcation indicating that it become hostile. "When the entry upon land has been by permission or under some right or authority derived from the owner, adverse possession does not commence until such permission or authority has been repudiated and renounced and the possessor thereafter has assumed the attitude of hostility to any right in the real owner."[16]

CLAIM OF RIGHT

One must also understand what a "claim of right" means. One California case indicated that a "[c]laim of right does not require a belief or claim that the use is legally justified. It simply means that the property was used without permission of the owner of the land."[17] A Connecticut

---

11 Galiher v. Johnson, 391 P.3d 1101, 1106 (Wyo. 2017).
12 Double J Farmlands v. Paradise Baptist, 999 So. 2d 826, 829 (Miss. 2009).
13 Gore v. Cambereri, 303 A.D.2d 551 (N.Y. App. Div. 2003).
14 Weaver v. Helm, 941 S.W.2d 801, 804 (Mo. Ct. App. 1997).
15 Mid-Valley Res. v. Engelson, 170 Or. App. 255, 260 (Or. Ct. App. 2000) (citations omitted).
16 Hinkley v. State of New York, 234 N.Y. 309, 316 (1922).
17 Felgenhauer v. Soni, 121 Cal. App. 4th 445, 450 (Cal. Ct. App. 2004) (citation omitted).

court held that "[a] claim of right does not necessarily mean that the adverse possessor claims that it is the proper titleholder, but that it has the intent to disregard the true owner's right to possession."[18] A New York court held that "[p]ossession under a claim of right is incompatible with knowledge or a belief that one does not own the land in question but that ownership rests in another."[19]

The definition of "claim of right" sometimes overlaps with "hostile." In North Carolina, it overlaps so much that the courts consider the two terms as synonymous.[20] This matches Nebraska's point of view: "Claim of ownership or claim of right means 'hostile,' and these terms describe the same element of adverse possession."[21] If that is true, it should mean (in theory) that the phrase "hostile and claim of right" has a redundancy. In Missouri, a court held they "are not two separate elements but are one in the same." The same court held "hostility" only means "that the claimant acts with the intent to occupy the disputed property as his own, exclusive of the rights of all others."[22]

Maine, on the other hand, has ruled that the concepts are separate, even after admitting most states define "hostile" and "claim of right" synonymously. One Maine court described "hostile" as meaning that "the possessor does not have the true owner's permission to be on the land," and that "permission negates the element of hostility." Then the same court held that to take property "under a claim of right" means that the claimant "is in possession as owner, with intent to claim the land as its own, and not in recognition of or subordination to the record title owner."[23]

Traditional Sets of Tests for Hostility or Claim of Right: Good Faith, Subjective, and Objective

One area of law that is somewhat in flux, depending on the situation or the state, is whether "good faith" is necessary for a claim of right. A critical question is whether the adverse possessor's state of mind has any relevance. Did he understand he was using someone else's property, and just threw caution to the wind, and set up shop there for years? Or did he have an honest, but mistaken, belief that he owned it? Must he

18 Eberhardt v. Imperial Constr. Services, LLC, 101 Conn. App. 762, 768 (Conn. App. Ct. 2007) (citation omitted).

19 Falco v. Pollitts, 298 A.D.2d 838, 839 (N.Y. App. Div. 2002).

20 Johnson v. Stanley, 96 N.C. App. 72, 75 (N.C. Ct. App. 1989).

21 Wanha v. Long, 255 Neb. 849, 859 (1998).

22 DeVore v. Vaughn, 504 S.W.3d 176, 183 (Mo. Ct. App. 2016).

23 Striefel v. Charles-Keyt-Leaman P'ship, 733 A.2d 984, 991 (Me. 1999) (citation and brackets omitted).

present evidence of what he was thinking? It reminds one of what Abbie Hoffman said, in a very different context: "I've never been on trial for my thoughts before."

Most states either require an adverse possessor to prove "good faith" as part of a claim of right, or they rule that nothing matters except for the claimant's objective actions. A comparison of how some states handle this issue follows.

In Iowa, a claim of right must be asserted in good faith, and there is no good faith if the claimant knows he had no title or basis for claiming an interest in the property.[24] As the Supreme Court of Iowa put it, to let simply anyone assert a claim of right "would put a premium on dishonesty."[25] The same is true in Georgia: "We hold that the correct rule is that one must enter upon the land claiming in good faith the right to do so. To enter upon the land without any honest claim of right to do so is but a trespass and can never ripen into prescriptive title."[26]

New York has an interesting history on this issue. At one point there were questions about what it would take to have an initial claim of right. Its high court had held in 1915 that it is immaterial "that the [occupant] knew all along that he was in the wrong."[27] Eventually some more modern cases started to ignore that rather ancient ruling, just as young people often ignore old people. At least one case broke the tradition entirely, holding that if a party understood he was not a record title holder from the beginning, he would never become a successful claimant. In *Joseph v. Whitcombe*, a couple had moved into a vacant house, cleared years of overgrowth of weeds from the property and invested considerable money and "sweat equity" into various improvements during 17 years of continuous and undisturbed occupancy of the premises. When the successor in interest to the titled owner sought to eject the defendants, they counterclaimed, seeking a declaration that they had established ownership by adverse possession. The First Department Appellate Division held that the defendants had failed to establish that their entry onto the premises had occurred under a claim of right. The court held that "they entered merely as expectant licensees, whose expectations had no objective basis in fact, and their subsequent possession does not even rise to the level of license. Never having had possessory rights, they may not now enjoy ownership rights."[28]

---

24 Clymer v. Shawd, 741 N.W.2d 823 (Iowa Ct. App. 2007) (citation omitted); Carpenter v. Ruperto, 315 N.W.2d 782, 785–86 (Iowa 1982).

25 315 N.W.2d at 785 (citation omitted).

26 Halpern v. Lacy Inv. Corp., 259 Ga. 264, 265 (1989).

27 Ramapo Mfg. Co. v. Mapes, 216 N.Y. 362, 370–71 (1915).

28 279 A.D.2d 122, 127 (N.Y. App. Div. 2001).

A few years later, in the context of the case *Walling v. Przvbylo*, the Court of Appeals (New York's highest court) disagreed, and decided to go back to the roots. In that 2006 case, defendants argued that they had evidence the adverse possession claimants had known they did not own the land that they had developed and occupied. The court analyzed more than a hundred years of common law, and held that a party seeking adverse possession could assert that he was acting under a "claim of right" regardless of whether he had actual knowledge of the true owner at the time of possession. The court held that "[c]onduct will prevail over knowledge . . . ."[29] It also held that "[t]he issue is 'actual occupation,' not subjective knowledge."[30] Therefore, the court held that evidence that the plaintiffs may have known they were trespassing was irrelevant.

But just as paper beats rock, the legislature beats common law. In 2008, New York's legislature reacted to that decision, and enacted changes to the adverse possession statutes. The Introducer's Memorandum to the proposed changes specified that "[a]dverse possession should be used to settle good faith disputes over who owns land. It should not be a doctrine which can be used offensively to deprive a landowner of their real property." These changes included drafting a statutory definition of "claim of right." Now, pursuant to RPAPL 501(3), "[a] claim of right means a reasonable basis for the belief that the property belongs to the adverse possessor or property owner, as the case may be." A cynic might claim that the people who pressed the legislature into reducing potential adverse possession claims had property and assets, and therefore had the ability to hire good lobbyists to persuade state senators. A cynic might also say potential claimants who wanted to retain the ability to obtain property from rich people, without paying for such property, had less ability to hire good lobbyists or fund those senators' campaigns. But I hate cynics.

Other states also battle with whether to require a claimant to show that his claim of right was in good faith. In Oregon, for example, prior to 1990, the common law controlled. The courts at that time did not review the claimant's subjective point of view. Apparently an intent to occupy and own the property was enough. But in 1990, its new legislation indicated that any new adverse possession case required the claimant also to have an honest belief of actual ownership that began at the time of first possession, continued for the relevant time period, and was objectively a reasonable belief.[31] Regardless, the law on this issue in Oregon was and is still not crystal clear.

29 7 N.Y.3d 228, 232–33 (2006).

30 *Id.* at 233.

31 Wood v. Taylor, 307 Or. App. 688, 698 (Or. Ct. App. 2020), citing OR. REV. STAT. § 105.620.

Kansas also changed its policies, but in a slightly different manner. At one point, it specifically required "hostility," in order for a party to obtain adverse possession. But then in its legislature enacted a statute,[32] becoming effective in 1964, that provides that an adverse possessor's case can be based either on a claim that was (1) "knowingly adverse" or (2) "under a belief of ownership." It would seem that so long as the other elements are met, the only reason a party would be unable to claim adverse possession would be if the claimant neither believed he owned certain land, nor that he wanted to adversely possess that land. For example, if a claimant believed the fence his contractor built had been put on the true boundary, but it was actually 20 feet over the boundary line, without the claimant's knowledge, then it would be theoretically possible for his opponent, the record title holder, to successfully argue against adverse possession on this basis.

Maine went through its own changes as well, claiming that it once followed the "minority rule," which it described as meaning that "one who by mistake occupies . . . land not covered by his deed with no intention to claim title beyond his actual boundary wherever that may be, does not thereby acquire title by adverse possession to land beyond the true line."[33] In 1993, its legislature enacted a statute[34] that provided that a mistake of a boundary line established hostility, and that so long as the other elements of adverse possession were proven, the hostile nature of the claim is established, and no further evidence of the knowledge or intent of the person in possession would be required. What is not so clear in Maine is whether one who mistakenly enters land, in a situation unrelated to a boundary dispute issue, has actually adversely possessed it.

In Hawaii, by statute, the claimant must show that he acted "in good faith," which is defined as meaning that "a reasonable person would believe that the person has an interest in title to the lands in question and such belief is based on inheritance, a written instrument of conveyance, or the judgment of a court of competent jurisdiction."[35] This is not a subjective test in the traditional sense of the word. Notably, the Hawaiian Constitution, Article XVI, Section 12, has specific rules for adverse possession concerning real property of over five acres—including the use of the term "good faith."

One of the states that has no subjective test is Washington. Its high court ruled that so long as the claimant treats the land and his own

32 Kan. Stat. Ann. § 60–503.

33 Dombkowski v. Ferland, 893 A.2d 599, 603 (Me. 2006).

34 14 Me. Rev. Stat. § 810-A.

35 Haw. Rev. Stat. § 669-1(b).

against the world through the statutory period, that is sufficient. His internal thoughts and subjective belief about what interest he has in the land, and whether he intends to dispossess the "true" owner, is irrelevant.[36] Washington's Supreme Court cited a law review article that described the issue bluntly: "Adverse possession revolves around the character of possession, and it is difficult to see why a man's secret thoughts should have anything to do with it. Maybe the idea originated in a confusion of permission or agreement between owner and possessor with unilateral intent in the possessor's mind. Whatever the reason, the court could yet perform a service by doing away with any requirement of subjective intent, negative or affirmative. Since a man cannot by thoughts alone put himself in adverse possession, why should he be able to think himself out of it?"[37] In making this ruling, the court also indicated it was reversing previous case law that had used the "confusing" method of analyzing the claimant's subjective belief.

Alaska has an objective test as well: "The hostility requirement . . . is determined by application of an objective test which simply asks whether the possessor acted toward the land as if he owned it, without the permission of one with legal authority to give possession."[38] Feelings are not important. Only what you do counts.

In theory, this objective standard should make it easier for the claimant to establish an adverse possession claim. After all, part of the reason the law exists is to make sure that parties who spend years of blood, sweat, tears, and money taking care of property and developing property should be able to keep it. In at least one state, one's subjective thoughts about why he might be deemed an owner are irrelevant. The only thing that matters is whether he intended to actually possess it. In one case that used colorful language, the court held that "[w]hile it is true that a 'black-hearted trespasser' can adversely possess land under claim of right, the fact remains that both a 'black-hearted trespasser' and a 'Good Samaritan' must go upon the land with the purpose of claiming it as his or her own to prosecute a successful claim of adverse possession."[39]

---

36 Chaplin v. Sanders, 100 Wn.2d 853, 860–61 (1984).

37 ITT Rayonier, Inc. v. Bell, 112 Wn.2d 754, 761 (1989), citing William Stoebuck, *The Law of Adverse Possession in Washington*, 35 Wash. L. Rev. 53, 80 (1960).

38 McDonald v. Harris, 978 P.2d 81, 84 (Alaska 1999) (internal quotation marks and citation omitted, emphasis added). This case concerned an easement, but the rule applies in the context of adverse possession cases too.

39 DeHertogh v. Beauregard, C.A. Nos. PC02–6318 Consolidated with PC02–6317, at *15 (R.I. Super. Aug. 5, 2010).

As that quote indicates, relevant subjective thoughts are not limited to whether one has "good faith," that is, a reasonable belief that one is actually the owner of property. There are other potentially relevant subjective thoughts as well. Wisconsin once heard an interesting case in which the adverse possessor's predecessors had apparently not even intended to make a claim of right over certain property. Although those predecessors' physical occupation and use of the property would have been sufficient to an adverse possession claim, the predecessors had once admitted they knew they did not own it. The lower appellate court held that the subjective intent of a possessor—that is, whether the possessor intended to claim title—was irrelevant. But its Supreme Court disagreed. It held that "the plain meaning of 'claim of title' is that a possessor must subjectively intend to claim ownership of the disputed property."[40] Interestingly, it indicated that if there were no evidence one way or the other about the subjective intent of the possessors, the hostility element would have been presumed. Unfortunately for the alleged adverse possessors, there was evidence on subjective intent, and it was against them. As the court held, "this presumption [about hostility] may be rebutted by evidence demonstrating that a possessor lacked the subjective intent to claim title to the property."[41]

One critical part of hostility in certain states, if not all states, is that one must not only occupy the land, but one must also actually want to claim that land as his own. In one Texas case,[42] the trial court ruled that one set of neighbors had adversely possessed a portion of their neighbor's land. The appellate court affirmed, indicating that "the property under dispute here was adversely possessed, despite the mutual mistake regarding the property lines."[43] The line was established as a true boundary line of this tract of land "by recognition and acquiescence in the line as the true line by all interested parties for a sufficient length of time."[44]

A dissent in that case indicated that the majority had failed to consider a critical issue: that even if the alleged adverse possessors did use certain property, there was nothing in the record to indicate that the claimants or their predecessors "ever intended to claim any property from the [neighbors] that was actually owned by the [neighbors]."[45]

This went to the Supreme Court of Texas, which generally agreed with the lower court's dissent. It held that "'hostile' use does not require an intention to dispossess the rightful owner, or even know that there is

40 Wilcox v. Est. of Hines, 355 Wis.2d 1, 18 (2014).

41 *Id.* at 287.

42 Tran v. Macha, 176 S.W.3d 128 (Tex. App. 2004).

43 *Id.* at 133.

44 *Id.* at 134.

45 *Id.* at 135.

one. But there must be an intention to claim property as one's own to the exclusion of all others; mere occupancy of land without any intention to appropriate it will not support the statute of limitations."[46] Since there was no evidence the claimants or their predecessors ever intended to exclude the neighbors from that property, or that neighbors used the property only with the claimants' express permission, there was no basis for an adverse possession claim. The court concluded that before taking a "severe step" of awarding property rights to one that has not purchased it, "the law reasonably requires that the parties' intentions be very clear."[47]

If the above rules were not confusing enough, there is yet another way of examining hostility and claim of right cases. Most cases rule that the court determines if there is a claim of right either by determining if the claimant had a subjective good faith reason to believe the property was his, or by simply looking at the person's actions objectively. But as indicated in the following section, at least some courts rule that one can only win an adverse possession claim if the claimant had bad faith, and that he knew all along that he had no legitimate right to the property at stake. This is the ultimate example of "Nice guys finish last."

Separate Tests for a Claim of Right: Bad Faith and the Effect of a Mistake

South Carolina actually required, or perhaps still requires, bad faith in certain circumstances from any adverse possession claimant. This made, or still makes, that state a *Star Trek* mirror universe, in which only the evil, brutal people prevail, and those who make innocent mistakes do not. This was articulated apologetically in one of its lower appellate cases, which held: "In South Carolina, unlike in most other jurisdictions, possession under a mistaken belief that property is one's own and with no intent to claim against the property's true owner cannot constitute hostile possession."[48] It held that the claimants in that case occupied the tract "thinking they were its rightful owners." It "reluctantly" reversed the lower court's decision which granted adverse possession "[b]ecause South Carolina's law on adverse possession apparently favors intentional wrongdoers . . . ."[49] This was partially based on a previous decision from its high court, which held that "a claim of adverse possession fails where an encroaching neighbor is under a mistaken belief as to

46 Tran v. Macha, 213 S.W.3d 913, 915 (Tex. 2007) (citation omitted).
47 *Id.*
48 Lusk v. Callham, 287 S.C. 459, 461 (S.C. Ct. App. 1986).
49 *Id.* at 462.

boundary location and therefore lacks intention to dispossess the true owner."[50]

That South Carolina court may have conflated various issues. One is whether a claimant has a mistaken belief that the particular piece of land is his own, and the other is whether the claimant intended to claim that the particular piece of land was his own, had he known of his mistake. Those may be related issues, but they do not always match up. Regardless, in that case, the South Carolina court seemed to be self-critical about its own common law, which had a backwards attitude toward good faith and bad faith. To put it another way, the court seemed to believe the adverse possessor must lose because he would not have claimed the land as his own had he known it belonged to his neighbor. Perhaps the adverse possessor should have prepared stronger evidence that the claimant had definitely decided where the boundary line was, and that he would have kept everyone off that space, no matter what.

In any event, South Carolina partially redeemed itself. It noted in a later case the main rule that a good faith mistake does not allow one to claim adverse possession. But it held that this was only in certain contexts. It held that this rule is applicable only to cases involving boundary disputes between adjoining landowners; only in that context will a good faith mistake be fatal to an adverse possession case. It held that if the dispute concerns an entire tract of land; the claimant can still succeed even if he had a good faith mistaken belief that he owned the property.[51]

Other states also wrestle with the concept of whether an adverse possessor who has made a mistake would be unable to claim possession in a hostile manner. North Carolina had one set of rules. But then in 1985 it did an about face. "We have concluded that a rule which requires the adverse possessor to be a thief in order for his possession of the property to be 'adverse' is not reasonable, and we now join the overwhelming majority of states . . . and hold that when a landowner, acting under a mistake as to the true boundary between his property and that of another, takes possession of the land believing it to be his own and claims title thereto, his possession and claim of title is adverse."[52]

Virginia sees the matter in a complicated way. Its courts have held that in certain circumstances, a mistake would negate hostile possession.

> Where a mistake occurs in determining the location of a boundary line described in a deed and the claimant has not proved the

50 Brown v. Clemens, 287 S.C. 328, 331 (1985).

51 Wigfall v. Fobbs, 295 S.C. 59 (1988); Perry v. Heirs at Law & Distributees of Gadsden, 316 S.C. 224, 225 (1994).

52 Walls v. Grohman, 315 N.C. 239, 249 (1985).

> definite and positive intention to occupy, use and claim as his own the land up to a particular and definite line on the ground then the claimant cannot establish adverse possession. However, when a claimant mistakenly believes that a particular line on the ground represents the extent of his or her own land and treats all the land within the line on the ground as his or her own in a manner that satisfies the other requirements of adverse possession . . . then the hostility requirement is generally satisfied.[53]

Illinois courts described the problem that arises if a court were to rule that adverse claimants cannot obtain success, if the basis for relief was that they made a mistake about where the boundary line was. The high court noted that "some jurisdictions have applied a subjective test, holding that the intention of the possessor is the controlling factor in determining whether possession to a mistaken boundary is hostile. Thus, if a landowner through mistake or ignorance takes possession to a boundary beyond the true line intending only to claim to the true line and not intending to claim the additional land if it should be ascertained that the boundary is not as he thought it, then such possession is not adverse or hostile." Illinois rejected that analysis, and used a simple test: "Occupancy to a visible and ascertained boundary for the statutory period is deemed the controlling feature in determining hostility in mistaken-boundary cases." It noted that "[t]he difficulty with the subjective test is that it affords no protection to the landowner who innocently and mistakenly occupies and improves land beyond his boundaries. He can never acquire title thereto. Conversely, he who deliberately sets out to steal adjacent land may succeed."[54]

CONSIDERATIONS FOR LITIGATORS

It is important for a litigator to understand the ocean of different kinds of cases, statutes, and attitudes toward hostility and a claim of right. At the beginning of the litigation, one must review the law on all potential hostile/claim of right issues if for no other reason than that it will help to see which rationale or rules in the state would be most helpful to one's own client. Other critical things to understand include what actually occurred, objectively, and what the subjective reasons were behind the client's decision to occupy and control the space. Other issues to

---

53 Quatannens v. Tyrrell, 268 Va. 360, 372 (2004) (internal quotation marks, citations, and emphasis omitted).

54 Joiner v. Janssen, 85 Ill. 2d 74, 82–84 (1981).

consider are what kinds of statements the claimant (or his predecessors) made about the land in issue. For example, did the claimant make comments to anyone about whether he actually believed he had the right to occupy the space? Of course, the record title holder will also need to ask pointed questions in depositions concerning why the claimant could ever have believed he owned the space in question.

In the context of handling cases and statutes, one cannot simply assume that because in one context a certain test is required, that this is necessarily required in all contexts. For example, in South Carolina (as indicated above), just because one must apparently prove bad faith in order to succeed in certain kinds of adverse possession cases does not mean that applies in others. There are many other ways of distinguishing cases on the claim of right issue; nearly every case has some unique aspects. Perhaps a court would be dead set against a person who encroached on a portion of land, but not against someone who encroached on the entirety of the land. Perhaps the court will accept a claim if the claimant occupied space originally by mistake, but then came to realize half way through the statutory period that he did not own the property of record.

Other issues to consider would arise if one's client is a claimant, but obtained that property from previous adverse possessors. In that case, evidence about their subjective intent or good faith may be impossible to obtain, so one will have to convince the court that an objective test is best. Other issues a litigator must consider are whether the state's courts sometimes hold that a claim of right is presumed in certain contexts, and as a corollary issue, what evidence it would take to rebut that presumption. A litigator may also have to consider whether the mistake of the claimant was that (for example) he meant to place a fence in one location but actually placed it at another, or whether he meant to place the fence at the boundary but he simply misunderstood where the legal boundary was. Whether the law in any particular state distinguishes between these kinds of errors may be unclear. Regardless, because hostility has so many branches, a smart litigator will try to find some way of distinguishing cases or statutes that appear to be against his client. Finally, unless the law clearly requires bad faith, it would always be best if representing a claimant to have him be able to articulate some explanation about why he believed in good faith that he owned the property at issue.

Another issue to consider is how to prove hostility in particularly tough circumstances. For example, if a claimant has taken possession of property from the title owner originally by permission, there still may be a way of ultimately claiming hostility. In that kind of situation, the party seeking to establish a claim of adverse possession must make an "unqualified and definite renunciation" of the owner's rights.[55] Similar strict rules apply when a party seeks to establish adverse possession against a close family member. In that case, possession will not be considered adverse to the family member unless there a clear showing of the hostile claim.[56]

Finally, one must even determine whether "hostility" is even an element in one's state, which to some degree rests on an issue of burdens, addressed in Chapter 33. In New Jersey, one court held that in 1969, "the New Jersey Supreme Court did away with hostility as an essential element of adverse possession."[57] But years later, another New Jersey court held that this element had a "continuing vitality."[58]

55 Southern Pac. Co. v. San Francisco, 62 Cal. 2d 50, 56 (1964).
56 Lobro v. Watson, 42 Cal. App. 3d 180, 186 (Ct. App. 1974).
57 Stump v. Whibco, 314 N.J. Super. 560, 576 (App. Div. 1998).
58 Yellen v. Kassin, 416 N.J. Super. 113, 120–21 (App. Div. 2010).

Chapter 4
Color of Title

An adverse possessor can cut through the Gordian knot of the claim of right element if he can prove he has color of title, such as an actual deed in his name for the property (even if the deed is defective). This is the gold standard for a good adverse possession case. It is also a complicated issue, which probably deserves a full book for proper analysis, if not a whole bookshelf. Some states, such as Iowa, consider a "color of title" to be a separate issue from a "claim of right" and only one of the two is necessary.[1] Other states, such as New York, still require a "claim of right," but in such states a color of title is a kind of "claim of right."[2] At least one state, New Mexico, requires color of title straight out; without color of title, do not collect $200 and do not pass Go.[3]

A quick and dirty definition of "color of title" is "[a] written instrument or other evidence that appears to establish title but does not in fact do so."[4] Another court gave a more detailed definition, stating that "[c]olor of title means something in writing which upon its face, professes to pass title, but which does not do it, either from want of title in the person making it, or the defective mode of conveyance that is used, but such writing must not be so plainly and obviously defective as that no man of ordinary capacity would be misled by it."[5]

An Arkansas court described the concept in an interesting way, by distinguishing fiction from nonfiction:

> Color of title is not, in law, title at all. It is a void paper, having the semblance of a muniment [document/record] of title, to which, for

1 Council Bluffs Sav. Bank v. Simmons, 243 N.W.2d 634, 636 (Iowa 1976).

2 *See generally* N.Y. R.P.A.P.L. §§ 501, 511–512.

3 *See* Williams v. Howell, 108 N.M. 225, 227 (1989).

4 Black's Law Dictionary (9th ed. 2009).

5 Pemberton v. Woodford, 2013 Ohio 214, ¶ 20 (Ohio Ct. App. 2013) (citation omitted).

> certain purposes, the law attributes certain qualities of title. Its chief office or purpose is to define the limits of the claim under it. Nevertheless, it must purport to pass title. In form, it must be a deed, a will, or some other paper or instrument by which title usually and ordinarily passes. Such qualities as are imputed to it by the law, for limited purposes, are purely fictitious and are accorded to it only to work out just results. Fictions are never used in procedure or law for any other purpose.[6]

As another court put it, "In general any instrument purporting to convey the land may be color of title, however defective or imperfect it is, and no matter from what cause it is invalid."[7]

The Supreme Court of South Carolina held that color of title means "any semblance of title by which the extent of a man's possession can be ascertained." It "is anything which shows the extent of occupant's claim . . . . The object of color of title is not to pass title. In that case it would be title, not color of title. The only office of color of title is to define the extent of the claim and to extend the possession beyond the actual occupancy to the whole property described in the paper . . . . It is by no means necessary that the paper should be in the form of a deed. A bond or even a receipt would be sufficient."[8]

There are several potential benefits to an adverse possession claimant that has color of title. (Some benefits depend on whether the statute at issue requires a deed, versus some other instrument that allegedly transfers title.) One benefit is that, depending on the state, the number of years one must act as an adverse possessor may be reduced. Wisconsin is one example in which, if one has a recorded written instrument, occupancy need only be for ten years, but if the case is based on a claim of right not based on a recorded written instrument, then one needs 20 years.[9] Another is that, instead of occupying entirety of the land at issue, one need only occupy a portion of it. (This is further discussed below.) A third is that, as indicated above, it is possible that the "claim of right" element may be avoided or easily met, and (as indicated in other portions of this book) hostility may be presumed. The fourth is that he may not

6 Weast v. Hereinafter Described Lands, 33 Ark. App. 157, 158–59 (1991) (citations omitted).

7 Van Meter v. Grice, 380 So. 2d 274, 280–81 (Ala. 1980) (italics omitted) (partially overruled on other grounds).

8 Graniteville Co. v. Williams, 209 S.C. 112, 121–22 (1946) (citations omitted).

9 Wis. Stat. Ann. §§ 893.25–893.27. If taxes are paid on the premises, there is a further reduction on the length of occupancy.

need to prove he paid taxes on the property, depending on the state. For example, in Alabama, in order to use the ten-year limitation period, a recorded deed (or other color of title) would suffice in lieu of having the land listed for taxation for that time period.[10]

Examples of instruments that have constituted color of title include a deed conveying property that had already been conveyed to another, or a deed from a cotenant purporting to convey a fee simple, and a void tax deed.[11] Another potential example would be "a deed purporting to convey title pursuant to a court decree . . . even though the decree may be erroneous or even void for want of jurisdiction."[12]

A deed void upon its face may suffice.[13] (Or it may not.[14]) Many other deeds would also work, such as a deed executed by a person who has no power to convey;[15] a deed executed by an alleged agent who had no authority;[16] or signed by one lacking mental capacity;[17] or by one having neither title nor possession;[18] or a deed secured by fraud of the grantee.[19] As yet another example, a void tax deed constituted color of title in a South Dakota case. It was void because the land at issue was not subject to taxation, since it was owned by an Indian.[20] That voidness was irrelevant because the court held that the instrument "purported to convey title, and that is sufficient to constitute color of title."[21]

Just because an adverse possession claimant has a piece of paper concerning property does not mean he has color of title. To some degree, it depends on how clear it would be to a layman that it does not pass title. It also depends on how clear the property description is. For example in one case, the court held that a deed containing an indefinite property description was void and did not constitute color of title for a claim,[22]

---

10 ALA. CODE ANN. § 6-5-200.

11 *See* Jones v. Barger, 67 Ark. App. 337 (1999); Welder v. Wiggs, 31 Ark. App. 163 (1990).

12 *In re* Estate of Tobin, 176 Ill. App. 3d 580, 586 (Ill. App. Ct. 1988).

13 *See, e.g.*, McMillan v. Wehle, 55 Wis. 685 (1882); Whittlesey v. Hoppenyan, 72 Wis. 140 (1888).

14 *See, e.g.*, Larkin v. Wilson, 28 Kan. 513, 514 (1882).

15 Sanborn v. French, 22 N.H. 246 (1850); Perry v. Perry, 99 N.C. 270 (1888).

16 Millen v. Stines, 81 Ga. 655 (1888).

17 Ellington v. Ellington, 103 N.C. 54 (1889).

18 Webber v. Clarke, 74 Cal. 11 (1887); Love's Lessee v. Shields, 11 Tenn. 405 (1832).

19 Oliver v. Pullam, 24 Fed. Rep. 127 (C.C.W.D.N.C. 1885).

20 This was the term of art the judge used to describe the person in the case.

21 Murphy v. Pierre 17 S.D. 207, 95 N.W. 925 (1903). *See also* Horn v. Blaney, 268 Ark. 885, 597 S.W.2d 109 (Ark. Ct. App. 1980) (holding that a void tax deed constituted color of title even though it conveyed land owned by the United States and thus was not subject to taxation).

22 Darr v. Lambert, 228 Ark. 16 (1957).

but in another the same state's court held that a deed constituted color of title because a surveyor was able to locate the tract from the description.[23]

There is no universal law as to whether color of title may be evidenced by a contract for sale of land. In one case, a party entered into possession of property under a contract of sale, and paid for the lots, but the defendants did not execute deeds to him. The Missouri court held regardless that he "possessed the lots under color of title."[24] Montana's Supreme Court also held that a contract for the sale of land does constitute color of title.[25] But one Georgia court held that "[a] writing that does not on its face profess to pass title, but expressly states that title will be conveyed at a future time and upon certain conditions, is not sufficient to constitute color of title."[26] This would seem to indicate that a mere contract of sale is insufficient, at least in that state.

As an aside, even if adverse possession does not work, but one has a contract of sale, some courts have held that the execution of a contract to purchase land causes an equitable conversion of the purchasers' contractual interest into an equitable interest in the realty itself.[27] In other words, the buyer under an executory contract for the conveyance of property becomes the equitable owner of the land sufficient to enable him to maintain a quiet title action.[28]

One must also review the relevant statutes and case law to see if the state has certain requirements such as recording the document, in order to claim color of title. In Wisconsin, the written instrument needs to be recorded within a set time limit with the register of deeds of the county.[29] A recording obligation also exists (for example) in Alabama,[30] Colorado,[31] and Florida.[32] In California, while the instrument need not be recorded, recordation does establish the intention to claim the property adversely to the owner.[33] Kentucky does not apparently need the document recorded either.[34]

---

23 Belcher v. Stone, 67 Ark. App. 256 (1999).

24 Thomas v. B.K.S. Dev. Corp., 77 S.W.3d 53, 60 (Mo. Ct. App. 2002). *See also* Carrington v. McNeil, 58 A.D.2d 719 (3d Dep't 1977); First Nat'l Bank v. McGinnis, 819 P.2d 1080, 1083 (Colo. App. 1991).

25 Long v. Pawlowski, 131 Mont. 91 (1957).

26 Shippen v. Cloer, 213 Ga. 172, 173–74 (1957) (superseded by statute).

27 Dyer v. Dist. Ct., 188 Colo. 41 (1975); Bent v. Ferguson, 791 P.2d 1241 (Colo. App. 1990).

28 Bent v. Ferguson, 791 P.2d 1241 (Colo. App. 1990); *see also* Jacquez v. Jacquez, 694 P.2d 1292 (Colo. App. 1984).

29 Wis. Stat. § 893.26.

30 Green v. Dixon, 727 So. 2d 781, 783–84 (Ala. 1999); Ala. Code § 6-5-200 (1975).

31 Wostenburg v. Karme, 53 Colo. 258, 258–59 (1912).

32 Fla. Stat. § 95.16(1) (1991).

33 Johns v. Scobie, 12 Cal. 2d 618 (1939).

34 Knott Coal Corp. v. Kelly, 417 S.W.2d 253, 255 (Ky. Ct. App. 1967).

Critical issues for a successful color of title claim revolve around good faith. One issue is how to define the term. Another issue is whether it is necessary. And if it is a necessary element, another issue concerns burdens.

Not all courts agree on what "good faith" means. In some jurisdictions good faith for the purposes of establishing a claim under color of title seems to just mean the absence of fraud or similar conduct.[35] Other courts hold that if an adverse possessor knows of a defect in title, then even if he is otherwise blameless, there is no good faith.[36] Other courts rule that the claimant must have had an honest belief based on reasonable grounds that he had valid title to the land when he entered it.[37]

If good faith is not needed for a color of title case, then in theory anyone can find a way to have a deed signed by someone to the alleged grantee. To allow that kind of leeway is like pouring gasoline throughout a building, and handing a Zippo lighter to a pyromaniac.

As indicated, one issue for a color of title case is whether the party claiming an adverse possessory interest had a good faith basis to believe that the deed at issue actually transferred title. In many cases, this is resolved by statutes, which specifically indicate that "good faith" is critical. This is true in the relevant statute in the state of Washington,[38] which expressly requires that the color of title claim be made in good faith. Other states, like New Mexico[39] and South Dakota,[40] also require "good faith" pursuant to a statute in the context of color of title. New York, which requires a "claim of right" in all circumstances, including ones based on color of title, has statutorily defined the term, as previously indicated in this book. Pursuant to its relevant statute, "[a] claim of right means a reasonable basis for the belief that the property belongs to the adverse possessor or property owner, as the case may be."[41]

Many states, if they do not include it in the statute, would likely require the good faith element anyway. But as indicated below, that is not universal.

Another issue concerns presumptions and burdens on a "good faith" issue. New Mexico, for instance, indicated explicitly that there is a

35 *See* Thurmond v. Espalin, 50 N.M. 109, 115–16 (1946).

36 *See* Fernandez Brothers v. Ojeda, 266 U.S. 144, 146–47 (1924); Facundo v. Yabucoa Sugar Co., 118 F.2d 1, 4–5 (1st Cir. 1941); Madden v. Alpha Hardware Supply Co., 128 Cal. App. 2d 72 (1954).

37 *See* Fife v. Barnard, 186 F.2d 655, 660 (10th Cir. 1951); Armstrong v. Cities Serv. Gas Co., 210 Kan. 298, 311 (1972); Williams v. Striker, 29 Wash. App. 132 (1981).

38 Wash. Rev. Code § 7.28.070.

39 N.M. Stat. § 37-1-22.

40 S.D. Codified Laws § 15-3-15.

41 N.Y. R.P.A.P.L. § 501(3).

presumption of good faith, but that this presumption "does not apply when evidence is presented that the deed was obtained with full knowledge of its invalidity."[42]

In one Florida case,[43] Luke Frazier and his mother, Connie Frazier, took real property owned by Richard Goszczynski without his consent. The court called the Fraziers' scheme (described next) as "brazen and mischievous."[44] Goszczynski owned real property, but when a co-owner died, and taxes were no longer paid on the property, he did not notice. The Fraziers, however, did notice. So Luke Frazier prepared a quitclaim deed and attempted to convey the property from himself, as grantor, to himself and his mother, as grantees. This is known as a "wild deed" because the grantor never had interest in the first place. The Fraziers then took possession of the property, paid the delinquent taxes, and rented the property to others, keeping the rental payments for themselves. When Goszczynski discovered the scheme, he filed suit to quiet title to his property. The Fraziers filed a counterclaim to quiet title, claiming that they adversely held possession of the property in excess of seven years under color of title (the wild deed) and that the property therefore belonged to them.

Goszczynski won the case, partially helped by the fact that Luke Frazier had been prosecuted for fraud in a matter concerning the same real property, and was convicted. The court held that "color of title requires that the deed of conveyance be accepted by the grantee in good faith and with the belief that it constitutes a legitimate conveyance of title." The court also added an amusing discussion of self-love. "There is also the rather unique notion adopted by the Fraziers, but foreign to us, that a valid consideration of a conveyance of land from oneself to oneself is the love and affection that one has for oneself. We reject this nonsensical assertion of good faith." The court finalized by explaining that "[t]he law of adverse possession under color of title was devised to address the perceived need to resolve the ever growing problem of individuals who took possession of property pursuant to a flawed conveyance that they in good faith believed was valid. It was enacted for salutary purposes. It was not enacted to give legitimacy to the actions of fortune hunters and mischievous interlopers who distort the law with the artifice of a wild deed prepared by themselves conveying the property to themselves for the purpose of taking the property of others for their own financial gain."[45]

42 *In re* Estate of Duran, 133 N.M. 553, 563 (N.M. 2003).

43 Frazier v. Goszczynski, 161 So. 3d 542 (Fla. Dist. Ct. App. 2014).

44 It sounds like something the *Key & Peele* substitute teacher would say.

45 161 So. 3d at 546.

Did any reader think this was a one of a kind situation? It wasn't. It reminds me of what one of my law school professors once said: "One day your client will tell you, 'I have a brilliant idea of how to make a lot of money.' You will listen to the idea and say, 'Yes, it's brilliant, and you could make a lot of money. But it's also illegal.'"[46] Other examples of this phony kind of color of title case include a New Mexico Supreme Court case called *Palmer v. Denver & Rio Grande Western Railroad Co.*[47] In that case, the defendant railroad company conveyed a tract of land to one of the plaintiffs, but specifically excepted a strip of land within its boundaries as not included in the conveyance. That plaintiff then conveyed the entire tract, including the specifically excluded portion of land, to his mother. She in turn conveyed the same property back to him and his siblings. No consideration changed hands between the mother and son during these transactions. The court found that the transactions were undertaken merely for the purpose of obtaining record title to the disputed property. This court decided that such maneuvering "clearly fell short" of the legal threshold to establish good faith.[48] The court agreed with the defendants' argument that "color of title was created by the conduct of the plaintiffs, and accordingly was not in good faith."[49] The court concluded that when "color of title is created and obtained with knowledge of its invalidity by one claiming title by adverse possession, there is an absence of that good faith required by the statute."[50]

Similarly, other states have found that some third party must transfer the document of title to the person claiming title by adverse possession. For example, in *Y A Bar Livestock Co. v. Harkness*, the Supreme Court of Montana decided that a cotenant of property, who was also the sole owner of a corporation, could not create color of title in the property for adverse possession purposes by conveying the property to the corporation.[51] There are many other cases indicating similar rules.[52]

In *State v. King*,[53] the Supreme Court of West Virginia distinguished the case in which a party who perpetrated a "wrongful act," from the "vastly different" situation of a party who "paid out his money" and obtained a fraudulent deed in good faith and who thereafter occupied

46 Don't ask if my professor's prediction came true.

47 75 N.M. 737 (1966).

48 *Id.* at 739.

49 *Id.*

50 *Id.* at 740.

51 269 Mont. 239, 887 P.2d 1211, 1216–17 (1994).

52 *See, e.g.*, Hyland v. Kirkman, 204 N.J. Super. 345, 498 A.2d 1278, 1292 (1985) ("The court first holds that a bona fide 'claim of ownership' in a quiet title action . . . may not be founded on a wild deed sworn by plaintiff himself.").

53 77 W. Va. 37 (1915).

and improved the land for the necessary period based on his good faith in his title.[54] If one has good faith, that would be acceptable, but there is no color of title "to individuals to fabricate paper title, with express intent and purpose to obtain what does not belong to them, or to make additions to what the law gives them as persons in possession under claim of title."[55]

Anyone reading the above and assuming it was a universal concept would be wrong. One example of a different way of addressing nearly the same issue was in the Maine case called *Estate of Stone v. Hanson*.[56] In that case, the court examined a statute concerning adverse possession of uncultivated lands, which in that state is treated differently from adverse possession of cultivated lands. The Hanson defendants were record title holders of certain land along the shore of a lake. Then in 1968, Lewis Stone prepared a wild deed, conveying the property to others. Eventually the grantees then issued Mr. Stone a deed back in his name. When he died, and his widow tried to sell it, she discovered that the Hansons were still the owners of that property, and she filed a quiet title action against them. The statute at issue required, among other elements, that there be a "recorded deed," which the Hansons claimed had an implicit good faith claim associated with it. The court disagreed. It held that there was no reason to go beyond the actual language of the statute, and that the statute did not require "good faith" and did not prohibit "a deed from the adverse possessor himself."[57] (However, as an aside, it did indicate that if there was "a showing of fraud or misrepresentation (e.g. a deed with forged signatures)" then the court might be permitted to determine there was no true "recorded deed.")[58]

There are other older cases, as well, that hint that the court should not examine a deed from the point of view of "good faith."[59] Examining issues about good faith in a color of title run into the issues about proving how a person could have known about a deed, whether that person should have known, and so on. Then the court may need to engage in certain kinds of mind reading exercises, or presumptions about how a rational person would think. But even if "good faith" is not necessary, one should also check if a "claim of right" is required in that state for a color of title claim, which may in effect include "good faith" concepts.

---

54 *Id.* at 47.

55 *Id.* at 48.

56 621 A.2d 852 (Me. 1993).

57 *Id.* at 853.

58 *Id.* at 854.

59 *See, e.g.*, McDaniel v. Ramsey's Adm'rs, 305 Ky. 536 (1947); Shutt v. Methodist Episcopal Church, 187 Ky. 350 (1920); Burns v. Stewart, 162 N.C. 360 (1913); Marky Inv., Inc. v. Arnezeder, 15 Wis. 2d 74 (1961).

Moving on from the good faith issue, another critical issue is whether the claimant actually possessed all of the land indicated in the document that allegedly gave him title. "Without color of title, the claimant would only be entitled to adversely possess the part of the tract that he has taken into his actual possession. However, if the claimant enters and actually possesses only part of a tract under color of title, a court may find that his possession will extend to the full tract described in the title."[60]

In other words, one benefit of a color of title case is that the claimant does not need to occupy the entire space. This is because the conveyance's description, and "not the physical use of the land by the claimant, that determines the boundaries of the land that may be acquired by adverse possession under color of title."[61] In New York, if adverse possession is based on a written document, the claimant generally only needs possess a portion of the land.[62]

If your client is the record owner of the property, and not the mere claimant, you can try to find an exception to the above rule. In Alaska, the doctrine of allowing the adverse claimant to occupy only a portion as a means of proving possession of the entire tract "does not apply where the owner is in actual possession of a part of the property. Under those circumstances the owner is said to constructively possess all of his property which is not in the adverse possessor's actual possession."[63] As an Alabama court put it, "one who adversely possesses a part of a tract of land and has color of title to the whole tract, gains possession of all the land provided no one else [is] in possession."[64]

Hostility may be an issue in a color of right case, but that may not be a difficulty, because in some states, a "color of right" is itself a form of hostility. In Oregon, the relevant statute requires proof of hostile possession. But it defines "hostile possession" as holding property "under claim of right or with color of title."[65] Maryland similarly indicates that one form of hostility is color of title.[66] Of course, when one is defending against an adverse possession case, one can still try to claim that the person with color of title lacked hostility. This seems to have had little attention in case law.

Another issue is how much detail is indicated in the defective deed that provides alleged colorable title. "[W]here the description in the

60 DeVore v. Vaughn, 504 S.W.3d 176, 184 n.4 (Mo. Ct. App. 2016).

61 Hubbard v. Curtiss, 684 P.2d 842, 847 (Alaska 1984).

62 N.Y. R.P.A.P.L. § 511; Hutton v. Townsend, 150 A.D.2d 972, 972 (N.Y. App. Div. 1989).

63 Ault v. State, 688 P.2d 951, 955–57 (Alaska 1984).

64 Long v. Ladd, 273 Ala. 410, 413 (1962).

65 Or. Rev. Stat. § 105.620(2)(a).

66 Yourik v. Mallonee, 174 Md. App. 415, 427–28 (2007).

deed, aided by extrinsic evidence, is insufficient to identify the property, the deed cannot serve as color of title."[67] Therefore, it may become an issue as to whether one's state allows using extrinsic evidence, or whether the evidence one might seek to present would be admissible.

One needs to carefully review the statutes for other benefits that may arise in the context of a color of title case versus a traditional claim of right case. For example, in New York, a color of title case would allow a valid claim of adverse possession even if the premises had not been enclosed, where the space "has been used for the supply of fuel or of fencing timber, either for the purposes of husbandry or for the ordinary use of the occupant."[68] The same rule would not apply for a traditional claim of right case not based on a written document.

Of course, just because there is color of title does not necessarily mean an adverse possession claimant has smooth sailing. At least in one state, the adverse possessor must show the elements as well, such as actual, exclusive, and continuous possession of the property in question.[69]

If one's client has color of title, there is yet another way he may obtain title, even if he does not meet the other elements for adverse possession, such as "actual" or "continuous" possession. At least one state, Washington, has a statute entitled "Color of title to vacant and unoccupied land."[70] That statute concerns a substitute method of obtaining relief. In order to be "deemed and adjudged" the legal owner of land under that statute, four elements must be established. The claimant to the land must prove (1) color of title to the land; (2) the claimed title to the land is made in good faith; (3) the land being claimed is vacant and unoccupied; and (4) the claimant paid all taxes legally assessed on the land for seven successive years.

I cannot help but conclude this chapter with a reference to a North Carolina case concerning color of title called *Justice v. Mitchell*.[71] This case explains why lawyers will always be necessary to explain peculiar logic sometimes involved in the law, and why (hopefully) AI will never replace us.

In that case, there was a dispute over the ownership of certain lands between the plaintiff, Susie Mitchell Justice, and the defendants, James R. Mitchell and John Mitchell. The lands were originally owned by Mollie J. Mitchell, who died in mid 1949. In her last will and testament, Mollie devised the lands to James for his lifetime, and after his death, the

---

67 Brylinski v. Cooper, 95 N.M. 580, 583 (1981).
68 N.Y. R.P.A.P.L. § 512.
69 Ginsberg v. Stanley Aviation Corp., 193 Colo. 454, 457 (1977).
70 WASH. REV. CODE § 7.28.080.
71 238 N.C. 364 (1953).

lands would pass to the plaintiff, Susie. However, shortly after Mollie's will was offered for probate, James presented a deed in his favor dated December 31, 1940, which appeared to be signed by the late Mollie. The only problem was that he had not registered it. It was just something he held onto.

He claimed that he had been in open, notorious, and adverse possession of the lands for over nine years prior to the lawsuit. But James lost the case, and the Supreme Court of North Carolina affirmed.

The court noted that in that state, adverse possession ripens into title after seven years of possession, if there is color of title. The court held that even if that particular deed could have been considered potentially color of title at some point, it was not considered color of title at the onset. In that state, an instrument which *actually* conveys title (which is what he claimed the deed did) is not color of title—at least not yet. That is because "color of title" means a document that only *appears* to pass title, but in fact does not.

For the first two years he had the right to register it—because it was a true and proper deed. But he did not. In that state, the relevant statute indicated the deed then became void ab initio, and therefore in an ordinary case, the title would revest to the grantor. So this deed he had hung onto could not become "color of title" (if at all) until those two years elapsed. And when those two years elapsed, it was January 1, 1943, and Mollie died in mid 1949. So he did not hit the required seven-year deadline.

He had another strike against him as well. Since the title reverted to the grantor due to the failure to register the deed; title became Mollie's again. Then after Mollie died, her will took effect. And he had the right to be on the premises as a life tenant pursuant to Mollie's will. The problem for James was that in that state, in order for colorable title to ripen into good title, he had to take an action as a quasi-trespasser, so that he would be liable to an action of ejectment. Since he had the absolute right to remain on the property pursuant to the will, he was not a trespasser, and could not have been ejected. So it appears the time never started ticking anyway.[72]

72 If someone can understand the logic of this case without having to reread it five times, he is superior to me.

Chapter 5
Exclusivity

As most Americans do not live in kibbutzim, we should have a good idea about a critical element of true landownership: exclusive dominion. As one court put it, "[e]xclusive dominion over land is the essence of possession, and it can exist in unused land if others have been excluded therefrom."[1] To put it another way, if your client is looking for advice about how to prove adverse possession, he should be told not to be neighborly. He should use the land solely on his own. If he cannot do so, at least he should keep everyone else out, to the best of his ability. Alternatively, if your client wants to let people onto his adversely possessed property, he should make sure that when they enter, he clarifies to the world that they are merely guests, and not theoretical owners.

"Exclusivity" is a requirement of adverse possession. However, "exclusive" does not necessarily mean exclusive use. For example, in one New York case,[2] the plaintiff only used the property seasonally, and he allowed family members and neighbors to use the premises. The court held that regardless, so long as their use did not interfere with plaintiff's activities during the statutory period, he could still claim exclusivity. Regardless, a litigator should address how his client uses the property: "Evidence of *use* is admissible because it is ordinarily an indication of *possession*."[3]

One court held that "[a] fence is the usual means relied upon to exclude strangers and establish the dominion and control characteristic of ownership."[4] In another case, a defendant claimed to adversely possess some land bounded by a fence. His neighbor, the plaintiff, claimed that he had accessed the disputed property periodically to fix the fence, and, therefore, the defendant adverse possessor could not establish exclusivity. The court disagreed, noting that "'exclusive' does

---

1 Wood v. Nelson, 57 Wash. 2d 539, 540 (1961).

2 Robinson v. Robinson, 34 A.D.3d 975 (N.Y. App. Div. 2006).

3 Huber v. Cardiff, 186 Ohio App. 3d 384, 388 (2009).

4 57 Wash. 2d at 540.

not mean absolutely exclusive, but only such use as would be expected of an owner under the circumstances."[5] In that case, since the plaintiff only went to the disputed property to get better access to maintain the fence, and since this was "nothing more than any neighboring land owner might do" then this did not undermine the defendant's claim of exclusive possession.[6] (Note that Chapter 11 indicates that to rely on a fence in every case may be a serious mistake.)

One revealing case about the definition of exclusivity was resolved by the Alaskan Supreme Court in 1974.[7] That was a time when the courts still felt comfortable using "Indian" instead of "Native American" to describe a person.

In that case, Mr. Peters, who claimed property by adverse possession, was 71 years old, and he claimed that his family's interest in the property dated from 1916. The property in dispute was a small section of beachfront in a protected cove and harbor, in a semi-wilderness area near Juneau. (The record title was held by another entity.) Mr. Peters drove to the property every weekend, and lived there off and on every year during seal hunting season. He also used his boats for sealing and for fishing, returning to his land at the property to process the seal and smoke the fish.

One amusing aspect of the case was in testimony, which reveals a difference between how lawyers think and how human beings think. There was a question about whether one of his predecessors had bought a building, or had also bought the land under the building. When asked about it, the plaintiff answered: "Well, I don't think it can go without it. The house can't be up in the air. I don't know about that one. I can't answer it."[8]

In any event the trial court held that he had not proven an adverse possession claim in part because of an alleged lack of exclusivity. The trial court held that "[c]lamdiggers, picnickers, and others have certainly occasionally made use of the beach area off and on through the years, and not necessarily with permission of plaintiff or anyone."[9]

Alaska's Supreme Court disagreed with that analysis, and held that Mr. Peters had a valid adverse possession claim. It reached that decision by indicating the reason this element of adverse possession exists, is that the adverse possessor must "put the record owner on notice of the existence of an adverse claimant. That purpose should, therefore, be kept in

5 Cook v. Eddy, 193 P.3d 705, 713 (Wyo. 2008) (citation and certain internal quotation marks omitted).

6 *Id.*

7 Peters v. Juneau-Douglas Girl Scout Council, 519 P.2d 826 (Alaska 1974).

8 *Id.* at 828 n.4.

9 *Id.* at 830.

mind when deciding whether any given set of circumstances satisfies the exclusive use requirement." The court cited a treatise's comments about "exclusive use," as follows: "In determining the exclusive character of the possession, the character and locality of the property and the uses and purposes for which it is naturally adopted are considered, and mere casual and occasional trespasses upon the land by a stranger are not generally considered as interrupting the continuity of adverse possession of land."[10]

The court therefore held that "[o]ccasional clamdiggers could not destroy the exclusive character of Peters' use since such casual intrusions were clearly not considered by Peters to interfere or conflict with his own use. In allowing strangers to come on the land to dig clams and in allowing friends, relatives and other members of the Tlingit tribe occasional use of the land, Peters was merely acting as any other hospitable landowner might."

On the other end of the scale is a case like *Raftopoulos v. Monger*,[11] in which the Colorado Supreme Court noted that "[a]ny sort of joint or common possession by the adverse claimant and the record owner prevents the possession of one claiming adversely from [attaining] the requisite quality of exclusiveness."[12] In that case, the record owner used the range land at issue to graze sheep on a regular annual basis in a manner consistent with the arid character of the land. The court therefore held that this type of use was sufficient to preclude an adverse possession claim by the joint user who had loosely fenced the disputed parcel and had used it to graze cattle and horses.

Another case addressing these issues was in Washington state, in which a man named Bell bought a houseboat and started periodically using land adjacent to it. When the record title holder filed an action to quiet title, Bell counterclaimed based on adverse possession. That counterclaim was dismissed because of a lack of exclusive use. Notably, it was not the plaintiff that had used the land. But luckily for the plaintiff, there were other people who also used the same land during times they used their own houseboat. The court held that their intrusion "cannot be said to be merely casual. The evidence shows that they moored their houseboat near the same property for a longer period than did Bell. During this period, they used the property in question along with Bell. Bell's acquiescence in their use of the land cannot be described to be simply the attitude of a good neighbor. It shows, rather, that there was a shared occupation of land.

10 *Id.*, citing 5 Thompson on Real Property § 2547 (1957 Replacement).

11 656 P.2d 1308 (Colo. 1983) *overruled on other grounds by* Gerner v. Sullivan, 768 P.2d 701 (Colo. 1989).

12 *Id.* at 1311.

This does not constitute the exclusive use of land necessary for adverse possession and, in our judgment, reasonable persons could not conclude otherwise."[13] The court pointed out that Bell's strategy, of showing off how much and to what degree he used the property, did not disprove the non-exclusive use. In other words, although Bell tried to throw the judges off the track of the critical issue, he failed.

In one interesting case from Oregon, *Sea River Properties, LLC v. Parks*,[14] there were two title owners, but because of how the land had changed over time, there were questions about who owned which part of the modern land. The court awarded to plaintiff title by accretion, meaning the slow addition of land next to water, due to the water's movement. "In deciding the question of accretion, the trial court heard extensive expert testimony about the geological development of the area since 1858 and made detailed factual findings."[15] These are issues that people like me, city boys, can barely conceive of. In any event, the defendant claimed that his adverse possession claim trumped the title by accretion. The Oregon Supreme Court disagreed. It held that the property at issue was an undeveloped grassy beach, and therefore "a natural place for walking or picnicking."[16] And defendant admitted, perhaps unwittingly, that other visitors to that beach area also used plaintiff's property for recreational purposes "[a]ll the time."[17] Even further destroying his own case, he admitted that "other people routinely camped on plaintiff's property, parked their trailers there, and went back on the trails that cross the property."[18] The court held that since other families used the same property in the same way that his family did, the defendant's use of the property was not exclusive.

13 ITT Rayonier, Inc. v. Bell, 112 Wash. 2d 754, 758 (1989) (citation omitted).
14 333 P.3d 295 (Or. 2014).
15 *Id.* at 302.
16 *Id.* at 314.
17 *Id.* at 311.
18 *Id.* at 314.

Chapter 6
Actual Possession

Many states require "actual possession" for an adverse possession claimant. Sometimes it appears as if "actual" is tied into another element, but sometimes it does not.

One state that indicates that "actual possession" is a separate element is Washington. In that state, one judge indicated that "despite being combined into one element the terms 'actual' and 'uninterrupted' are distinct concepts. Actual possession is established only if possession is of such a character as a true owner would make considering the nature and location of the land in question. One could possess property as the true owner periodically rather than uninterruptedly."[1]

Some courts see "actual" as a kind of offshoot of the concept of "exclusive." For example in Missouri, "[a]ctual possession is the present ability to control the land and the intent to exclude others from such control."[2] In that state, the courts also indicate what steps are sufficient (and insufficient) for "actual possession": "A mere mental enclosure of land does not constitute the requisite actual possession."[3] In Missouri, at least in the context of a case where a claimant lacks color of title, "there must be continual acts of occupying, clearing, cultivating, pasturing, erecting fences or other improvements and paying taxes on the land."[4] (This issue of erecting an enclosure, or cultivating land, is also addressed in Chapter 11.)

In Kentucky, to prove actual possession, the claimant must demonstrate that "such use and occupation of the claimed property as to establish a clear dominion over it."[5] In Maine, to prove actual possession, claimants must prove that the disputed property is in their "immediate occupancy and physical control" by demonstrating "an actual use and

---

1 LeBleu v. Aalgaard, 193 Wash. App. 66, 81 (Wash. Ct. App. 2016) (citation omitted).
2 Eime v. Bradford, 185 S.W.3d 233, 236 (Mo. App. 2006).
3 Harris v. Lynch, 940 S.W.2d 42, 45 (Mo. Ct. App. 1997).
4 *Id.*
5 Moore v. Stills, 307 S.W.3d 71, 78 (Ky. 2010).

enjoyment of the property that is in kind and degree the same as the use and enjoyment to be expected of the average owner of such property."[6]

In Maryland, "[d]etermination of whether a claimant is in actual possession of the claimed land is a fact-intensive inquiry . . . something more than mere occasional use of land is needed. But, the character, location, and use of lands vary, and the type of possessory acts necessary to constitute actual possession in one case may not be essential in another."[7]

A potential adverse possession claimant may hope to be in a state which has looser rules about what "actual possession" means. For example, in Tennessee, "[t]here may be actual possession in law without actual occupation or cultivation."[8]

Notably, at least in one state, Alabama, it is "not necessary to physically reside upon land to establish title by adverse possession."[9] One need simply use the property "in a manner consistent with its nature and character."[10]

If one is in a state that specifically indicates that "actual" possession is necessary, then one may need to determine what kind of land is being "actually" possessed, as the burden to prove "actual" possession may change. In Missouri, "[t]he 'actual possession' element of adverse possession is less strict for wild, undeveloped land than it is for developed land, because the nature, location, and possible uses for the property may restrict the type of affirmative acts of ownership that may be appropriate for the land."[11] Somewhat conversely, in Pennsylvania, if contested property is woodland, a claimant must meet a high standard of proving he has resided upon or cultivated the property; the general and lower standard for actual possession in a non-woodland case is just to "maintain dominion" over it. In one case,[12] this was a critical issue, and the court spent a great deal of ink on the definition of "woodland."

There is a long list of kinds of incidental uses of land that are insufficient for "actual possession" in the context of adverse possession. For example, cutting timber in wild lands may not be sufficient to establish actual possession of the land.[13] Uses such as allowing hogs to fatten up,

6 Harvey v. Furrow, 2014 ME 149, ¶ 12, 107 A.3d 604, 611 (internal quotations omitted).

7 Senez v. Collins, 182 Md. App. 300, 325–26 (2008) (citations and internal quotation marks omitted).

8 Tidwell v. Van Deventer, 686 S.W.2d 899, 902 (Tenn. Ct. App. 1984).

9 Hand v. Stanard, 392 So. 2d 1157, 1160 (Ala. 1980) (citations omitted).

10 *Id.*

11 Luttrell v. Stokes, 77 S.W.3d 745, 749 (Mo. App. 2002).

12 Gruca v. Clearbrook Cmty. Servs. Ass'n, 2022 Pa. Super. 209, 7–14, 286 A.3d 1273 (Pa. Super. Ct. 2022).

13 *See, e.g.*, Noland v. Wise, 259 S.W.2d 46 (Ky. 1953); Marsee v. Colson, 307 Ky. 328 (1948).

the ranging of cattle, the operation of a water mill, the cutting of bushes and hay, the occasional sowing of grass, and the intermittent holding of church services and meetings are all insufficient to establish the actual possession of another's land, at least in Kentucky.[14] Maintenance of trails is insufficient.[15] Seasonal hunting, allowing cattle and hogs to roam, planting trees, and so on, can also be held to be insufficient.[16]

If your client is the claimant and cannot prove "actual" possession, he may be able to claim the next best thing—constructive possession. There may be some overlap as to whether "actual" includes "constructive" in some courts. The New York Court of Appeals held long ago that "[p]ossession means simply the owning or having a thing in one's own power; it may be actual, or it may be constructive. Actual possession exists where the thing is in the immediate occupancy of the party; constructive is that which exists in contemplation of law, without actual personal occupation."[17]

If one represents a title holder, one may first try to allege that the alleged adverse possessor only had constructive possession, and that this kind of possession is insufficient. There may be some theoretical support to that argument.[18]

But it appears most courts would rule that constructive possession would be sufficient. There are at least two workable methods: "(1) when the claimant is operating under color of title and (2) when the land is marked by clear and definite boundaries."[19] The latter may work if the claimant has occupied at least a portion of the property at issue.

---

14 Moore v. Stills, 307 S.W.3d 71, 78 (Ky. 2010).

15 Est. of Welliver v. Alberts, 278 Ill. App. 3d 1028 (1996); Nome 2000 v. Fagerstrom, 799 P.2d 304 (Alaska 1990).

16 Hardt v. Eskam, 218 Neb. 81 (1984); Pierz v. Gorski 88 Wis. 2d 131 (Wis. App. 1979); Rowland v. McLain, 86 Ga. App. 140 (1952).

17 Brown v. Volkening, 64 N.Y. 76, 80 (1876).

18 *See, e.g.*, Rohrer v. Allen, 415 So. 2d 1054, 1058 (Ala. 1982) (dissenting opinion).

19 N.A.S. Holdings v. Pafundi, 169 Vt. 437, 441 (1999).

Chapter 7
Open and Notorious Possession

A critical element is that the claimant must have possessed the property in an open and notorious manner. I cannot help but get an earworm every time I hear the word "notorious." There was a Duran Duran song that used that word over and over and over again; it is even stuttered. If one practices in a state in which both "open" and "notorious" are elements, one may not need to worry about proving both. "Despite discrete meanings, Washington courts unify the two constructs of 'open' and 'notorious' as if the words are synonyms."[1] But a litigator must check the state's law to be sure.

Some of the critical issues to consider for this element are (1) what persons need to know that the claimant has openly used the property? the title owner? or the public?; and (2) whether the nature of the property affects what steps the claimant should have taken to prove his "open" use.

One court described this element as meaning the "claimant's claim of ownership is evidenced by such acts and conduct sufficient to put a man of ordinary prudence on notice of the fact that the land in question is held by the claimant as his own."[2]

New York courts indicated that what people actually think in the neighborhood is crucial. "Notorious possession" was described by a New York appellate court as "so conspicuous that it is generally known and talked of by the public or the people in the neighborhood. Possession or character of holding in its nature having such elements of notoriety that the owner may be presumed to have notice of it and of its extent."[3] If one believes the court will apply this standard, it may be helpful at trial for a party to bring in witnesses willing to explain who they thought the owner of the property was, and why. If that is the

1 LeBleu v. Aalgaard, 193 Wash. App. 66, 81 (Wash. Ct. App. 2016).

2 *Id.* at 80.

3 Seward Park Hous. Corp. v. Cohen, 287 A.D.2d 157, 164 (N.Y. App. Div. 2001) (citation omitted).

true definition, then if one lives in community in which people do not generally discuss who possesses what piece of property, then in theory one could claim the adverse possessor's use was not "notorious." If the people in the community have more interesting things to gossip about than landownership, then in theory the alleged adverse possessor could have trouble proving his case. The same could be said for a claimant who occupies property that is hidden from view, or far from neighbors.

Another court described this element as being demonstrated by "proof that the claimant's occupancy was conspicuous, widely recognized and commonly known."[4] The open and notorious element of adverse possession "is satisfied by visible acts of ownership exercised over the premises, such as maintaining and improving the property."[5]

Other courts define the term as concerning what the owner knows, or should have known. The Supreme Court of Montana held that the term "open and notorious use" is defined as "a distinct and positive assertion of a right hostile to the rights of the owner and brought to the attention of the owner."[6] If that is taken literally, all the record title owner need say, presumably, is that the assertions were not brought to his attention. But presumably, in many cases, the court will hold that constructive notice is good enough.

Judges can be confused by what "notorious" means. In one Illinois case, the defendants had claimed to have adversely possessed property in part by fencing in the property, and using it for 20 years. The trial judge concluded that they had not acquired the land by adverse possession, because defendants could not prove "that the true landowner knew of defendants' possession or had constructive knowledge of defendants' continued use of the land." The appellate court held that this was not the correct standard for "open and notorious." It cited Black's Law Dictionary, which defines "open and notorious" as "[a]cts on the land of another sufficient to alert the owner of a claim to his land which may ripen into title under adverse possession." The court held: "We find the correct test for open and notorious is whether the community in the vicinity of the land at issue is or could be apprised of defendants' possession and exclusive use and enjoyment." It concluded by ruling that the 20 years of fencing in property met that requirement.[7]

In case anyone still believed that defining "open and notorious" was a piece of cake, he should reconsider. In an Indiana case called

4 Williams v. Frymire, 186 S.W.3d 912, 920 (Mo. App. 2006) (internal citations and quotation marks omitted).
5 *Id.* (internal quotation marks omitted).
6 Amerimont, Inc. v. Gannett, 278 Mont. 314, 323 (1996).
7 Beverly Trust Co. v. Dekowski, 216 Ill. App. 3d 732, 739 (Ill. App. Ct. 1991).

Greene v. Jones,[8] the Joneses claimed to adversely possess a seven-foot strip of land that the records indicated were owned by their neighbors. The Joneses improved it, including by grading and planting grass and trees there. The trial court held that the Joneses had adversely possessed the property, and granted relief in their favor. But an appellate court disagreed because there was not enough of a delineation for people in the neighborhood to tell where the claimants believed the boundary line was. The court held that notorious means "[i]t must be so conspicuous that it is generally known and talked of by the public—at least by the people in the vicinity of the premises. It must be manifest to the community. In the course of twenty years a visible occupancy naturally ought to become notorious. It ought to be so well known and commonly understood that the people residing in the neighborhood could testify with substantial unanimity concerning its existence."[9]

However, there was a well-thought-out dissent, which has rationale useful to consider in arguing the other side. That judge indicated that the only relevant issue was that the Joneses' neighbors, who actually owned the property at issue, knew that the Joneses claimed that property for the statutory period. Being "notorious" to the community at large therefore was irrelevant, at least according to the dissenting judge. The dissent argued that possession does not need to be notorious when the owner has actual notice of the adverse claim. The dissenting judge went on to note that "[t]he majority of jurisdictions has consistently held that openness and notoriety are unnecessary if the owner has actual knowledge of the adverse claim."[10] But in Indiana, apparently, this belt and suspenders ruling is necessary. It is not enough just for the claimant to argue that the actual owner is aware of his use; the general public must be able to be aware as well.

In accordance with the dissenting judge from that case, there is indeed case law indicating that if the titled owner has "actual knowledge of the adverse possession" then the adverse possessor needs not prove open and notorious possession, because that knowledge is "equivalent to" open and notorious possession.[11] One might also consider that it would seem that the purpose of this element in an adverse possession case is not to ensure that neighbors reach any particular conclusion, but is instead to make sure the claimant would, at the very least, provide constructive notice to the title owner. One would arguably not even need to

8 490 N.E.2d 776 (Ind. Ct. App. 1986).
9 *Id.* at 778 (citation omitted).
10 *Id.* at 780.
11 United States *ex rel.* Zuni Tribe of New Mexico v. Platt, 730 F. Supp. 318, 322 (D. Ariz. 1990).

provide constructive notice to the title owner, if one had provided actual notice to the title owner. Therefore, if all else fails in terms of proof, an attorney representing the alleged adverse possessor, during depositions, should at least attempt to have the title owner admit that he was aware of what the adverse possessor was doing.

It is not enough to just analyze what was done on the land in question, to resolve whether there was open and notorious possession. One must also analyze what kind of land is in question. As one court held, meeting the element of open and notorious possession, like the other adverse possession elements, depends upon the particular land in question: "No particular act or series of acts is necessary to demonstrate an intention to claim ownership. No particular act or series of acts is necessary to demonstrate an intention to claim ownership. Such a purpose is sufficiently shown where one goes upon the land and uses it openly and notoriously, as owners of similar lands use their property, to the exclusion of the true owner."[12] "In determining what will amount to actual possession of land, considerable importance must be attached to its nature and to the uses to which it can be applied, or to which the claimant may choose to apply it."[13]

Case law helps to explain what "notorious" is and what it is not in this context. For example, in one Oregon case a party made a claim over a certain woods area. He put up signs on trees outside the portion he allegedly adversely possessed, but the evidence indicated those signs had not existed for years. And although the claimant allegedly put up barbed wire around the space he claimed, an objective witness alleged that there were only a few strands of barbed wire tacked to trees. The court held that "[i]n a wooded area these indistinct markings would not, without more, give notice of an adverse claim." Therefore, he lost the case in part on the lack of "notorious" possession.[14]

A somewhat opposite end of this issue concerns open and notorious use of land in a case where virtually no outsider even knew the land existed. In that case, the claimant sought a claim over nearly 15 acres of land in Delaware. He had simply discovered it magically while boating, like in a scene from an old Disney movie. The property was secluded: a wooded, marshy, landlocked parcel of land that was bounded on four sides that would make it difficult for anyone passing by to notice the claimant occupied it. The property was not enclosed by a fence, and no permanent structures were added. The claimant only installed a few "No Trespassing" signs, which apparently no outsider ever saw. But

12 Marvel, et al. v. Barley Mill Road Homes, Inc., 34 Del. Ch. 417, 422–23 (Del. Ch. 1954).
13 Taylor v. Johnston, 289 N.C. 690, 711 (1976) (citation omitted).
14 Wales v. Lester, 267 Or. 379, 382 (1973).

because of the nature of the land, and the fact that the claimant had visited the property many times, much more so than neighbors visited their own land, and that he hunted the land, made trails, fished, and camped there, this was enough for a valid adverse possession claim. "Given the nature of the Property as a wild, secluded piece of land, it is difficult to imagine more suitable—and feasible—usages."[15] It makes one think of the tree falling when no one is around to hear it—does it really make a sound? Except here, if someone adversely possesses property and there is no one who might conceivably be given the chance to find out, is it really adversely possessed? In this particular case, the answer is "yes."

15 Tumulty v. Schreppler, 132 A.3d 4, 29 (Del. Ch. 2015).

Chapter 8
Continuous Possession

"Continuous" would seem to be the easiest element to understand. But there are always unresolved issues even for apparently simple words.

The term "continuous" in this context means stretching on without break or interruption.[1] "The law does not require the possession to be evidenced by persons constantly from day to day performing acts of ownership. It is sufficient if the land is used continuously for the purposes to which it may be naturally adapted."[2]

New York has a helpful explanation of the concept: "[T]he requirement of continuous possession is satisfied when the adverse claimant's acts of possessing the property, including periods during which the claimant exercises dominion and control over the premises or is physically present on the land, are consistent with acts of possession that ordinary owners of like properties would undertake. In other words, the character of disputed property is crucial in determining what degree of control and what character of possession is required to establish adverse possession."[3] (As indicated throughout this book, the character of the land may be a critical issue for other elements of adverse possession too.)

One Missouri judge made a joke[4] when explaining the law: "[One] required element of adverse possession is that such possession must be 'continuous for a period of ten years.' 'Continuous' means without lapse, uninterrupted, for the entire statutory period. Ten years means ten years."[5]

At least one state has implied that this is not really a separate category from "actual possession" and that all one need to do to prove "actual" and/or "continuous" possession is to show "the use to which the land

1 Nye v. Fire Grp. P'ship, 265 Neb. 438, 443 (2003).
2 *Id.* (citation omitted).
3 Ray v. Beacon Hudson Mountain Corp., 88 N.Y.2d 154, 159–60 (1996) (internal brackets, citations, and quotation marks omitted.)
4 Or at least as close to a joke as you might find in case law.
5 Flowers v. Roberts, 979 S.W.2d 465, 470 (Mo. Ct. App. 1998).

has been put is similar to that which would ordinarily be made of like land by the owners thereof."[6]

Since "continuous" is generally an element for an adverse possession case, one needs to really understand its meaning. Two cases from the same state help to clarify the word. In one case, *Hardt v. Eskam*,[7] there was a claim of adverse possession to certain river land, which was suitable for hunting, fishing, and livestock pasture year-round. The adverse possession claim was based on use of the property for intermittent cattle grazing and limited seasonal hunting. The Nebraska Supreme Court reversed the trial court, which had ruled in favor of the plaintiff adverse possessor claimants. In doing so, the Supreme Court stated that, generally, seasonal and recreational use is merely occasional use—and not continuous use. Therefore, under that theory, at least in that context, even if a claimant uses property for decades, but during each year for only short periods of time, this cannot ripen into title for the real estate.

Less than 20 years later, the same court gave further direction on the issue in *Nye v. Fire Group Partnership*.[8] In that case, the disputed property was suited for either residential or agricultural uses. The adverse claimant plaintiffs had planted and maintained grass during warm weather, and erected a snow fence in the winter. But for obvious reasons, the snow fence did not remain erect year-round, and the grass was not mowed year-round. The trial court had granted summary judgment in favor of the defendant title owners, but the Nebraska Supreme Court reversed, finding material issues of fact about whether the plaintiffs' use of the property met the elements of adverse possession. With respect to the element of continuous use, the Supreme Court determined that the plaintiffs' use was consistent with residential use year-round. Unlike the intermittent use of the property in *Hardt* for a few weeks or months each year, the use in *Nye* "left the property in a continuous state of use for purposes of determining adverse possession."[9] Accordingly, the Nebraska Supreme Court concluded that there was an issue of fact whether the plaintiffs' use of the property was continuous.

Some states require "uninterrupted" use, which seems to either be a synonym, or a close synonym, to "continuous." In West Virginia, both are required. The term "continuous possession" means that an adverse possession has not been abandoned by the claimant during the period;

6 Anthony v. Searle, 681 A.2d 892, 897 (R.I. 1996) (citation omitted).
7 218 Neb. 81 (1984).
8 265 Neb. 438 (2003).
9 *Id.* at 444.

"uninterrupted possession" means that no other party, unrelated to the party claiming adverse possession, has broken the chain of possession.[10]

A seasonal break alone may not be the tipping factor. "Continuous use or possession . . . may be established notwithstanding seasonal breaks from the use of the property . . . . Continuity may be maintained by intermittent or seasonal use of land which is primarily or obviously adapted to such use . . . . It is enough that the land be devoted to the ordinary uses of the adverse claimant provided they are such as to put the true proprietor on notice."[11]

In Vermont, for example, using property only at certain times of the year for certain activities and not using it for the rest of the year can constitute sufficiently continuous use for adverse possession.[12] The same state indicated in another case that "[t]he kind and frequency of acts of occupancy depend on the condition of the property, the uses to which it is adapted, and the intentions of the claimant . . . . Whether the amount of time between acts of occupancy interrupts the running of the period depends on circumstances and intention of occupier."[13]

In another case, alleged adverse possessors of a certain strip of contested land tried to argue that they held barbecue events, softball, and volleyball games as regular activities there. The Mississippi court held that this was not enough, citing the law that "[m]ere sporadic, noncontinuous use is insufficient to establish continuous and uninterrupted possession."[14]

In one Minnesota case, the adverse possessors, who won the case, claimed to have "continuously" possessed wooded property by doing such things as erecting a fence, installing a septic system running under the dog-pen area, and replanting shrubs and bulbs in the area near their home. The losing side claimed on appeal that "'occasional plantings in the woods, spring clean up, [sic] pulling down vines, and trimming branches on a few occasions over many years' is too irregular to be considered continuous."[15] The appellate court affirmed, holding that "[a] bright-line test for how much activity constitutes continuous

10 State v. Davis, 140 W. Va. 153, 174 (1954).

11 Larson v. Tonneson, 933 N.W.2d 84, 95 (N.D. 2019) (citations and internal brackets omitted).

12 Thibault v. Vartuli, 143 Vt. 178, 181 (1983) (using island only in summer for recreational activities); Montgomery v. Branon, 129 Vt. 379, 386 (1971) (using hunting camp only during season); Amey v. Hall, 123 Vt. 62, 67–68 (1962) (using logging camp only during cutting times).

13 N.A.S. Holdings v. Pafundi, 169 Vt. 437, 443 (1999).

14 Winters v. Billings, 281 So. 3d 75, 82 (Miss. Ct. App. 2019) (citation and internal quotation marks omitted).

15 *In re* Application of Ganje, 659 N.W.2d 261, 268 (Minn. Ct. App. 2003).

possession of a property for adverse-possession purposes does not exist. Instead, the rule of thumb used is that the disseizor must be using the property as his or her own, i.e., regularly and matched to the land's intended use. Under this standard, [the adverse possessors'] more sporadic use of the wooded area, as compared to the area near their house, is reasonable."[16] The court also pointed out that the adverse possessors apparently used the wooded areas in the disputed property similarly to the way they treated the wooded portions on their "true" own property.[17]

There are many other cases concerning these issues. For example, in a Wisconsin case, *Kraus v. Mueller*,[18] the continuous occupancy of a hunting shack during hunting season was sufficient for an adverse possession claim. In another, a Washington state case called *Booten v. Peterson*,[19] weekend summer use of a beach place was held sufficient to establish peaceable adverse possession to an adjacent parcel of real property used for a recreation center and camping. In a Michigan case called *Nechtow v. Brown*,[20] the use of property for a summer home for recreational purposes was sufficient adverse possession; in the Massachusetts case *Mahoney v. Heebner*,[21] seasonal physical absence from a summer residence did not break the chain of continuous peaceable possession for the purpose of establishing adverse use.

Grazing also comes up periodically in the world of adverse possession. Case law indicates that there is "continuous" use if the land for grazing is occupied and used in the manner during the full period of the growing season.[22]

---

16 *Id.*

17 *Id.*

18 12 Wis. 2d 430, 107 N.W.2d 467, 472 (1961).

19 47 Wash. 2d 565 (1955) *overruled on other grounds by* Chaplin v. Sanders, 100 Wash. 2d 853, 676 P.2d 431, 436 n.2 (1984).

20 369 Mich. 460 (1963).

21 343 Mass. 770 (1961).

22 Shores v. Lindsey, 591 P.2d 895, 900 (Wyo. 1979); Lantry v. Parker, 37 Neb. 353 (1893); Springer v. Durette, 217 Or. 196, 342 P.2d 132, 134 (1959); Adams v. Lamicq, 118 Utah 209 (1950); Niles v. Churchill, 29 Colo. App. 283 (1971).

Chapter 9
Adversely Holding the Property for the Required Time Period

Geçmiş olsun. It's Turkish. It means, "May it pass quickly."
—*Midnight Express*, Oliver Stone

One of the many non-universal aspects of adverse possession law is a critical one. How long does it take before an adverse possessor can claim ownership? Every state has its own policy. But not only does every state have its own policy, but even within states there are often varying rules, depending on whether the claimant has paid taxes, has a deed in his favor, what kind of property is at stake, whether it is cultivated, and even the size of the property.

A New Jersey court provided an interesting background into the history of limitation periods in British adverse possession cases: "Before 1237 claimants had been required to prove seisin [possession] on the day in 1135 when King Henry I died; then they were restricted to the day in 1154 when Henry II was crowned; in 1275 the boundary was moved forward to the coronation of Richard I in 1189 and there it remained for many years. Indeed, the length of the period progressively enlarged until in 1541 a claimant might be obliged to establish an adverse holding for over 300 years in order conclusively to sustain his title."[1] This is no longer the law, obviously. Now we have a policy of setting a standard specific number of years a claimant must have occupied the space.

One might believe that of all the issues in adverse possession cases, this issue would be the easiest to grasp, without even needing to review case law. That assumption is incorrect. For example, in *J M Land Co. v. First Union National Bank*,[2] the New Jersey Supreme Court analyzed four different statutes that apply to claims of adverse possession. Two were for 20-year periods, one concerned a 30-year period, and another

1 Predham v. Holfester, 32 N.J. Super. 419, 422 (App. Div. 1954).
2 166 N.J. 493, 500 (2001).

was for a 60-year period. Until that decision was issued, many lower courts had believed that 20 years was sufficient. But its Supreme Court held that it was not. After an extensive review of historical precedents, including colonial statutes, the court determined that the 20-year statutes of limitations applied to a deadline to seek ejectment, but that those ejectment statutes had been superseded and were no longer in effect. In New Jersey, if the tract of land is cultivated, there is a 30-year period for perfection of claims to adverse possession, and if it is uncultivated, there is a 60-year period of time.[3]

Another example of how one can misunderstand a statute arose in Arizona. In that state, there are various statutes defining the relevant time periods. One statute indicates, in pertinent part: "When a party in possession claims real property by right of possession only, actions to recover possession from him shall be commenced within two years after the cause of action accrues" by a "plaintiff who shows no better right."[4] An internet search reveals that some people list "two years" as the shortest time period by which a party can claim adverse possession. But case law indicates that this is a "sparsely-used" statute because of that limiting language.[5]

Other matters to investigate include the quality of title. For example, Colorado Revised Statute section 38-41-108 provides a shortened time period of possession if the claim is based on color of title: seven instead of the 18 years prescribed by section 38-41-101. Some other states also distinguish the statute of limitations between adverse possessors who pay taxes and/or have some sort of written instrument, on the one hand, from those that do not, on the other.

Every state seems to have its own rules. For example, in Pennsylvania, one statute[6] indicates that the period of 21 years is reduced to ten years if the adverse possessor files an action seeking relief and files and serves appropriate notices ahead of time.

One always has to check not only the statute and common law on adverse possession, but also must check the particular circumstances, such as whether the adverse possessor is coterminous, meaning he is seeking relief from his neighbor. This can affect not only what elements must be proven, but also can affect what period of time is at issue. For example, in Alabama, "there are basically two types of adverse

---

3 N.J. Stat. Ann. § 2A:14-30 & 31.

4 Ariz. Rev. Stat. § 12-522.

5 Chabrowski v. Bank of Am., No. CV-17–08111-PCT-JAT, at *10 n.5 (D. Ariz. Aug. 28, 2018).

6 42 Pa. Cons. Stat. § 5527.1.

possession; statutory adverse possession, and adverse possession by prescription." The

> statutory version, which requires possession for only ten years rather than the twenty years required by the prescription version, also requires that the possessor hold under color of title, have paid taxes on the property for ten years, or have derived his title by descent or devise. However, in cases . . . where adverse possession is claimed by a conterminous owner [an owner who shares boundaries], the three latter requirements do not apply. Thus, a conterminous landowner . . . must prove open, notorious, hostile, continuous, and exclusive possession for only ten years. He need not prove either a deed or color of title to the property, annual listings for taxation, or descent or devise from a predecessor in order to maintain his claim.[7]

Texas has various kinds of distinguishments. For example, the default period is ten years, meaning the true owner must seek to eject the adverse possessor within ten years of his possession.[8] But that statute does not apply to an adverse possessor who has no title instrument, to the degree that he occupies more than 160 acres, unless those acres are "actually enclosed."[9] There are further exceptions. There is a three-year time period needed if the adverse possessor has color of title.[10] There is a five-year period if the adverse possessor cultivates, uses or enjoys the land, pays applicable property taxes, and has a "duly registered deed."[11] (One wonders why property under a duly registered deed should have a five-year time period, but a mere color of title would have a three-year time period.) There is also a special statute if the record owner has a disability: the statute indicates such a person "regardless of whether the person is or has been under a legal disability, must bring suit not later than 25 years after the day the cause of action accrues to recover real property held in peaceable and adverse possession by another who cultivates, uses, or enjoys the property."[12]

---

7 Tidwell v. Strickler, 457 So. 2d 365, 368 (Ala. 1984) (citations omitted).
8 Tex. Civ. Prac. & Rem. Code § 16.026.
9 Arizona has a similar rule. Ariz. Rev. Stat. § 12-526.
10 Tex. Civ. Prac. & Rem. Code § 16.024.
11 *Id.* § 16.025.
12 *Id.* § 16.027.

Part 3

Other Potential Elements

Chapter 10
Peaceful Occupancy

Dr. Leo Marvin: "I want some peace and quiet!"
Bob Wiley: "Well, I'll be quiet."
Siggy: "I'll be peace!"[1]

—*What About Bob?*, Tom Schulman

I only talk about peace.

—Malala Yousufzai at the 2023 Academy Awards ceremony

In certain states, one of the elements for a successful adverse possession case is that the possession must be "peaceful." One Mississippi court defined "peaceful" with tautology: that it is "marked by, conducive to, or enjoying peace, quiet, or calm."[2]

Mississippi makes this a requirement for an adverse possession claimant.[3] Rhode Island does as well: "The possession of the property must be uninterrupted and peaceful during [the statutory] period, and under a claim of right."[4]

In Georgia, pursuant to statute, a party may establish title by adverse possession where the possession, is, among other things, "peaceable."[5]

---

1 Siggy was played by the child actor Charlie Korsmo, who 15 years later got a JD from Yale Law School, and is now a professor of corporate law and corporate finance at the Case Western Reserve University School of Law. For those who love the "Six Degrees" game, I went to film school with Harry Elfont, who achieved the dream and became a director; Harry Elfont directed pre-Professor Korsmo in *Can't Hardly Wait*, Korsmo was in *Dick Tracy* with Dustin Hoffman, and Dustin Hoffman was in *Sleepers* with Kevin Bacon.

2 *See* Biddix v. McConnell, 911 So. 2d 468, 477 (Miss. 2005) (citation omitted).

3 Rice v. Pritchard, 611 So. 2d 869, 871 (Miss. 1993); Winters v. Billings, 281 So. 3d 75, 80 (Miss. Ct. App. 2019).

4 Taffinder v. Thomas, 119 R.I. 545, 549 (1977).

5 Ga. Code Ann. § 44-5-161(a).

New Jersey's relevant statute indicates that to make a claim of title which is under dispute, one must be in "peaceable possession" of the land.[6]

Texas also requires proof that the possession is "peaceable" for the duration of the statutory period.[7] Texas has legislatively defined the term. "'Peaceable possession' means possession of real property that is continuous and is not interrupted by an adverse suit to recover the property."[8] By that standard, the title owner could constantly threaten to file suit, and yell on a bullhorn 24 hours a day that the claimant had improperly taken the title owner's property, but the claimant's occupancy would still be "peaceful." Technically, even having the title owner grab a bat and knock people out of his property might still mean there is "peaceable possession," but if a title owner did that, he might eliminate a different element of adverse possession.

In one case, a Mississippi court seemed to believe "peace" meant the absence of a dispute: "When the record reflects no dispute over the subject property, there is sufficient evidence to support the chancellor's determination of possession peaceful. In this case, there was no testimony in the record of any dispute over the subject property during the relevant period of claimed adverse possession, and we find sufficient evidence to support a finding of peaceful use."[9]

To clarify, "peaceful" in the context of adverse possession cases may not really mean "peaceful." Peaceful also may not mean there was never any dispute at all, because "[s]imple disputes often arise between neighboring landowners, but do not rise to the level of destroying the peaceful existence between them."[10]

On the other hand, in certain states, certain steps one can take, other than filing a suit, can reach the breach of peace level. In one case, the uncontested proof was that one neighbor called 911 when a car was over the property line, after which an officer arrived at the property. This invocation of legal authority was deemed to disrupt peace.[11] That court cited a case[12] in which a property owner battling a golf course was "picking up the out-of-bounds markers and throwing them back onto the course and also painting over the white lines put on his property by the golf course with green spray paint." There was no "peace" in that case either.

6 N.J. Stat. Ann. § 2A:62-1.
7 *See* Glover v. U. Pacific R, 187 S.W.3d 201, 213 (Tex. App. 2006).
8 Tex. Civ. Prac. & Rem. Code § 16.021(3).
9 Anderson v. O'Neal, 338 So. 3d 629, 645 (Miss. Ct. App. 2022) (citation omitted).
10 Hill v. Johnson, 27 So. 3d 426, 432 (¶ 29) (Miss. Ct. App. 2009) (citation omitted).
11 Edwards v. Williams, 292 So. 3d 586, 593 n.4 (Miss. Ct. App. 2019).
12 Biddix v. McConnell, 911 So. 2d 468, 477 (Miss. 2005).

Other states do not concentrate much on defining "peace." One example is a Georgia Supreme Court case from 1978.[13] In that case, in 1937, when a house was built upon lot 75 and a survey made, the claimants learned for the first time that their driveway encroached onto their neighbor's land. The title owner of lot 75 demanded payment for the land and threatened suit, but the claimants refused to pay, and essentially called the title owner's bluff. The title owner lost the game of chicken, and did not carry out his threat. Eventually the claimants filed their own case, because they needed marketable title to the encroaching portion of the driveway. The majority implied that "peace" had been proven, but the dissent argued that "[t]he evidence shows that the possession was not peaceable since suit was threatened soon after the error was discovered . . . ."[14] Therefore if a litigator represents a title owner, the title owner should be told that once one makes a threat of a suit, one has to carry it out. Otherwise, peace is deemed to reign again.

An attorney who believes that "peace" is a requirement for his state must carefully check all related laws. For example, in New Jersey, the peaceful occupation element is not a requirement in the context of an adverse possession claimant who is paying real estate taxes on it.[15] Real estate tax obligations are discussed further in Chapter 13.

13 Brown v. Wilson, 240 Ga. 856 (1978).
14 *Id.* at 857–58.
15 N.J. Stat. Ann. § 2A:62-1.

Chapter 11
Cultivation, Improvement, Substantial Enclosures, Ouster, and Other Odds and Ends

In some states, merely claiming "possession" is not enough. There are some specific statutes or case law defining what is necessary for "possession." And these rules can also differ within a state, depending on whether the claimant is using the claim of right method, which is not based on a written instrument, or the color of title method, which relies on a written instrument.

In New York, as one example, the statute RPAPL 512 describes how to prove possession based on the color of title method, meaning a document or judgment appears to give the claimant title. In such a case, the claimant has three choices: (1) to prove there have been "acts sufficiently open to put a reasonably diligent owner on notice," (2) to prove the area "has been protected by a substantial enclosure," or (3) "it has been used for the supply of fuel or of fencing timber, either for the purposes of husbandry or for the ordinary use of the occupant." Conversely, if the adverse possession claim is based on a claim of right, then possession must be proven under RPAPL 522. Either of the first two options are sufficient under that statute, but using it for the supply of fuel or fencing timber would not be.

There is also a statutory exception in that state concerning acts across a boundary line. In New York one has to consult RPAPL 543, which indicates in part that "[n]otwithstanding any other provision of this article, the existence of de minimus [sic] non-structural encroachments including, but not limited to, fences, hedges, shrubbery, plantings, sheds and non-structural walls, shall be deemed to be permissive and non-adverse." Some of these issues are addressed in Chapter 35.

Prior to 2008, New York also used "cultivation" or "improvement" of property as being a basis for possession. That is no longer the case, although the old law still applied to claimants seeking rights for their actions prior to 2008.

Many other states have statutes that indicate that New York's old method was proper. In many states, one must also prove (for example) that there was a "substantial inclosure" or that the claimant cultivated or improved it, in many contexts. This is true in South Dakota,[1] Wisconsin,[2] North Dakota,[3] Idaho,[4] California,[5] Nevada,[6] Montana,[7] and Florida.[8] ("Inclosure" is often used as the statutory form of the word "enclosure." I use the words interchangeably here.)

Those kinds of laws could provide a difficult situation for an adverse possessor who lived in a house, if he did little of relevance with the land, and did not place any kind of enclosure around it. In theory, the adverse possessor could claim that the building itself was an enclosure, or could hope that repairs he had made to the house over the years count as "cultivation." Otherwise, someone who walks into a home and just claims "This is mine," may be out of luck in such a state, even if he lives there peacefully for 100 years.

At least one state, Georgia, does not necessarily require this kind of additional element, but considers it to be just one way of proving actual possession: its relevant statute[9] provides that "[a]ctual possession of lands may be evidenced by enclosure, cultivation, or any use and occupation of the lands which is so notorious as to attract the attention of every adverse claimant and so exclusive as to prevent actual occupation by another."

If a substantial enclosure is needed, one should try to find out what that truly means. The Wisconsin Supreme Court explained that "[a]n inclosure having no purpose of physical exclusion of outside interferences" would still be sufficient.[10] In other words—so long as it shows where the boundary is, it does not actually have to keep people out. The Supreme Court of South Dakota held that planting and maintaining a line of trees on disputed property is deemed a substantial enclosure.[11] On the other hand, in a Pennsylvania case, the court held that when "land had been partially enclosed by a single strand of wire which had broken and fallen to the ground in several places," then this was "insufficient to show an inclosure of a substantial character."[12]

1 S.D. Codified Laws §§ 15-3-11 & 15-3-13.
2 Wis. Stat. §§ 893.25 & 893.26.
3 N.D. Cent. Code § 28-01-11.
4 Idaho Code § 5-210.
5 Cal. Civ. Proc. Code § 325.
6 Nev. Rev. Stat. § 11.140.
7 Mont. Code Ann. § 70-19-410.
8 Fla. Stat. Ann. § 95.18.
9 Ga. Code Ann. § 44-5-165.
10 Illinois Steel Co. v. Bilot, 109 Wis. 418, 446, 85 N.W. 402, 408 (1901).
11 *See* Lewis v. Aslesen, 2001 S.D. 131 (2001).
12 Niles v. Fall Creek Hunting Club, Inc., 376 Pa. Super. 260, 267 (Pa. Super. Ct. 1988).

In one Wisconsin case, the titled owners tried to define terms narrowly, to avoid a valid adverse possession claim. They claimed the element of "cultivation" meant the raising of crops, and claimed "improvement" meant the erection of permanent structures or a garden. The court disagreed, and held "cultivation and improvement" should be defined broadly as putting the land "to the exclusive use of the occupant as the true owner might use such land in the usual course of events." Since the claimants alleged that they had conducted "plant-related activities," the court held that this could "constitute a usual and exclusive use of residential land."[13]

Another Wisconsin case, from its high court, addressed similar issues. It defined "usually improved" as "ordinary use to which the land is capable and such as an owner would make it," but that such use must also be sufficiently visible to give notice of exclusion to the true owner.[14] In that case, the adverse possessors built a cottage, put in a septic tank, cut out and burned the dead trees and brush, and dug out and burned the stumps. They spaded the entire area and planted blue grass. This activity, the court held, was planting a "flag of hostility." While not "every square foot" of the land was used, the court held that it was clear that the land as a whole was visibly changed by the adverse possessor from wild lands to a house and yard.

In Connecticut, one of the elements of an adverse possession case is ouster of possession.[15] In Chapter 24, this book discusses the ouster element in the context of co-owners, but in Connecticut, it is an element in every adverse possession case. In that state, ouster has a particular meaning. "By ouster is not meant a physical eviction, but a possession attended with such circumstances as to evince a claim of exclusive right and title, and a denial of the right of the other tenants to participate in the profits . . . . An entry upon the land of another, is an ouster of the legal possession arising from the title, if made under claim and color of right, otherwise it is a mere trespass. The intention guides the entry, and fixes its character."[16]

---

13 Stahlnecker v. Vieth, 2023 WI App 6, 985 N.W.2d 457 (Wis. Ct. App. Dec. 22, 2022 (citation omitted).

14 Burkhardt v. Smith, 17 Wis. 2d 132, 139, 115 N.W.2d 540, 544 (1962).

15 Roberson v. Aubin, 120 Conn. App. 72, 74 (2010).

16 Lucas v. Crofoot, 95 Conn. 619, 623–24 (1921) (internal quotation marks and ellipses omitted).

Chapter 12
Tacking

In certain circumstances, a party who has adversely possessed real property for less than the statutory time period may satisfy that period by "tacking" his possession to that of a prior adverse possessor. As a South Carolina Supreme Court case noted, "Tacking is the legal principle whereby successive adverse users in privity with prior adverse users can tack successive adverse possessions of land so as to aggregate the prescriptive period . . . ."[1] Tacking has also been defined as "successive, uninterrupted possessions by persons between whom privity exists. If such tacked possessions constitute one continuous adverse possession for the statutory period it will be sufficient."[2] If there are multiple successive adverse possessions for the required time period, there will need to be an unbroken chain between all of them, for that time period.

A practical description of tacking was given in the Nebraska case *Kelley v. Long*.[3] The court in that case indicated that "[t]o permit tacking of successive adverse possession of grantees of an area not within the calls of a deed . . . but contiguous thereto, among the ultimate facts to be established is the intended and actual transfer and delivery of such area to the grantees as successors in ownership, possession and claim. Privity means privity of possession. It is the transfer of possession, not title, which is the essential element."[4]

To put it another way, the "determinative question" for tacking "is whether there is evidence that the [original possessor] intended to transfer any rights in the disputed property that they may have acquired by adverse possession."[5]

An adverse claimant must therefore either produce evidence of this intent, or try to claim that the property is presumed to have been

1 Dickinson v. Pake, 284 N.C. 576, 585 (1974) (citation omitted).
2 Sears v. Catholic Archdiocese of Washington, 5 A.3d 653, 662 (D.C. 2010) (citation, italics, and internal quotation marks omitted).
3 3 Neb. App. 467, 473 (1995) (citation omitted).
4 *Id.* (citation omitted).
5 Timber Serv. Co. v. Ellis, 163 Or. App. 349, 354 (1999).

successively conveyed. In one Alabama Supreme Court case, the court held that the presumption in favor of the adverse possession claimant applied: "For the purpose of effecting title by adverse possession, where all the traditional elements are present, tacking of periods of possession by successive possessors is permitted against the coterminous owner [meaning a title owner sharing the boundaries with the claimant] seeking to defeat such title, unless there is a finding, supported by the evidence, that the claimant's predecessor in title did not intend to convey the disputed strip."[6]

Courts in many states, if not the majority of states, allow tacking when a grantor adversely possessing property beyond the bounds of a parcel he owns by deed, conveys the parcel to a grantee who continues adversely possessing the same additional property.[7] The Supreme Court of Arizona held that "any conveyance, agreement, or understanding which will refer the several adverse possessions to the original entry and which is accompanied by a transfer of possession will create such a privity as to permit a tacking. The ordinary solemnities for the transfer of land are not required; no written instrument is necessary, a parol transfer will suffice."[8]

A recent District of Columbia case[9] has good guidance for understanding tacking. It involved a church that was the record title holder of a driveway, and its new neighbors only had a recorded easement to use that driveway. But a previous neighbor to the church had allegedly adversely possessed the driveway, including putting a fence around it and not allowing the church to use it. When the previous neighbor transferred title to the new neighbors, the recorded deed did not indicate that the driveway was being transferred; it only indicated that a right to use it as an easement was being transferred. Finally, the new neighbors claimed adverse possession to that driveway in part due to the alleged tacking.

The lower court in the District of Columbia dismissed that claim, finding that since the recorded deed did not specifically indicate that the

---

6 Watson v. Price, 356 So. 2d 625, 627 (Ala. 1978).

7 *See, e.g.*, Bryan v. Reifschneider, 181 Neb. 787, 792, 150 N.W.2d 900, 904 (1967) ("It is the generally accepted rule . . . [that] the taking of possession of contiguous lands, some of which are not within the calls of the deed, which have been used by the grantor as a unit . . . , and the transfer of possession pursuant to a deed or contract has evidentiary value as to the existence of privity."); *see also* James A. Webster, Jr., Webster's Real Estate Law in North Carolina § 14.09 at 14–18 (Patrick K. Hetrick et al. eds., 6th ed. 2017) ("The general rule is that tacking is allowed in such a fact situation."). These cases and secondary source were cited with disapproval in Cole v. Bonaparte's Retreat Prop. Owners' Ass'n, Inc., 259 N.C. App. 27, 34–35 (2018).

8 Santos v. Simon, 60 Ariz. 426, 428 (1943), citing 2 C.J.S., Adverse Possession § 131, at 694.

9 Gan v. Van Buren St. Methodist Church, 224 A.3d 1205 (D.C. 2020).

new neighbors were being transferred that driveway, then they could not claim rights to it. The Court of Appeals of the District of Columbia, which is its highest court, reversed. It held that that it had previously ruled tacking is proper where "(1) there was continuous adverse possession of the disputed property by two successive occupants who owned an adjacent property, and (2) the first occupant sold the adjacent property to the second occupant."[10] It held (as indicated above) that this is the majority view across the United States: it is irrelevant for tacking purposes if the deed does not expressly indicate the piece of property at issue is being transferred.

The court went on to note that a number of states allow "tacking in the absence of express conveyance [but that they] carve out an exception to that general rule where (a) the deed at issue expressly excludes the disputed parcel or (b) the seller did not intend to turn over possession of the disputed parcel to the buyer."[11] It held that its own rule somewhat followed that one. Its rule was that "a period of adverse possession by a prior owner may not be tacked if (1) the prior owner expressly disavows transfer of an interest in the disputed property to the subsequent owner, or (2) the party claiming adverse possession fails to show by clear and convincing evidence that the prior owner intended to turn over to the subsequent owner possession of the property in dispute."[12] Since, in that case, the deed indicated that the driveway was an easement, but did not expressly exclude the driveway as being transferred to the claimant, then the claimant still had a chance of success.

The dissent saw the law differently. It cited a number of cases from the United States indicating what some call the "minority view." It stated that "[p]ossession generally cannot be tacked to make out title by adverse possession where the deed by which the last occupant claims title does not include the land in dispute."[13] It indicated that there were only a few exceptions to that rule, including when "the disputed parcel was inadvertently omitted from the deed and there is a subsequent deed correcting the oversight."[14] The dissent indicated that "[i]n cases where, as here, there is a conveyance by deed and the deed refers to the disputed parcel, the deed is the touchstone with respect to that parcel and we should resist going beyond the deed to permit a broad-ranging review of extraneous evidence of the grantor's subjective intent as the majority proposes."[15] The dissent also indicated that the court's deci-

10 *Id.* at 1208.
11 *Id.* at 1210.
12 *Id.* at 1211.
13 *Id.* at 1214–15.
14 *Id.* at 1215.
15 *Id.* at 1219.

sion was problematic from a policy perspective because rules about transferring a "right to ownership by adverse possession should be in harmony with and not undermine the important purposes underlying the requirement of recordation of deeds: notice, stability, clarity, and certainty."[16]

As the dissenting judge properly pointed out, there are a number of states that follow what seems to be known as the "minority view" concerning tacking. For example, the North Carolina Supreme Court has repeatedly departed from the majority rule. In one case it decided, *Ramsey v. Ramsey*,[17] the plaintiff brought an ejectment action against the defendant, an adjacent landowner, over the defendant's use of a spring located on the plaintiff's property. The defendant and his predecessors in title had used and maintained the spring for more than 50 years, and the defendant raised adverse possession as a defense to the ejectment claim. The defendant had adversely possessed the spring for only 17 years at the time of the action, but argued that his adverse possession should be tacked to his predecessor in title in order to satisfy the requisite 20-year statutory period. In determining whether the defendant and his immediate predecessor had the necessary privity to allow tacking, the North Carolina Supreme Court reviewed what property was actually conveyed to the defendant as set forth in the deed. Since the deed did not indicate that the predecessor conveyed the spring or the tract of land on which it was located, the defendant's claim failed. In short, in North Carolina, privity through a deed does not extend beyond the property described in that deed. There are other states which may follow this minority rule as well, such as California, Maryland, Michigan, Wyoming, and Pennsylvania.[18]

Michigan has perhaps a slightly different rule from the majority. One of its courts has held that privity of estate "may be shown in one of two ways, by (1) including a description of the disputed acreage in the deed, or (2) an actual transfer or conveyance of possession of the disputed acreage by parol statements made at the time of conveyance."[19]

Another issue for tacking is how the final claimant of the adversely possessed property obtained his rights. If he obtained it by deed or by descent, that may be sufficient. But if it is just a matter of that various

16 *Id.* at 1219–20.

17 229 N.C. 270 (1948).

18 *See* Gan v. Van Buren St. Methodist Church, 224 A.3d 1205, 1215 (D.C. 2020) (dissenting opinion), citing Messer v. Hibernia Sav. & Loan Soc'y, 149 Cal. 122 (1906); Senez v. Collins, 182 Md. App. 300 (2008); Sheldon v. Michigan Cent. R. Co., 161 Mich. 503, 126 N.W. 1056, 1059 (1910); Baylor v. Soska, 540 Pa. 435 (1995); Tissino v. Mavrakis, 67 Wyo. 560 (1951).

19 Killips v. Mannisto, 244 Mich. App. 256, 259 (2001) (citations omitted).

different persons entered on the land in succession without privity of estate, then tacking is unlikely to work.[20]

One relevant case from Alabama entitled *Bean v. Mitchell*[21] concerned tacking rights, originating from a person whose name sounds like it comes out of a farmer's daughter joke. In that case, there were two neighboring landowners, each of which owned property. The claimants alleged that they had also adversely possessed an additional eight-acre parcel of land, which their neighbor actually had record title to. The court noted that the adverse possession claimant's predecessor in title, Viron Turnipseed, had purchased the property at issue, including what he had believed included the eight acres, which were surrounded by a fence. Turnipseed continued in possession of lands up to that fence, claiming it was the boundary line, until his death in 1951. The claimant had been in possession since his death, claiming title up to the fence. The judge worked overtime on that case; he actually went to the property at issue, and saw with his own eyes that the fence claimed by the adverse possessors to be the boundary, had been in that location for more than 20 years as evidenced by the fact that trees along that fence had grown around the wire and in some instances the wire was embedded up to six inches in some trees.

The title holders of those eight acres, however, argued that when Turnipseed's widow conveyed the real property to the adverse possession claimants, in 1964, the conveyance did not include the legal description of the disputed property. According to the title holders, this meant the claimants could not avail themselves of the tacking doctrine. However, the court held that in the context of a coterminous owner, that is, a neighboring owner, tacking would apply unless there was specific evidence "that the claimant's predecessor in title did not intend to convey the disputed strip."[22] Therefore, the court upheld the ruling in favor of the adverse possessors.

In reaching this conclusion, the court cited a previous Alabama case, which indicated rationales for that kind of ruling, including that if cases such as this were handled in any other way, "the number of small, landlocked parcels of land throughout the state—the title to which in most cases would be impossible to trace—would stagger the imagination."[23]

This kind of language would seem to be very positive for adverse possessor claimants who wished to take advantage of tacking, even if the deed did not describe the property at issue. However, there may

20 *See* Gore v. Hall, 206 Md. 485, 112 A.2d 675, 678 (1955).
21 372 So. 2d 14 (Ala. 1979).
22 *Id.* at 16 (citation omitted).
23 Watson v. Price, 356 So. 2d 625, 627–28 (Ala. 1978).

be a way around it for the title holder. The title holder may claim that "the deed of conveyance expressly excludes conveyance of the disputed parcel." If that argument works, then the alleged adverse possessor will not be able to claim tacking applies.[24]

West Virginia's high court decided the case *Brown v. Gobble*,[25] revealing critical issues about tacking, and also revealing that some neighbors will spend inordinate amounts of time, effort, and legal fees on a relatively small amount of space. This is good for attorneys of course; how would we survive without people like this?

In that case, the plaintiffs, who were the record title owners of the disputed two-feet-wide tract of land, sought to keep their neighbors, the defendants and adverse possession claimants, from using that space. The adverse possession claimants had bought the neighboring property, which they believed included that two-feet-wide space, less than ten years before the date the plaintiffs exercised their ownership rights. Since ten years was the magic statutory time period, the defendants had to prove their rights through tacking. The court noted that "'tacking' permits adding together the time period that successive adverse possessors claim property, and that should this period of time added together be more than ten years, adverse possession may be allowed."[26]

The defendants produced evidence on every element of an adverse possession case. For the "tacking" element, they presented evidence of when their predecessors in title had purchased the property, which was decades before. They presented evidence of "hostile" or "adverse" possession by tacking, by calling witnesses who testified that the two-feet-wide tract was fenced off decades earlier, that the predecessors placed the fence along the tract, and that the predecessors claimed the tract as theirs. To establish the element of "actual" possession by tacking, the defendants called witnesses who testified that the defendants' predecessors periodically repaired the fence surrounding the two-feet-wide tract, and that they constructed and maintained a shed along a portion of the tract. To establish the element of "open and notorious" possession by tacking, the defendants called witnesses who testified that during the period that their predecessors owned the defendants' property, the reputation of the tract was that it belonged to those predecessors. To establish the element of "exclusive" possession by tacking, the defendants presented testimony by two of the original owners of plaintiffs' property. Those witnesses testified about

24 Sears v. Catholic Archdiocese of Washington, 5 A.3d 653, 662 (D.C. 2010).
25 196 W. Va. 559 (1996).
26 *Id.* at 567.

lack of objections to the predecessors' claims. To establish the "continuous" possession element, the defendants presented testimony that their predecessors enclosed, maintained, and claimed ownership of the two-feet-wide tract up until they sold their property to the defendants. Finally, to establish the element of "claim of title" the defendants presented evidence to show that no party had "actual title" to the two-feet-wide tract.

Unfortunately for the defendants in that case, the trial court found that this evidence did not establish adverse possession. Fortunately, for the defendants, the high court noted that the trial court's decisions indicated he had improperly focused on the defendants' actions, instead of the defendants' predecessors' actions. The high court also noted that the trial court had violated the rule that required it to make findings and conclusions of law that would be sufficiently detailed to permit a reviewing court to ascertain the factual core of, and the legal foundation for, the ruling below. Therefore the matter was reversed and remanded.

Finally, an attorney also has to check the statutes concerning tacking. For example, Louisiana has extremely intricate and complicated law within its statutes differentiating kinds of tacking,[27] which is beyond the scope of this book. And, in South Carolina, tacking only "counts" if it is between ancestors and heirs in the context of the ten-year statute of limitations, but under the 20-year presumption of grant, tacking between other parties is permitted.[28] See Chapter 31 for more on the presumption of grant.

27 *See* Brown v. Wood, 451 So. 2d 569, 574 (La. Ct. App. 1984).
28 Getsinger v. Midlands Orthopedic Profit Sharing Plan, 327 S.C. 424, 429–30 (1997).

Chapter 13
Paying Real Estate Taxes
A Potential Shortcut and, in Certain States, a Requirement

Since our society has determined that landowners cannot avoid real estate taxes, then for even more reason, adverse possession claimants should not be able to avoid that obligation. Depending on the state, the pressure to pay taxes for adverse possession claimants can either be a carrot or a stick. The government does not want a successful adverse possessor to get away without paying real estate taxes. This government's attitude is what led Al Capone to prison; he was only convicted for tax evasion. As *Catch-22*'s Milo Minderbender says, "everyone gets his share." This is especially true for the man at the top.

A cynical way of looking at law is that the government writes its own statutes, and therefore has the power to protect itself. This can be true even from the prism of the little world of adverse possession. One way it protects itself is by preventing private citizens from using adverse possession to make claims against certain government land, regardless of the length or character of that use. But there is another way that that the government protects itself—taxes. The government forces people to pay real estate taxes; even adverse possession claimants are not immune.

There is another way of looking at that situation—to put an extra level of protection for landowners against adverse possessors. For example, in Indiana, the landowners apparently complained to the legislators about this possibility. "The Indiana adverse possession tax statute, enacted in 1927, followed great agitation . . . caused principally by 'squatters' who were obtaining original titles to land by adverse possession."[1] Since then, one cannot obtain rights as an adverse possessor in that state without the claimant or predecessor paying taxes on the land. However, the Indiana Supreme Court interpreted this element as being fulfilled so long as the adverse possessor has "substantially" complied with the

1 Fraley v. Minger, 829 N.E.2d 476, 488 (Ind. 2005), citing James H. Neu, *Adverse Possession in Indiana*, 16 Notre Dame Law. 216, 219 (1941) (quotation marks omitted).

requirement to pay those taxes.[2] This "substantial" issue in the context of real estate tax payment in Indiana is further discussed in this chapter, below.

There are three different rationales on why a party (or his predecessors) must pay taxes in order to claim adverse possession: "(1) to require further evidence of good faith and intent on the part of the adverse occupant; (2) to give further notice to the record owner of the existence of the adverse claim and of the time it would mature into title; and (3) to insure that the taxing authority will receive its property tax."[3]

A litigator handling an adverse possession case will need to review many issues concerning real estate taxes, including what that state's laws indicate on the matter, and, if the claimant has not paid the taxes, why he did not do so. Other issues include whether it is just a portion of a lot that the claimant did not pay taxes for, or whether it was the entirety of it.

In many states, the law gives people a choice on how long they must adversely possess property before their rights have ripened in full. In those states, paying taxes is a shortcut; the time period necessary will be reduced by years. In yet other states—apparently a minority—one must pay taxes to obtain adverse possession rights—without paying those taxes, a potential claimant may have to start from scratch. And in other states, there is no absolute requirement to pay real estate taxes. But even in those states, one should expect that if the claimant has indeed paid taxes over a period of years, it will make his allegation of a claim of right much more convincing.

One example of a state with a shortcut method, which requires color of title, is Illinois. In that state, one must meet the traditional elements of an adverse possession case for 20 years in order to succeed.[4] Alternatively, a claimant can be deemed to adversely possess lands for about a third of that time, seven years, under certain qualifications. Its statute on that issue indicates that "[e]very person in the actual possession of lands or tenements, under claim and color of title, made in good faith, and who for 7 successive years continues in such possession, and also, during such time, pays all taxes legally assessed on such lands or tenements, shall be held and adjudged to be the legal owner of such lands or tenements, to the extent and according to the purport of his or her paper title."[5]

---

2 *Id.* at 490.

3 Trappett v. Davis, 102 Idaho 527, 534 (1981), citing Comment, *Payment of Taxes as a Condition of Title by Adverse Possession: A Nineteenth Century Anachronism*, 9 SANTA CLARA LAW. 244 (1969).

4 735 ILL. COMP. STAT. 5/13-101.

5 735 ILL. COMP. STAT. 5/13-109; *see also* Malone v. Smith, 355 Ill. App. 3d 812, 816 (2005).

In *Kerlin v. Tensaw Land Timber Co.*, the Alabama Supreme Court recited its state's law regarding adverse possession and taxes:

> In Alabama there are basically two types of adverse possession, these two types being statutory adverse possession and adverse possession by prescription. Adverse possession by prescription requires actual, exclusive, open, notorious and hostile possession under a claim of right for a period of twenty years. Statutory adverse possession requires the same elements, but the statute provides further that if the adverse possessor holds under color of title, has paid taxes for ten years, or derives his title by descent cast or devise from a possessor, he may acquire title in ten years, as opposed to the twenty years required for adverse possession by prescription.[6]

As just indicated, some states indicate that paying tax is an absolute requirement in order to make a successful adverse possession claim. For example, in Nevada, if one wants to make an adverse possession claim, the claimant must pay all taxes assessed against the property for five years.[7] California follows the same rule: "In no case shall adverse possession be considered established . . . , unless it shall be shown that the land has been occupied and claimed for the period of five years continuously, and the party or persons, their predecessors and grantors, have timely paid all state, county, or municipal taxes that have been levied and assessed upon the land for the period of five years during which the land has been occupied and claimed."[8]

This is a similar statute in Utah: "Adverse possession may not be established unless it is shown that the land has been occupied and claimed continuously for seven years, and that the party and the party's predecessors and grantors have paid all taxes which have been levied and assessed upon the land according to law."[9]

A tough and confusing issue, which seems to come up over and over again, concerns when one has occupied just a portion of one's neighbor's space, and does not pay taxes for that strip of land. One Idaho Supreme Court case discussed that issue, and held that the "majority" view is that where the legal description of the adverse claimant's primary land does not include that additional strip of land, and taxes are assessed in accordance with the legal description, then the claimant's payment of such taxes on his land, does not constitute payment of taxes

6 390 So. 2d 616, 618 (Ala. 1980) (citations omitted).

7 Nev. Rev. Stat. § 11.150; Nev. Rev. Stat. § 40.090.

8 Cal. Civ. Proc. Code § 325(b).

9 Utah Code Ann. § 78B-2-214 (1987).

on the strip of land for the purpose of adverse possession.[10] However, Idaho disapproved of this majority view, and held, basically, that in the context of lots arranged by number, if an adverse possession claimant had believed that the disputed portion was within the portion he was paying taxes for, that is sufficient.

A few years later, a similar issue was heard by the Idaho Supreme Court again,[11] but it did not work out as well for the claimants. In that case, certain parties had met the elements of adverse possession, except for the tax requirement. The lower court concluded that the county's tax plat was in error, causing an illegal double tax on certain space of the claimants' neighbor's property. Both sides paid for taxes on a portion of the same property. The lower court awarded the claimants only for the particular space that both the title owner and the adverse possessors had paid for and not the portion the claimants incorrectly believed was theirs but had not paid taxes for. Both sides appealed. The high court affirmed, ruling that the properties were assessed based on metes and bounds descriptions in the deeds, so the lot number corollary did not apply.

The high court also held that "[t]he resolution of this conflict depends primarily on what is perceived as the primary purpose of the tax requirement."[12] The court held that its state focused more on the conduct of the adverse claimant, rather the "notice" rationale. Therefore, in a case of double taxation, it would favor the adverse possession claimant, or at least for that portion the claimant paid for.

The same court also held that "[a]lthough payment of property taxes is required in adverse possession cases, there is, as a practical matter, no tax requirement in agreed boundary cases."[13] Unfortunately for the claimants there, that was not an agreed boundary case. (Agreed boundary cases are addressed in Chapter 29.)

Other states have addressed the same issue—when a claimant owns one parcel and pays taxes for his own parcel, but because there is a boundary line dispute, he is actually occupying a portion of the neighboring parcel of land. In Indiana, so long as a claimant believed (mistakenly) that his tax payments also covered that portion of land over the boundary that (in reality) he was actually adversely possessing, the court will not require the claimant to prove he paid taxes for that portion of the neighboring parcel. In that state, such a "reasonable and

10 Scott v. Gubler, 95 Idaho 441, 443 (1973).
11 Trappett v. Davis, 102 Idaho 527 (1981).
12 *Id.* at 534.
13 *Id.* at 532.

good faith belief substantially complies with the statutory tax payment requirement."[14]

In at least one state, this boundary line exception is written into the statute. One example is Minnesota. An adverse claimant there must possess the land for at least 15 years. But for land separately assessed as tracts or parcels, in addition to the 15-year requirement, the claimant or his predecessor must have paid taxes for five consecutive years while occupying them. However, one portion of that statute has exemptions to that exception—notably for boundary line disputes. No tax payment is required when the adverse possession claim involves boundary line disputes between adjoining lands.[15]

The traditional view of certain states (like Montana and California) with a tax payment requirement, which is unlike that of, say Indiana and Idaho, is that where the legal description of the adverse claimant's land does not include the disputed parcel, and taxes are assessed in accordance with the legal description, then "payment of such taxes does not constitute payment of taxes on the claimed parcel for the purpose of adverse possession."[16]

In California, the adverse possession claimant must either prove (1) no taxes were assessed against the land, or (2) that he paid them during the appropriate time period.[17] In California, if a party is seeking to possess an adjoining lot to the one he already owns, this would normally make adverse possession impossible because he would be unable to prove he paid those taxes.[18]

California has two exceptions to the ordinary rule that those whose taxes are assessed by lot number cannot establish the payment of taxes on a portion of another's lot. First, the claimant may show "that there is an error in the description on the assessment roll" to establish the error and his payment of taxes. The second would be "[W]here the claimant by construction of buildings or other valuable improvements or by the building of fences has visibly shown occupation of a disputed strip of land adjoining the boundary, several cases have reasoned that the 'natural inference' is that the assessor did not base the assessment on the record boundary but valued the land and improvements visibly possessed by the parties."[19]

---

14 Celebration Worship Ctr., Inc. v. Tucker, 35 N.E.3d 251, 255 (Ind. 2015).

15 St. Paul Park Ref. Co. v. Domeier, 950 N.W.2d 547, 550 (Minn. 2020), citing Minn. Stat. § 541.02.

16 Scott v. Gluber, 95 Idaho 441, 443 (1973), citing Townsend v. Koukol, 148 Mont. 1 (1966); Ernie v. Trinity Lutheran Church, 51 Cal. 2d 702 (1959).

17 Glatts v. Henson, 31 Cal. 2d 368, 372 (1948).

18 Gilardi v. Hallam, 30 Cal. 3d 317, 326 (1981).

19 *Id.* at 327.

A somewhat amusing and definitely confusing California case was *Sorenson v. Costa*, in which several neighbors discovered that they had been occupying lots that were shifted a half-lot to the west compared to the legal descriptions found in the relevant deeds. Similarly, the county's assessment rolls contained mistaken descriptions of the property. When one neighbor had the land surveyed, everyone discovered the error. Then two neighbors filed cross-actions seeking to quiet title and other relief. One neighbor was found to have met the elements of adverse possession, including payment of taxes. The court held that "[w]here a claimant of title by adverse possession has paid the taxes actually assessed on the property occupied, a misdescription on the tax assessment roll or in the tax receipts will not generally affect the efficacy of payment under statutes requiring the payment of taxes in order to establish title by adverse possession."[20]

Moving on to a new issue, in New York, tax payments are not the be all and end all. "[T]he failure to pay taxes is not conclusive evidence" on a claim for adverse possession.[21] However, it could be a "significant circumstance," which would weaken a claim.[22] In some circumstances in New York, the lack of payment would be "irrelevant."[23] In other states, like Oregon, the courts hold that the payment of taxes is not essential to establish adverse possession, but failure to pay the taxes is important evidence tending to refute the claim. In one Oregon case, the defendants contended that they did not know that their tax statement did not include the taxes for the disputed tract. The trial court was permitted to deem this claim as plausible.[24] In *Doenz v. Garber*, the Wyoming Supreme Court explained that nonpayment of taxes by the adverse possessor or the payment of taxes by the owner of record, while a consideration, does not circumvent an adverse possession claim. In fact, "[n]onpayment of taxes by the claimant is usually the case where use to a fence line rather than deed line is the primary basis of the claim."[25] In Wyoming, an adverse possession claimant's failure to pay taxes on the disputed property is simply "a fact to be weighed along with the other circumstances in the case and tends to weaken a claim of ownership by adverse possession."[26] In Tennessee, payment of taxes does not establish adverse possession, but there is a statutory presumption that the adverse claimant owns the land in such a case if the claimant or predecessor has done

---

20 32 Cal. 2d 453, 466 (1948).

21 Gerwitz v. Gelsomin, 69 A.D.2d 992, 993 (N.Y. App. Div. 1979).

22 *Id.*

23 Robinson v. Robinson, 34 A.D.3d 975, 977 (N.Y. App. Div. 2006).

24 Mattoon v. Clayborn, 42 Or. App. 893, 897 (Or. Ct. App. 1979).

25 665 P.2d 932, 937 (Wyo. 1983).

26 Braunstein v. Robinson Family Ltd. P'ship LLP, 226 P.3d 826, 833 (Wyo. 2010).

so for a 20-year period or longer. In such a case, the claimant would be "presumed prima facie to be the legal owner of such land."[27] This is a rebuttable presumption, and not an absolute.[28]

On the other end of the telescope, in at least one state, Alabama, "the legal title holder may use proof of his payment of the property taxes to controvert an element of the claimant's *prima facie* case of adverse possession."[29]

Anyone representing an adverse possession claimant who had an obligation to pay outstanding real estate taxes, but did not, would probably come up with the same bright idea—pay them now. Perhaps one might even consider paying them off right before the litigation starts. Courts have evaluated this idea in various ways.

For example, in one California case, the appellate court ruled that the trial court had erroneously ruled that defendants had extinguished the plaintiff's easement by adverse possession. This is because they had only made a lump sum payment of several years' worth of delinquent property taxes, but the statute required "timely" payment of taxes.[30] On the other end is a relatively recent Nevada case. In that case, the statute required the payment of taxes against the property during the period of five years preceding the filing of the complaint, but the claimant had made tax payments on the property for only four calendar years. Yet, during those four years, he paid more than five years' worth of taxes against the property. The court held that this was sufficient under its statute.[31] In a Utah case, there was an issue because certain taxes were not timely paid; the adverse possessor conducted a "redemption of taxes," which the trial court ruled was technically different from "payment of taxes." The appellate court disagreed; apparently in that state, so long as the state gets its money, all else is forgiven.[32]

One might consider the issue of paying taxes in the context of adverse possession cases to be as dry as sand in the Sahara,[33] but every once in a while there is an argument about the matter that almost becomes amusing. Cases like *Hagman v. Meher Mount Corp.*[34] (also discussed in Chapter 21) show that there is no end in creative lawyering about certain issues. In that case, an estate sought adverse possession rights over a portion of land owned by a religious corporation, but the estate had not

27 Tenn. Code Ann. § 28-2-109.
28 *See* Corrado v. Hickman, 113 S.W.3d 319, 324 (Tenn. Ct. App. 2003).
29 Lilly v. Palmer, 495 So. 2d 522, 527 n.2 (Ala. 1986).
30 McLear-Gary v. Scott, 25 Cal. App. 5th 145 (2018).
31 Selig v. Selig, 531 P.3d 605 (Nev. App. 2023).
32 Martin v. Kearl, 917 P.2d 91, 93 n.5 (Utah Ct. App. 1996).
33 Don't call it the "Sahara desert," as I used to; "Sahara" means "desert."
34 215 Cal. App. 4th 82 (Cal. Ct. App. 2013).

paid for that portion's real estate taxes. As indicated earlier, in that state, an adverse possessor is required to prove that he timely paid all state, county, or municipal taxes that have been levied and assessed upon the land. This must have been done for at least five years. The religious entity argued the estate failed to comply with this requirement for two reasons: (1) he never paid the property taxes on the disputed half acre; and (2) he never paid the mosquito assessments. The estate admitted it paid no taxes, but it won the case because it properly and convincingly responded that (1) no property taxes were ever levied or assessed on the property due to the religious entity's tax-exempt status; and (2) the mosquito assessment is not a tax.

One also has to carefully review the statutes of one's state, because payment of taxes may mean, in certain cases, a claimant has also proved other elements of his adverse possession case, like color of title or possession, automatically. For example, in Arkansas, "[u]nimproved and unenclosed land shall be deemed and held to be in possession of the person who pays the taxes thereon if he or she has color of title thereto, but no person shall be entitled to invoke the benefit of this section unless he or she, and those under whom he or she claims, shall have paid the taxes for at least seven (7) years in succession."[35] In the same state, "[p]ayment of taxes on wild and unimproved land in this state by any person or his or her predecessor in title for a period of fifteen (15) consecutive years shall create a presumption of law that the person, or his or her predecessor in title, held color of title to the land prior to the first payment of taxes made as stated and that all the payments were made under color of title."[36]

35 Ark. Code § 18-11-102.
36 *Id.* § 18-11-103.

Chapter 14
Known and Visible Lines and Boundaries

Some elements for adverse possession cases only seem to exist in a few states. For example, in North Carolina, if one seeks an identified portion of property owned by another, the claimant's possession must be under "known and visible lines and boundaries."[1] That state has reiterated this element in many cases. In one case concerning amusing facts, a defendant claimed that she had proven this element because the house and other buildings at issue "were on a part of the lot that she described as generally corresponding to a buried electronic dog fence marked with some flags apparently protruding from the ground for the edification of the dog."[2] The court did not accept that argument. It noted that even if it were to assume that described a known and visible line or boundary, the line did not correspond to her claim, because, "[w]hen specifically asked, defendant instead testified that she claimed property extending beyond the buried fence, but gave the jury no additional guidance as to where the property should be divided. As a result, she failed to meet her burden of establishing a claim under known and visible lines and boundaries."[3]

North Carolina is not the only state in which known and visible boundaries may be relevant. Chapter 29 discusses title by acquiescence, in which such issues become relevant. And in at least some states, "occupancy to a visible and ascertained boundary for the statutory period is deemed the controlling feature in determining hostility in mistaken-boundary cases."[4]

On a somewhat related topic, if the element of the location of the boundaries is needed, one must also remember there will be a burden of proof attached to that element, too. The claimant "must prove with reasonable certainty the location of the boundaries of the tract to which

1 Wallin v. Rice, 232 N.C. 371, 373 (1950).
2 Minor v. Minor, 266 N.C. 526, 531 (N.C. 2013).
3 *Id.* at 531–32 (internal quotation marks omitted).
4 Joiner v. Janssen, 85 Ill. 2d 74, 83–84 (1981).

he seeks to apply the five elements of adverse possession, and all of the elements must extend to the tract so claimed throughout the statutory period."[5] Further, "the boundaries must be susceptible of specific and definite location."[6] In other words, before the claimant asserting adverse possession can establish the five elements, the claimant must establish the boundaries of the land at issue with reasonable certainty.

5 Tapley v. Peterson, 141 Ill. App. 3d 401, 404–05 (1986).
6 *Id.* at 405.

Part 4

Defenses and Disruptions to Adverse Possession Claims

Chapter 15
Disrupting a Claimant's Continuous Use Claim

Observant people in Manhattan who roam the streets long enough will eventually discover that hypervigilant landowners close off private spaces that the public normally can access. Such spaces include portions of Rockefeller Plaza and College Walk at Columbia University. This is done for one day every year.[1] Why? Anyone who has read this far can probably guess the answer: to avoid the "continuous" element of a potential adverse possession case. "An interruption in the running of the statutory period for even one day ends it and it must begin anew."[2] Conversely, a "single instance of attempted interruption of an adverse user resulting in no actual interruption and followed by no attempt to test the right, does not necessarily destroy its continuity."[3]

To understand the continuous element, one must also understand the other side of the equation—the disruption or interruption. Case law reveals a number of methods that work, and what methods will not work. The interruption doctrine also may work in the context of challenging prescriptive easements.

The most obvious way of disrupting the continuous element of use is to file a legal action before the limitation period has expired. To a man with a hammer, everything looks like a nail. For attorneys, every problem looks like a potential lawsuit. But some potential adverse possession claims can be warded off without litigation.

Another method is "physical ouster" of the claimant or that a "substantial interruption" occurred during the statutory period.[4] The Restatement of Property (First) section 459(2) also indicates that adverse use is interrupted if the title holders "cause a cessation of the use without the aid of legal proceedings." A landowner's actions to break a claimant's

1 David W. Dunlap, *Closing for a Spell, Just to Prove It's Ours*, N.Y. Times, Oct. 28, 2011.
2 Gen. Iron Indus., Inc. v. A. Finkl & Sons Co., 292 Ill. App. 3d 439, 446 (1997).
3 Reed v. Wolyniec, 323 Pa. Super. 550, 558 (Pa. Super. Ct. 1983) (citation and internal ellipses omitted).
4 Carnevale v. Dupee, 783 A.2d 404, 410 (R.I. 2001) (citations omitted, and emphasis added).

continuous use of a disputed area "must be such as to actually interfere with and interrupt substantially the claimant's use of the land."[5]

Unfortunately for title holders seeking a quick fix, judges do not usually appreciate the idea of someone taking the law into his own hands, and physically forcing occupants out of claimed space. On the other hand, if the court decides that the title holder was a milquetoast, and that he did not try hard enough to defend his rights, he may be left without his real property.

Just to take an extreme, in theory, one kind of ouster would be a title holder taking a sledgehammer and destroying everything built by the adverse possessor on the title holder's property, and then building his own new structures there. This could subject the title holder to liability, but at least he might have a better chance of proving interruption in comparison with the sitting back and waiting approach.

Before giving advice to one's client about taking the law into his own hands, one may want to review the West Virginia criminal case *State v. Cook*.[6] In that case, the defendant and her husband built a fence along the edge of their property. The defendant's neighbors tore down the fence, placed roofing nails in the defendant's driveway, and bulldozed dirt and rocks onto the property. Upon learning that defendant had called the police, one neighbor, standing six feet four inches and weighing more than 300 pounds, began to violently beat the defendant's husband, who was five feet six inches and weighed about 140 pounds. In defense of her husband, the defendant shot and killed the neighbor. (The appellate court vacated the conviction, as the state had not proved beyond a reasonable doubt that she did not act in defense of her husband.)

In any event, the easiest method of handling this issue, just like anything in life, will usually not work. That is, making an oral protest against the adverse holder, without any overt action, interrupts nothing.[7] It may even have the opposite effect—because it could confirm the occupation is hostile. In a New Hampshire Supreme Court case, the title holders made many phone calls and emails to the claimant, stating that the claimant's fence encroached against their property. But the court held that such demands are not "ouster," whether by phone, email, letters, or by raising one's voice. Therefore, the court held that there was no interruption of the adverse possession.[8] The Vermont Supreme Court similarly held that "[m]ere verbal protestations without action to reassert control or dominion over the disputed land does not interrupt the adverse

5 LaFreniere v. Sprague, 108 R.I. 43, 53 (1970).
6 204 W. Va. 591, 515 S.E.2d 127 (1999).
7 *See* Crone v. Nuss, 263 P.3d 809, 818 (Kan. Ct. App. 2011).
8 O'Malley v. Little, 170 N.H. 272, 277 (2017).

possessor's interest in the property."[9] In one Mississippi case, its Supreme Court held that "a party must do something more than merely verbally protest; there must be a physical interruption or a court proceeding or some unequivocable act of ownership which interrupts the exercise of the right claimed and being used by the opposite parties."[10]

If oral protests do not work, and emails or letters have limited effect, one can try more than one approach at once. In one Kansas case, the court held that sending claimants a certified letter notifying them that they were trespassing, and placing a "No Trespassing" sign on the disputed land constituted an "overt act" that "exhibited a specific declaration of purpose to protect [the owner's] rights of ownership against the [claimants] and were sufficient to put the [claimants] on notice and toll the statute of limitations."[11]

In other cases, "No Trespassing" signs do not amount to much. In a Pennsylvania case, putting up a "No Trespassing" sign for 24 hours was deemed not to interrupt anything relevant.[12] Similarly in a Rhode Island case,[13] when one party placed "a saw horse with a sign reading 'Road Closed' at the entrance to the road once a year," and "the saw horse only covered a small portion of the road" and "[v]ehicles desiring access would simply go around the sign," this such an action did not constitute substantial interruption.

As one Colorado court put it, "To disrupt the adverse possession claim, the record owner must assert a claim to the land or perform an act that would reinstate him in possession."[14] Some courts indicate something very strong is necessary. For example, the California Supreme Court held that "[t]o interrupt the adverse user the re-entry of the legal title holder must be open, notorious and under claim of right and must equal in dignity and character that required to initiate an adverse possession."[15] Texas courts similarly hold that "[t]o constitute an interruption of an occupant's adverse possession, an entry by the owner must be made with the intention of taking possession. Such an entry by the owner, in order to defeat another's adverse possession, must clearly indicate to the occupant that his possession is invalid and his right challenged. It must be open and notorious and bear on its face an unequivocal intention to take possession. It cannot be accidental,

9 Brown v. Whitcomb, 150 Vt. 106, 110 (1988).
10 Board of Ed. of Itawamba Cnty. Miss. v. Loague, 405 So. 2d 122, 126 (Miss. 1981) (citation omitted).
11 Crone v. Nuss, 263 P.3d 809, 818 (Kan. Ct. App. 2011).
12 Reed v. Wolyniec, 323 Pa. Super. 550, 557–58 (Pa. Super. Ct. 1983).
13 Jerry Brown Farm Ass'n, Inc. v. Kenyon 119 R.I. 43, 48 (1977).
14 Bushey v. Seven Lakes Reservoir Co., 37 Colo. App. 106, 109 (1975).
15 Smith v. S. Pac. R.R. Co., 1 Cal. 2d 272, 275 (1934).

casual, secret, or permissive."[16] A Kansas court, citing a treatise, held that if the true owner openly entered the disputed property with intent to take possession and effectively exclude the claimant, this would also disrupt the claimant's "continuous" occupation.[17]

A survey of property by the title holder may or may not be sufficient to disrupt a continuous claim, depending on the state, and the obviousness of the surveyor's work. In one Ohio case, *Montieth v. Twin Falls United Methodist Church, Inc.*, the Montieths claimed ownership by adverse possession to a strip of land abutting their eastern property line. The Montieths acquired property, with the belief that a particular strip of land was part of the property. However, the strip of land was actually part of a church's property. Eventually, the church had its property surveyed for the purpose of grading the property, and the church's trustee then informed the Montieths that the strip of land did not belong to them. Thereafter, the Montieths initiated an action to quiet title to the disputed property, claiming ownership by adverse possession. The trial court found that the Montieths had satisfied the requirements for adverse possession and that the church's 1969 survey had not sufficiently interrupted the running of the statute of limitations for adverse possession. The appellate court reversed, indicating that, "[T]he statute was tolled at the time when the survey was conducted for the purpose of grading the property. This entry upon the disputed land by the [church], evokes a positive interruption of the statutory period and an unequivocal manifestation of intent to reclaim the property."[18]

Not every state handles surveys (in this context) in this manner. For example, in one Rhode Island Supreme Court case,[19] the court held that performing a survey and giving notice to claimants of the proper boundary line did not constitute a sufficiently substantial interruption to halt the continuous use of the area. However, in that case, the claimants removed surveyor's stakes and continued to use the area in a similar manner. Therefore, the title holder relying on a survey should at least try to make sure the stakes stay in place.

Many cases indicate that surveyors' stakes and marks have limited effect.[20] However, there are some cases indicating that if the surveys are done in a manner that truly clarifies that the title owner is still claiming ownership, the surveys may do the trick. For example, in a Missouri case placing stakes connected by string and posting a sign notifying

16 Kirby Lumber Corp. v. Smith, 305 S.W.2d 829, 830 (Tex. Civ. App. 1957) (citations omitted).

17 Crone v. Nuss, 46 Kan. App. 2d 436, 446 (2011).

18 68 Ohio App. 2d 219, 225 (Ohio Ct. App. 1980).

19 LaFreniere v. Sprague, 108 R.I. 43, 52 (1970).

20 *See* Pugatch v. Stoloff, 41 Mass. App. Ct. 536, 542 (1996).

adverse possessors that they could not use the area which was fenced off, was held sufficient to interrupt adverse use.[21]

Having a title owner enter the adversely possessed property alone may not be sufficient, depending on the context and circumstances of how it is entered. For example, in one Colorado case, it was held that if the claimant is using property for pasturing livestock and farming, and the title holder's employees occasionally enter the property for specific and limited purposes, then this is not a true interruption, and does not destroy the adverse possession.[22]

As one Maryland court put it, "The mere act of going upon the land is not enough. The owner must assert his claim to the land or perform some act that would reinstate him in possession, before he can regain what he has lost. The conduct claimed by an owner to work an interruption of adverse possession must be such as would put an ordinary prudent person on notice that he actually has been ousted. Not every act by the owner on the land interrupts actual adverse possession."[23]

Lawn mowing (also discussed in Chapter 35) is a likely ineffective method of claiming ouster. In a Washington state case heard by its Supreme Court, a claim for adverse possession was not defeated by the true owner's occasional mowing of the disputed property.[24] The claimant asserted a right to 30 inches of lawn and maintained the area up to that boundary. In contrast, the true owner mowed a ten-foot swath of lawn between the two properties, including the 30 inches claimed by adverse possessor. The court found this did not disrupt a claim for adverse possession, because "[t]he cutting of the entire lawn between the two houses could well have been an act of neighborly accommodation and does not evidence any intent to claim any right of ownership in the 30-inch strip with which we are concerned."[25]

If a record owner thinks an adverse possession claim is a possibility, it is important to confront the trespasser and develop evidence showing the elements of adverse possession were not met (e.g., there was an interruption to the trespasser's continuous possession). This might include timestamped photos of posted no trespassing signs or blockades to the claimant's ability to use or occupy the space, written correspondence with the trespasser (e.g., texts, emails, and letters) granting permission to the trespasser to use the disputed land for an agreed upon length of time, or timestamped photos showing the title owner's actual

---

21 Pierce v. Austin, 651 S.W.2d 161, 162–63 (Mo. App. 1983).
22 Bushey v. Seven Lakes Reservoir Co., 37 Colo. App. 106, 109 (Colo. App. 1975).
23 Senez v. Collins, 182 Md. App. 300, 335 (2008) (citation omitted).
24 Mesher v. Connelly, 63 Wn.2d 552 (1964).
25 *Id.* at 556.

possession by erecting a fence along boundary lines. If one can obtain evidence that the claimant is aware of the title holder's use, and did nothing to stop it, that is even better.

As a means of last resort, a title holder can also argue that the adverse possessor interrupted his own continuous possession "by acting in a way that acknowledges the superiority of the real owner's title."[26] Before the litigation begins, and during the statutory time period of possession, a title holder can hopefully get the potential occupant to orally admit that the title holder's rights are superior. Better yet to get it in writing. Even better would be video evidence indicating that the potential claimant had taken steps to allow title owner access and occupancy. The same actions might also work to disprove hostility; this is further discussed in the next chapter.

Another critical issue is abandonment. The element of continuity can be disrupted "where the adverse possessor interrupts the period of possession by abandoning the premises."[27] What does "abandonment" by an adverse possessor mean? One Illinois case addressed that issue. As a background, the court indicated that "[t]his litigation arose from an incident . . . in which Ketchens blockaded the McNeils' driveway—or what the McNeils had always assumed was their driveway. Leslie McNeil came home in the evening and found that Ketchens had parked his car in the driveway next to her and her husband's house . . . . The McNeils asked him to leave, and he refused. He invited the McNeils to sue him."[28] That invitation was accepted, making two sets of lawyers rich; the decision is approximately 28 pages long, even though the whole decision seems to address just a portion of one driveway.

In any event, one claim against the adverse possessors was that a certain tract known as Tract A had been left vacant by former adverse possessors for approximately one month. The court held that this did not destroy continuity: "Abandoning Tract A would have broken the continuity of possession, but by leaving the house vacant for approximately a month—which was merely the interim between moving out of the house and turning it over to the new owners—the [former adverse possessors] did not, by any reasonable view, *abandon* the property. In order to destroy the continuity of possession, the vacancy must not be merely occasional, such as occurs in every case where a party, from

26 Allen v. Johnson, 79 Conn. App. 740, 746 (2003).

27 Ray v. Beacon Hudson Mountain Corp., 88 N.Y.2d 154, 159 (1996).

28 McNeil v. Ketchens, 397 Ill. App. 3d 375, 377 (Ill. App. Ct. 2010).

some cause, shuts up his property for a short time, or, indeed, for a long time."[29]

Note that although an adverse possessor may be deemed to have abandoned his claims, a title owner is never deemed to have "abandoned" his real property so that anyone else can just claim it.[30] This makes real property unlike certain other kind of personal property. An interesting case on abandonment of property concerned an investor who paid Lee Harvey Oswald's widow for the rights to the rifle used to assassinate President Kennedy. The government had retained the rifle and would not return it. The investor could not recover compensation from the government, because a jury determined the assassin had abandoned that rifle.[31]

29 *Id.* at 396 (citation, ellipses, and internal quotation marks omitted).

30 *See* Rogers v. Ricane Enters. Inc., 772 S.W.2d 76, 80 (Tex. 1989).

31 *Pay for Oswald Rifle Is Denied*, Wash. Post, Feb. 25, 1969, at A3; *Jury Bars Payment for Oswald's Rifle*, N.Y. Times, Feb. 25, 1969, at 18.

Chapter 16
Disproving Hostility

Fans of Jimi Hendrix know about a conceptual "freak flag." Adverse possession fans know about a separate conceptual flag. As one court held, an adverse possession claimant "must unfurl his flag on the land, and keep it flying, so that the owner may see, if he will, that an enemy has invaded his domains, and planted the standard of conquest."[1] As indicated in Chapter 3, if the adverse possession claimant can prove the other elements of his claim, many states indicate that the hostility aspect will be presumed. However, there may be ways to overcome that presumption. If one is trying to prove an adverse possession claimant had lowered the hostility portion of this flag, there may be a few questions to ask of one's client, the title holder, in the hopes that the facts will help his case.

First one has to determine if the presumption really applies. For example, one New York court held that "where it is shown that the user and the landowner are related by blood or part of a select group of friends, the proponent is not accorded the benefit of the presumption," and then then the proponent of the adverse possession must come forward with evidence of hostile use sufficient to raise a triable issue of fact.[2] In such a case, the "party asserting the adverse possession claim must come forward with affirmative facts to establish that the use [of the property] was under a claim of right and adverse to the interests of [the true owner]."[3]

Similarly, in Minnesota, a "close family relationship between the claimant of land and the record owner . . . [creates] an inference, if not [a] presumption" that the possession was merely permissive.[4] A number of other cases seem to confirm that this is universal law.[5] Another basis to

1 Rutar Farms & Livestock, Inc. v. Fuss, 651 P.2d 1129, 1134 (Wyo. 1982) (citation omitted).

2 Wechsler v. New York State Dep't of Env't Conservation, 193 A.D.2d 856, 860 (N.Y. App. Div. 1993).

3 Est. of Becker v. Murtagh, 19 N.Y.3d 75, 82 (2012) (citation omitted).

4 Norgong v. Whitehead, 225 Minn. 379, 383 (1948).

5 Totman v. Malloy, 431 Mass. 143, 148 n.5 (2000) (citing numerous cases).

defeat the presumption of hostility, would be if the claimant "s[ought] permission for use [of the property] from the record owner."[6]

Then there are also cases indicating that hostility is never to be presumed. The high court of Alabama held that "[a]dverse possession becomes a perfect title on the theory that the true owner has by his own fault and neglect failed to assert his right against the hostile holding, but all presumptions and intendments are favorable to the title, and possessions are not presumed to be hostile thereto."[7] Oregon's Supreme Court held that no presumption of hostility arises from open and continuous possession in an adverse possession case.[8] And, in Minnesota, at least one court indicated that whether a presumption applies one way or the other on permissive use, is an unresolved issue.[9]

Some of the potential arguments to avoid hostility presumptions are in Chapter 3, such as whether the entry on the land was a mistake. But there are other methods to disprove hostility as well.

One question to ask a title owner (before the trial, hopefully) is whether the adverse possession claimant ever offered to buy the title owner's property, before the claimant's rights were solidified. In one New York case, the court held that "[a]n offer made by one in possession without title to purchase from the record owner during the statutory period is a recognition of the record owner's title and prevents adverse possession from accruing[.]"[10] This is because New York's high court has held that if the claimant acknowledges superior title in the record owner during the statutory period, this negates an essential element of an adverse possession claim, that is, possession with a claim of right throughout the time period.[11]

On the other hand, at least one case has indicated that if the elements of adverse possession had been established, then if the adverse possessor later takes steps to even further prove his ownership, those steps would be irrelevant. The Michigan Supreme Court held: "We do not think that an attempt by one who has acquired title by adverse possession to secure a deed of the land for the purpose of avoiding litigation in the future as to the validity of the title thus acquired, or to make his title one of record, should, in the absence of other proof, be treated as a

6 *Est. of Becker*, 19 N.Y.3d at 82 (internal quotation marks and citation omitted).
7 Prestwood v. Hunt, 285 Ala. 525 (1970).
8 Hoffman v. Freeman Land & Timber, LLC, 329 Or. 554 (1999).
9 Compart v. Wolfstellar, 906 N.W.2d 598, 603 n.4 (Minn. Ct. App. 2018).
10 Manhattan Sch. of Music v. Solow, 175 A.D.2d 106, 107 (N.Y. App. Div. 1991) (citation omitted).
11 Van Gorder v. Masterplanned, Inc., 78 N.Y.2d 1106, 1108 (1991).

recognition of the superior title of the owner or an admission that the possession enjoyed by him was permissive only."[12]

Another issue to consider is whether the title holder can prove that he allowed the adverse possession claimant to use the land at issue as a neighborly accommodation. If so, the title holder should succeed.

Two Wyoming Supreme Court cases show how small issues make a difference to resolve whether there was such an accommodation. In *Gray v. Fitzhugh*, that court relied on a neighborly accommodation to deny a claim of adverse possession. As the court put it, a neighborly accommodation should defeat a claim of adverse possession and "to hold otherwise would be to adjudge that common neighborliness may only be indulged under penalty of encumbering one's property."[13] In that case, the claimants had constructed a pond and recreational development that traversed the neighbor's irrigation ditches. The evidence at trial showed that the neighbors had an "unwritten 'neighborly' agreement" that they would exchange use of certain lands on each other's property. The court determined that "neighborly agreement" covered the property at issue and, therefore, the claimant lost.

But 40 years later, in *Galiher v. Johnson*,[14] the result was different. Some testimony in the trial indicated that the space was being used by the adverse possession claimants as a "reasonable accommodation," but the court held that this testimony alone was not conclusive. In that case, since the neighbors had no communication for over a decade, and there was no evidence of a "special relationship" that might normally occur between neighbors, the court held that there could not have been a mutual understanding about how certain land was used. As the court held, "A 'neighborly accommodation' simply cannot be assumed—there must be evidence of communication or joint activity which demonstrates such an accommodation."[15] Because there was no implicit agreement about the use of land, the court did not apply the "neighborly accommodation" concept to the situation, and held that the lower court properly awarded adverse possession rights to the claimants.

In a New York case[16] addressing similar issues, a plaintiff was an adverse possession claimant, arguing she had the right to certain parking access in neighboring property to her own. The plaintiff had claimed that the presumption of hostility should apply. However, the court noted that this presumption does not exist "where there is a close

---

12 Munroe v. Pere Marquette Ry. Co., 226 Mich. 158, 164 (1924).
13 576 P.2d 88, 90 (Wyo. 1978) (parentheses and citation omitted).
14 432 P.3d 502 (Wyo. 2018).
15 *Id.* at 512.
16 Millington v. Kenny & Dittrich Amherst, LLC, 124 A.D.3d 1108 (N.Y. App. Div. 2015).

and cooperative relationship between the record owner and the person claiming title through adverse possession."[17] In that case, defendant had moved for summary judgment to dismiss the action, arguing that the plaintiff could not prove hostility. This was in part because the plaintiff had been on "good terms" with the prior owners of the subject space, and did not dispute that the prior owners had been "accommodating" for the parking needs of every business on the block. The plaintiff also did not produce an affidavit from the former owner of the space, her own father, who could have theoretically claimed that the previous method of parking was done with hostility. Therefore, the court held that the lower court properly granted summary judgment to defendant and dismissed the adverse possession claim.

Another way of disproving that the adverse possession claimant has occupied the premises with hostility, and indeed a manner of defending an adverse possession claim entirely, would be in a rare case in which the claimant had already issued a deed to the title owner. In that kind of case, the title owner could claim estoppel by deed, meaning that the adverse possession claimant was estopped from making the claim pursuant to that deed. To put it another way, if the grantor has executed a deed conveying land to another, but simply remains on the land, then the grantor's possession is deemed subservient to the title held by the grantee. In such a case, the limitations period does not even commence running until and unless the grantor officially gives notice to the record owner that he has repudiated the deed.[18] However, if the grantor only entered into possession after the deed was executed, this law may possibly not apply.[19] In other words, the grantor would not be required to repudiate the deed before the grantor could claim adverse possession.

17 *Id.* at 1109 (citation omitted).

18 *See* Texas Co. v. Argo Oil Corp., 277 S.W.2d 308, 310 (Tex. Civ. App. 1955), writ refused NRE (July 6, 1955), citing Kidd v. Young, 144 Tex. 322 (1945); Sweeten v. Park, 154 Tex. 266, 270 (1955).

19 McLaren v. Beard, 811 S.W.2d 564, 568 (Tex. 1991).

Chapter 17
Statute of Frauds as a Defense

A typical affirmative defense to include in an action concerning real property is the statute of frauds. This is the statute that indicates that a contract for the transfer of real property must be in writing and signed in order to be enforceable.

However, adverse possession cases, on one end, and cases concerning the intentional transfer of land, on the other, are in different universes. Using a statute of frauds defense for an adverse possession case would be like using a bulletproof shield to combat noise pollution. As one state Supreme Court put it in a concurring opinion, "[A]cquisition of land by way of adverse possession completely bypasses the statute of frauds. The formalities generally required to prove and transfer land ownership do not exist when a person acquires legal title through adverse possession."[1] As another court put it, if a party claimed that it owned real property based on an oral promise, that might be barred by the statute of frauds. But when a "claim is based on adverse possession and not on the validity of the gift itself, the statute of frauds is irrelevant."[2]

In one Montana Supreme Court case, a defendant tried to use the statute of frauds defense to an adverse possession case. The defendant argued that the plaintiff adverse possessor's claim was based on an alleged oral conveyance of land. Therefore, according to the defendant, the statute of frauds barred the plaintiff from obtaining title under adverse possession. The Montana court disagreed, indicating that there were two methods of obtaining adverse possession. One was through color of title, which meant the claimant had sought rights under a written document. In Montana, one cannot use an oral gift as a means of claiming color of title. The other was through claim of title, which meant the possessor sought relief not founded on a written document. Under this ground, an oral grant of real property can serve as a foundation for

1 Gorman v. City of Woodinville, 175 Wash. 2d 68, 80 (2012).
2 Vezey v. Green, 35 P.3d 14, 23 (Alaska 2001).

a claim of title by adverse possession, notwithstanding the statute of frauds.[3]

As that Montana court indicated, where the applicable statute requires color of title for an adverse possession claim, "parol gifts of realty cannot ripen into title by adverse possession."[4] The statute of frauds may not precisely be the defense for such an adverse possession claim; a better description might be that the title owner will claim that the alleged recipient of the gift lacks one of the crucial elements for a valid adverse possession case.

Regardless, most attorneys have nothing to lose by including the statute of frauds in the response to an adverse possession case. It is highly unlikely that a court would sanction a defending attorney who claimed that the statute of frauds protected his client, even if the statute does not apply. But without some explanation or background in the answer, and especially if the claimant is not claiming color of title, then the defense may get easily dismissed.

3 Swecker v. Dorn, 181 Mont. 436, 438–40 (1979).

4 *Id.* at 439.

Chapter 18
Unclean Hands May Be a Defense to Adverse Possession by Claim of Right

One potential affirmative defense to an adverse possession case is "unclean hands." When non-attorneys hear the term "unclean," they might think of exorcisms or treif food, but those of us in the little world of adverse possession have something else in mind. This doctrine comes into play "when the one seeking relief in equity has violated conscience, or good faith, or other equitable principle, in his prior conduct."[1]

At first, this might seem to be a misnomer because, as the typical person on the street might say, one who adversely possesses his neighbor's property is already acting in a dirty manner. Regardless the defense survives. Just as with any other issue, a review of various cases can help understand in what context it fits.

In one California case, *Aguayo v. Amaro*,[2] a party seeking adverse possession over property argued she had a claim of right. In that case, plaintiff Sofia Aguayo and her husband Jesus Duran Aguayo regularly obtained properties by adverse possession. The property at issue had been owned by Isabel Infante. After Isabel died, the Aguayos recorded a wild quitclaim deed[3] that purported to transfer the property from "Jesus Duran" to the Aguayos, and directed the tax collector's office to mail property tax statements to Sofia Aguayo, to allow her to make the payments. A few years later, Sofia filed an action to quiet title to the property based on adverse possession. The court held that even though Sofia met the statutory elements of adverse possession, her act of recording a wild deed for the purpose of diverting tax bills from the true owner and to her address constituted unclean hands, defeating her equitable action; this decision was affirmed on appeal.

The court first noted that in certain contexts, unclean hands would not apply. For example, the wrongful act of trespass could not be the basis

1 General Elec. Co. v. Super. Ct., 45 Cal. 2d 897, 899–900 (1955) (citation and internal quotation marks omitted).

2 213 Cal. App. 4th 1102 (2013).

3 Wild deeds are also discussed in Chapter 4.

for an unclean hands defense to adverse possession by claim of right. "This is because if such a defense existed, adverse possession by claim of right would not be possible."[4]

However, in that case, the court upheld the unclean hands defense, and held that the trial court properly ruled against the adverse possessor. The basis for the unclean hands defense was that the alleged adverse possessor had committed a "deceitful act of recording a wild deed for the purpose of diverting tax bills to her address."[5] In other words, the adverse possessor had recorded the wild deed in order to prevent the "actual owner" from paying real estate taxes. Notably, the adverse possessor needed to make sure she paid the real estate taxes. Otherwise, the adverse possessor would not have met one of the critical elements of adverse possession in that state.

Other cases from California in the mid-20th century also indicate that it is critical to resolve who the fraudulent transactions were directed against and in what context, when evaluating an unclean hands defense. For example, in one case,[6] a property owner, Dr. Friedman, recorded a fraudulent deed of trust (a quasi-mortgage) in favor of the plaintiffs. This was intended to protect the property from claims by third party creditors. The defendant, Dr. Friedman's wife, later purchased the same property at a foreclosure sale. Eventually, she sought to quiet title to the property through adverse possession. The plaintiffs argued that unclean hands barred relief. The trial was unbelievably long—the transcript covered 2,341 pages. In any event, the court rejected this unclean hands argument. "The misconduct which brings the 'clean hands' doctrine into operation must relate directly to the transaction concerning which complaint is made. The misconduct must infect the cause of action before the court. Relief is not denied because the plaintiff may have acted improperly in the past or because such prior misconduct may indirectly affect the problem before the court. A party may have relief in connection with a transaction itself untainted although his original title may have been tainted by improper conduct."[7] In other words, the original unclean hands matter was unrelated to the adverse possession.

Back to the other coast, in one New York federal case, defendants had claimed a right to ownership of land, and the plaintiff argued that

4 213 Cal. App. 4th at 1112.

5 *Id.*

6 Treager v. Friedman, 79 Cal. App. 2d 151 (1947).

7 *Id.* at 173 (citation omitted).

this claim was barred by "unclean hands" for an odd reason. Plaintiff claimed that that defendants' cabin, placed on the allegedly adverse property, violated the local building and land use code. The court did not agree with plaintiff's analysis, and held that merely because possession may violate a statute does not indicate there is "unclean hands."[8]

Unclean hands can also work the other way—that is, a party who wishes to *challenge* an adverse possession claim might be barred from doing so under the "unclean hands" doctrine. In one case,[9] various parties from the same family fought over ownership of real property. One party named Rosie sought to challenge Levon's claims of adverse possession to property. In response, Levon claimed that Rosie, as the administrator of the underlying estate, had plundered the estate of certain property. So he claimed she had unclean hands. But the court noted that the adverse possession/tax title action was completely separate from the alleged plunder, which had been heard decades before in a separate case. The issues in the adverse possession case were unrelated to wrongful acts by Rosie described in that previous case. Therefore, the higher court overruled the trial court's decision, which had improperly allowed the adverse possessor to raise that defense.

8 Sullivan v. Snider, 8:19-CV-0129 (GTS/DJS), 2021 WL 1294595, at *13 (N.D.N.Y. Apr. 7, 2021).

9 Anderson v. O'Neal, 338 So. 3d 629 (Miss. Ct. App. 2022).

Chapter 19
Statute of Limitations and Laches as Defenses

The standard operating procedure of attorneys is to raise a statute of limitations defense in the answer to any lawsuit, almost without regard to how long ago the issue at stake took place. However, in the context of defending a title holder from an adverse possession case, the statute of limitations is a non sequitur. As one court put it, if an adverse possession claimant were to argue that the title holder had waived anything simply because he did not raise the defense of the statute of limitations, the claimant would have it "entirely backwards."[1]

The statute of limitations is not a defense to an adverse possession case, or at least not in its traditional sense. There is no specific deadline by which an adverse possessor must file an action to claim ownership. In other words, holding onto adversely possessed property for "too long" without filing an action is generally a legal impossibility. The law does not even require a party to bring an action to perfect his claim of adverse possession. "Rather, it is the record owner—not the intruder—who must bring an action [within the set deadline] after adverse possession commences in order to recover the property."[2] Some courts do, however, use the term "statute of limitations" in the context of adverse possession cases. They do not do so for an outside deadline for one to file an adverse possession case, but instead for the deadline to dispute an adverse possession claim.[3] The use of the same nomenclature for two different issues is confusing.

The only kind of relevant deadline a title owner cares about is one that indicates the adverse possession claimant must use the property for at least a certain number of years. Without hitting the full number of years, the adverse claimant cannot obtain those rights. This is to be raised by the title holder, and not the adverse possession claimant. But even in that case, at least one case has indicated a defendant need not

1 Roy v. Woodstock Cmty. Tr., Inc., 195 Vt. 427, 444 (2014).

2 Connolly v. Trabue, 204 Cal. App. 4th 1154, 1163 (Cal. Ct. App. 2012) (citation omitted).

3 *See, e.g.*, *In re* Colarusso, 295 B.R. 166, 173 (B.A.P. 1st Cir. 2003).

raise an affirmative defense that the adverse possessor failed to reach the meet the years-long requirement of continuous possession. An argument about the lack of continuous possession is unlike a true statute of limitations defense; only a statute of limitations defense needs to be raised in order to preserve it.[4]

The only time, in theory, a statute of limitations would bar an adverse possessor from seeking to enforce his rights is if a new adverse possessor (which theoretically could include the record title holder) were to take over that same property for the correct number of years.

Just to make a complicated issue even more complicated, there is at least one quasi exception to the preceding rules, but it only applies to a claimant seeking adverse possession rights, if that claimant is not in current possession of the property. In Wisconsin, there is a statute[5] that indicates that a person who claims ownership rights as the result of an event, loses the right to bring a claim based on that event if an instrument or notice of claim is not recorded within 30 years of the event. Adverse possession is considered to be such an "event." This means that if a claimant has a legitimate adverse possession claim, then once that claimant's rights have solidified, the 30-year period commences, and he must then take appropriate steps within the next 30-year period.[6] However, as indicated earlier, there is a statutory owner-in-possession exception to the 30-year recording requirement.[7] Presumably, this means that if the claimant had established a legitimate adverse possession claim so that as of 1990, he would have been deemed the owner, but then he (1) failed to seek formal relief in his favor by 2020 and/or failed to file a notice of claim by that date, and (2) when he finally filed an action for formal declaratory judgment relief after 2020, he was no longer in possession, he could lose his case on that ground.

Laches has a slightly different definition from the statute of limitations. Laches "requires a showing of unreasonable delay on the part of the plaintiff in bringing the action, which may show abandonment or waiver of a right, or the acquiescence by the plaintiff in the defendant's fault."[8] Usually, if laches is asserted, it is by the defendant adverse possessor "as an additional defense against a plaintiff record owner's action to recover the property."[9]

So that leaves the question of whether the title owner can use laches to bar his neighbor's claim of adverse possession. Just as is true for the

4 Chiodini v. Lock, 2014 Ark. App. 219, at * 5 (Ark. Ct. App. 2014).
5 Wis. Stat. § 893.33(2).
6 O'Neill v. Reemer, 259 Wis. 2d 544, 551 (2003).
7 Wis. Stat. § 893.33(5).
8 City of Highland v. Cnty. of San Bernardino, 4 Cal. App. 4th 1174, 1192 (1992).
9 Marriage v. Keener, 26 Cal. App. 4th 186, 190 (1994).

statute of limitations, generally this argument would not work.[10] The reason for this is that, especially in a state in which title vests in the adverse possessor by operation of law at the moment the requisite conditions for adverse possession have been established for the statutory period, then the adverse possessor has no obligation to seek relief to formally declare himself the adverse possessor. As one court put it, "upon expiration of the [statutory limitation] period, the holder of land by adverse possession obtains the title which can only be divested by the conveyance of the land to another or by a subsequent disseisin [i.e., dispossession by a new adverse possession claimant] for the statutory limitation period."[11]

In one case, the title owner claimed that certain witnesses had died, which would make that party's position more difficult, and that therefore laches should apply. However, the court disagreed, holding that, "Since all doubts are resolved against the adverse possessor, it appears any prejudice resulting from the loss of these [witnesses'] testimony will cause detriment to [the claimed adverse possessor], not [record owners]."[12]

The concept behind this is that one who has a valid adverse possession claim does not need to file an action to obtain those rights. So any laws about limitations do not affect that claimant once he has already gone through the statutory time period of control, because the claimant already has the ownership rights—automatically. The Illinois Supreme Court held that a claimant of title to land by adverse possession is not guilty of laches in not promptly resorting to legal proceedings to remove cloud on title.[13] As an Oregon court put it, "A plaintiff in possession under a claim of title is entitled to wait until possession is invaded or the title attacked before taking steps to vindicate it, and a mere lapse of time will not bar the action. Nor is laches a defense where the plaintiff claims title by adverse possession."[14]

10 *Id*. at 191 (citations omitted).

11 Applebey v. Lenschow, 144 Ill. App. 3d 208 (1986).

12 *Marriage*, 26 Cal. App. 4th at 192.

13 Sheaff v. Spindler, 339 Ill. 540, 557–58 (1930).

14 Eichner v. Anderson, 229 Or. App. 495, 500–01 (Or. Ct. App. 2009), citing 74 C.J.S. Quieting Title § 55 (2002) (footnotes and internal ellipses omitted).

Chapter 20
Affidavits of Interruption and Torrens Title

This chapter concerns two methods of potentially preventing a party from making an effective adverse possession claim. One is through an affidavit of interruption, and the other is through Torrens title.

On the first subject, the Wisconsin legislature enacted a method to respond to an anticipated adverse possession claim.[1] A brief description of the basics is that the title holder can file an affidavit of interruption with the register of deeds in the county where the property is located, along with a survey of the property. Then the owner has to provide notice to the potential adverse possessory claimant. In effect, it resets the clock, and would add another 20 years to the time required for the potential claimant to wait before filing his own adverse possession claim.

Rhode Island has a similar law, except that no survey needs to be prepared. It indicates that such a notice "shall be deemed an interruption of the use and prevent the acquiring of any right thereto by the continuance of the use for any length of time thereafter."[2]

In Massachusetts, if a landowner seeks to prevent someone from acquiring a right of way or other easement in or over his land, he may post, serve, and record a notice to prevent the acquisition of easement by custom, pursuant to Mass. Gen. Laws Ann. chapter 187, section 3. Under this statute, a person "may give public notice of his intention to prevent the acquisition of such easement, by causing a copy of such notice to be posted in a conspicuous place upon the premises for six successive days, and such posting shall prevent the acquiring of such easement by use for any length of time thereafter; or he may prevent a particular person or persons from acquiring such easement by causing a copy of such notice to be served upon him or them . . . ." Notably, this statute does not specifically address adverse possession claims; it only affects a right to a potential easement. Maine has a similar statute, but that one specifically refers to a notice to prevent the acquisition by "adverse possession."[3]

---

1 Wis. Stat. § 893.305.

2 R.I. Gen. Laws § 34-7-6 (2013).

3 Me. Rev. Stat. tit. 14, § 812.

On the second subject, the great unsung hero of people who wish to preserve their title ownership, without fear of a potential adverse possessor, is Sir Robert Richard Torrens (1812–1884). Although born in Ireland, he became a land reformer in Australia. He originated Torrens title, which was a system of land registration that spread to other countries. Under that system, the state creates and maintains a register of what parties own certain lands. It can serve as absolute evidence concerning the identity of the owner, and prevent a successful adverse possession claim. At one point, many states used the system, but there are relatively few states in which the law has not been repealed to some degree. At least two states seem to have it in place in full still to this date: Hawaii and Minnesota. There are some modern cases from those courts that indicate that this system can bar an adverse possession claim. (Other states may allow for this system as well; if one represents a party in such a state, then an attorney should provide proactive suitable advice to such a client.)

One of Hawaii's systems for recording title to real property is through the "Land Court," which was created by the legislature with the passage of the Torrens Land Act in 1903. Today, it is codified in HRS chapter 501.[4] The purpose of the system created by the Torrens Land Act "is to conclusively establish title to land through the issuance of a certificate of title."[5] In one Hawaiian case, the court granted summary judgment, dismissing an adverse possession case. The title owner had presented evidence concerning its registration, and the court cited HRS § 501-87, which indicates that "[n]o title, right, or interest in, to, or across registered land in derogation of that of the registered owner shall be acquired by prescription or adverse possession[.]"[6]

Minnesota has a number of cases concerning the Torrens system and how it affects adverse possession claims. In one case, the appellant had tried various methods of claiming ownership of portions of property. One of those theories failed outright: "Appellant's theory relies on outdated cases addressing the doctrine of adverse possession, which the legislature has explicitly precluded in the Torrens Act."[7] The court cited Minn. Stat. section 508.02, which provides in relevant part that "[n]o title to registered land in derogation of that of the registered owner may be acquired by . . . adverse possession."

4 Wells Fargo Bank, N.A. v. Omiya, 142 Haw. 439, 446 (2018).
5 Aames Funding Corp. v. Mores, 107 Haw. 95, 101 (2005).
6 Smith v. Smith, 128 Hawai'i 130 (Ct. App. 2012).
7 Britney v. Swan Lake, 795 N.W.2d 867, 873 (Minn. Ct. App. 2011).

Part 5

Special Kinds of Adverse Possession

Chapter 21
Private Parties Adversely Possessing Government Property

There are probably many nonlawyers who think lawyers sit around their office all day and use Latin phrases like "Nullum tempus occurrit regi." We do not, but in the right case it might be fun to throw around. This phrase occurs in hundreds of reported cases across the United States. The restriction on the application of adverse possession to public property is rooted in the ancient doctrine that time does not run against the king (which is what is expressed in that Latin phrase).

There are various reasons why the rationale still makes sense in modern times among those rare people who use English instead of Latin. For example, in effect government land is public land, and the public should not suffer from the negligence of its agents who fail to check on the status of that land. One might also argue that since the state holds that property in trust for its own people, then only the legislature can divest the land to others. To allow a private person to possess and thereafter claim ownership of public lands, should be considered a public nuisance, and no matter how long the state acquiesces, the law will not justify such a nuisance.[1]

Now that rationales are out of the way, we are still left with the question—can a private citizen adversely possess government property? The answer is not black or white.

In at least two states, the legislatures potentially exposed their states to adverse possession claims because of the breadth of the statutes. The statutes in some states permit adverse possession of "any real property" held by the state.[2]

In other states, the state-owned land is statutorily protected from claims of adverse possession. For example, under Washington's relevant statute, "the statute of limitations for adverse possession will not run

1 *See* Devins v. Borough of Bogota 124 N.J. 570, 574 (1991).
2 N.C. Gen. Stat. § 1-35; N.D. Cent. Code § 28-01-01.

against the State or city acting in its governmental capacity."[3] At least one reason Washington courts have ruled this way is that a relevant statute indicates that "no claim of right predicated upon the lapse of time shall ever be asserted against the state."[4] The Wisconsin state legislature enacted Wis. Stat. section 893.29(1), which prevents land held by the state and local government entities from being adversely possessed (with certain exceptions). An Arizona statute[5] provides that the state shall not be barred by the limitations of action relating to real property. Therefore, adverse possession does not run against the state.

At least one state even included a specific clause in its constitution to prevent losing public property through adverse possession. Article VIII, section 10 of the South Dakota Constitution provides in part that "[n]o claim to any public lands by any trespasser thereon by reason of occupancy, cultivation or improvement thereof, shall ever be recognized . . . ."

In other states, the answer to whether a private party may adversely possess government is an attorney's favorite response—"it depends." For example, Massachusetts permits adverse possession of state land generally, but permits no adverse possession of state land "held for conservation, open space, parks, recreation, water protection, wildlife protection, or other public purpose."[6]

There is another kind of real property that certain states consider a special case—if the real property is both (1) municipally owned, and (2) not dedicated to or used for a public purpose. In certain states, that kind of property may be treated like property owned by private owners, meaning it is capable of being adversely possessed.[7] The reason for this rule is that it will encourage municipalities to actually use such property. If not, then the property should be returned to the public in part as a measure to increase income to the state through real estate taxes.[8] In New York, one court described the distinction between lands held by the state as sovereign and those held as proprietor in *People v. Baldwin*.[9] The court held that "[t]here is a well-recognized distinction between lands held by the State as sovereign in trust for the public and lands held as proprietor only, for the purpose of sale or other disposition . . . such lands only as the state holds as a proprietor may be lost to the state; it cannot lose

3 Gorman v. City of Woodinville, 175 Wash. 2d 68, 72 (2012), citing Wash. Rev. Code § 4.16.160.
4 Wash. Rev. Code § 4.16.160.
5 Ariz. Rev. Stat. § 12-510.
6 Mass. Gen. Laws ch. 260, § 31.
7 *See* Siejack v. City of Baltimore, 270 Md. 640 (1974).
8 *See* Devins v. Borough of Bogota 124 N.J., 578–579 (1991).
9 197 App. Div. 285 (N.Y. App. Div. 1921), *aff'd*, 233 N.Y. 672 (1922).

such lands as it holds for the public, in trust for a public purpose, as highways, public streams, canals, public fairgrounds."[10]

In one interesting New York case, *Monthie v. Boyle Road Associates*,[11] a school district acquired title to 48 acres of land in the late 1960s. It used 19 of those acres for school buildings and the like, and left the other 29 acres undeveloped. Then in 1986, it offered to sell the 29-acre parcel. After a private party purchased that land in 1998, neighboring homeowners claimed to have been using some of those 29 acres in an adverse manner for years while it was owned by the municipality. Therefore, they claimed to have superior rights. The court held that those private citizens had the right to pursue their case, despite the fact that the property was owned by a municipality, and despite the fact that a portion of the entire parcel was still owned in a "governmental capacity."

Another example of the New York method is in a case in which the plaintiffs claimed to adversely possess property owned by a state entity, which was a part of parcels of other land which had been transferred from a county to a village entity. There was a dispute about what the county and/or village had ultimately intended to do with the parcel plaintiffs possessed. But what the court considered critical is that at trial, there was testimony concerning other conveyances to private individuals of other parcels of the land. Therefore, the court held that even if the present plan of the defendant was to use the disputed parcel for additional village parking, "the evidence of such conveyances is sufficient to establish its alienability and thus render it susceptible to adverse possession."[12] The court affirmed the award of title to certain property to the plaintiffs.

Another New York case concerned a tenant who claimed that after the owner of the property died, she adversely possessed it. However, when her landlord died, without a will and without heirs, the title vested "at once" to the state. It did not matter how long the former tenant lived in the premises afterward, or in what manner, because the state was the unknowing owner of it the entire time. And in New York, since generally one cannot claim adverse possession against the state, she could not obtain title, no matter what evidence she had about the post-death "hostility" or a "claim of right."[13]

Connecticut and Maryland are other examples of states that hold that municipal land not used for a public purpose is subject to adverse

10 *Id.* at 288 (citations omitted).
11 281 A.D.2d 15 (N.Y. App. Div. 2001).
12 Lewis v. Vill. of Lyons, 54 A.D.2d 488, 491 (N.Y. App. Div. 1976).
13 *In re* Haynes, 283 B.R. 147, 153 (Bankr. S.D.N.Y. 2002).

possession. In *Goldman v. Quadrato*,[14] the plaintiff claimed title by adverse possession to an adjacent lot owned by the City of Waterbury, which had acquired title through a tax-foreclosure proceeding. Noting that the city lot "was neither used for nor dedicated to any public purpose," the Connecticut high court held that the land was subject to adverse possession.[15] In one Maryland case, the plaintiff had operated for many years a dump on land owned by the City of Baltimore. The City had acquired the property, but had never used the land for any purpose. Because the City had never "devoted [the land] to public use and . . . it is unlikely it ever intends to do so," the court held that the plaintiff could maintain an action seeking title by adverse possession.[16]

One reviewing statutes against adverse possession of government property does not need to stop there. There can still be exceptions to the rules. In an interesting case in the state of Washington, a party had claimed title to certain real property through adverse possession—the property that a private owner had dedicated to a city. Although the city sought to dismiss the case, the claimant explained that his claim was based on adverse possession that transpired while the land was still in private hands, and before it was dedicated to the city.[17] The court held that the claimant could pursue his case. As the court held, it would be "absurd" to allow a prior owner to extinguish a valid adverse possession case against him by just transferring record title to the government. It would be like money laundering, except with real property. One should not be able to "clean" the property just by transferring the property to the government.

Another interesting case analyzed a federal statute, which concerns the Alaska Native Claims Settlement Act[18] (ANCSA). The ANCSA, signed into law in 1971, was intended to resolve issues surrounding aboriginal land claims in Alaska. It transferred titles to Alaska Native regional corporations and local village corporations. One portion of the act provides that "all land and interests in land conveyed in Alaska by the Federal Government pursuant to [ANCSA] to a Native individual or Native Corporation . . . shall be exempt, so long as such land and interests are not developed or leased or sold to third parties[,] from . . . adverse possession."[19] In the Alaskan Supreme Court case *Snook v. Bowers*, a particular lot at issue was indeed ANCSA land. However, that lot was "developed" within the meaning of the statute, and therefore the party

14 142 Conn. 398 (1955).
15 *Id.* at 403.
16 Siejack v. City of Baltimore, 270 Md. 640, 645 (1974).
17 Gorman v. City of Woodinville, 175 Wash. 2d 68, 70–71 (2012).
18 43 U.S.C. §§ 1601 *et seq.*
19 *Id.* § 1636(d)(1)(A).

seeking to avoid adverse possession could not rely on that statute to bar the claim.[20]

An example of creative legal thinking on this issue, which did not work, took place in California. In that case,[21] the late actor Larry Hagman's land was at issue. In 1987, one of the fences marking the boundary of his property was built in the wrong place. Hagman treated the fence as being accurately placed, and occupied and improved a .44-acre (about one-third of the size of a football field) portion of the 173-acre parcel owned by his adjoining neighbor, the Meher Mount Corporation (Meher Mount). The court noted that "Meher Mount is a religious group whose 'primary purpose' is to 'provide for the betterment of mankind by implementing the teachings of Meher Baba.'"[22] Its land was allegedly dedicated to that purpose. Meher Baba, in turn, was an Indian spiritual master who modestly claimed to be God in human form.

In any event, to avoid the adverse possession claim, Meher Mount noted that title to property owned by a public entity cannot be obtained by another through adverse possession.[23] So Meher Mount claimed that it was a public benefit corporation, and that this was the same thing as a public entity. Therefore, under this logic, the Hagman estate could not adversely possess the religious entity's property. The court disagreed and held that the term "public corporation" is a "term of art used to designate certain entities that exercise governmental functions." It also noted that "public benefit corporations are not public entities." A public benefit corporation has no sovereignty, and that made it highly unlike a public entity.[24] The estate of Hagman had its wish[25] fulfilled, and judgment in its favor was affirmed on appeal.

Finally, if one's client is seeking adverse possession claims against a government entity, and all options seem to be roadblocked, one may consider a claim based on a presumed grant, which is addressed in Chapter 31.

---

20 12 P.3d 771, 779–80 (Alaska 2000).
21 Hagman v. Meher Mount Corp., 215 Cal. App. 4th 82 (Cal. Ct. App. 2013).
22 *Id.* at 85.
23 *Id.* at 87, citing Cal. Civ. Code, § 1007.
24 *Id.* at 87–88.
25 If you got this reference, you must be (1) old and (2) a TV fanatic.

Chapter 22
Government Adversely Possessing Private Property

The Fifth Amendment to the Constitution of the United States provides in relevant part: ". . . nor shall private property be taken for public use, without just compensation." This clause, known as the Takings Clause, is "applicable to the States through the Fourteenth Amendment."[1] Regardless, some state constitutions have similar language.[2] As one court put it, "The Takings Clause was meant to protect private individuals from excessive government intrusion on their property rights."[3]

Does this right take effect when the government claims it has adversely possessed private property? In 1893, the U.S. Supreme Court implicitly held that officers of the United States, sued for trespass, could raise a defense of lawful title by adverse possession.[4] The Court did not address whether that was considered a taking without compensation, because the issue was trespass. But what the Court actually held is perhaps not as relevant as how modern courts interpret it, which is apparently that if the federal government has a valid adverse possession claim, then the Takings Clause is moot.

Another U.S. Supreme Court decision might also imply what the federal position is on adverse possession by the government. In *Texaco, Inc. v. Short*, a relevant statute indicated that if a party did not use a mineral interest in the property, then it would lapse and revert to the current surface owner of the property. When parties lost that interest due to failing to meet the requirements of the statute, they claimed such a result was unconstitutional. But the Supreme Court held that "[s]tates have the power to permit unused or abandoned interest in property to revert to another after the passage of time."[5]

---

1 Palazzolo v. Rhode Island, 533 U.S. 606, 617 (2001).

2 *See, e.g.*, art. I, § 18 of the Alaska Constitution and art. 1, § 17 of the Texas Constitution.

3 Pascoag Reservoir Dam, LLC v. Rhode Island, 217 F. Supp. 2d 206, 225 (D.R.I. 2002).

4 Stanley v. Schwalby, 147 U.S. 508 (1893).

5 454 U.S. 516, 526 (1982).

In any event, whether based on U.S. Supreme Court rulings or otherwise, many courts have indicated that even beyond the federal government, other public or governmental entities may acquire title to land by adverse possession, at least in dicta, if not in a holding.[6] A number of cases have also indicated, either explicitly or implicitly, when taking the private party's property by adverse possession, the government has no obligation to pay funds to the private party.[7]

This may seem unfair in light of constitutional protections from having the government take land without compensation. But one court explained it like this: "In the case of adverse possession, property is not taken. Rather . . . the former titleholder has lost his claim of ownership and the adverse possessor is thereafter maintaining its possession, not taking property."[8] That explanation probably will not satisfy one's client who loses real property worth millions of dollars.

But at least one case has indicated that the Takings Clause obligates the government to pay for land it claims to have adversely possessed. In a Rhode Island federal case, the court indicated in dicta that "[t]he government cannot escape the Takings Clause by opting to sit by until title is transferred to it, and then claim that it is not subject to the United States Constitution."[9]

Other cases have other methods of trying to claim why the government should be able to obtain property without payment. In one Nebraska case, a city had claimed an adverse possession interest in a certain portion of property, even though certain records indicated it was owned privately. The plaintiffs argued that the Constitution prohibits the taking of property without just compensation, and essentially that the only means by which the city could obtain rights was through eminent domain. The court, to some degree, sidestepped the issue. First, it noted that the adverse possession did not destroy the owner's rights during the running of the statutory period of limitation. Then it argued that "the public" obtained the right to that part of the land, and the members of "the public" did not have the power of eminent domain. As

---

6 *See, e.g.*, Roche v. Fairfield, 186 Conn. 490 (1982); Nyman v. Eugene 286 Or. 47 (1979); Drainage Dist. No. 1 v. Green Valley, 69 Ill. App. 3d 330 (1979); State, *ex rel.* Remy, v. Agar, 559 P.2d 1235 (Okla. 1977); United States v. 202.76 Acres of Land, 439 F. Supp. 483, 486 (D.N.D. 1977).

7 *See* Bd. of Cnty. Comm'rs v. Flickinger, 687 P.2d 975, 983–85 (Colo. 1984) (en banc); Commonwealth v. Stephens, 407 S.W.2d 711, 712 (Ky. 1966); Rogers v. Marlin, 754 So. 2d 1267, 1273 (Miss. Ct. App. 1999); City of Ashland v. Hardesty, 23 Or. App. 523 (1975); Petersen v. Port of Seattle, 94 Wn.2d 479 (1980).

8 State, *ex rel.* A.A.A. Investments v. Columbus, 17 Ohio St. 3d 151, 152 (Ohio 1985).

9 Pascoag Reservoir Dam, LLC v. Rhode Island, 217 F. Supp. 2d 206, 225–26 (D.R.I. 2002) *aff'd*, 337 F.3d 87 (1st Cir. 2003).

the court saw it, since "the public" acquired the land adversely, the city was merely holding title "for the benefit of the public."[10] Presumably, the plaintiffs were not thrilled with that logic, but it was issued by that state's highest court.

If all else fails, there is another way of arguing that the government should not be entitled to adversely possess your client's property. In Indiana, one must prove one has paid real estate taxes on the property in order to obtain an adverse possession right. The State of Indiana tried to prove it had adversely possessed certain land. So the private owner argued that the State had not paid the real estate tax. But, the State responded, the State is exempt from property taxation, and so if that rule were followed, it would be legally impossible for the State to adversely possess property. The court did not accept the State's argument—it held that this legal impossibility was just too bad. "There is no exception in the adverse possession tax statute for governmental units that are exempt from paying taxes. If an exception is to be made, it is for our legislature to so provide."[11]

10 Dunnick v. Stockgrowers Bank of Marmouth, 191 Neb. 370, 373 (1974).
11 State v. Serowiecki, 892 N.E.2d 194, 203 (Ind. Ct. App. 2008).

Chapter 23
Terminating an Easement through Adverse Possession

Adverse possession can also achieve another goal. That is, a party owning a servient estate may extinguish an easement through adverse possession. (For those needing a refresher course, an easement is a right to use another person's property for limited purposes, such as to cross over it. A servient estate is the land that is subject to the easement, and whose owner is required to provide access. A dominant estate is the opposite—the land whose owner has the right to the easement against the servient estate. In other words, the easement holder "dominates" and rules over the servient landowner, forcing that servient owner into giving the easement holder access. Cases often indicate that the dominant estate is the "easement owner," or the "easement holder.") This chapter concerns terminating an easement; Chapter 26 concerns obtaining an easement.

A quick and dirty way of explaining how adverse possession in this context works is that for the statutory time period, the "owner of the servient estate must use his land in a manner that is adverse to the exercise of the easement."[1] This kind of claim is "variously called termination of an easement by adverse possession, termination of an easement by prescription, extinguishment of an easement by adverse possession, and extinguishment of an easement by prescription."[2]

The party seeking to extinguish the easement would have to meet certain elements, which follow the elements of an adverse possession claim to some degree. New York's high court indicated that the servient estate "must establish that [its] use of the easement has been adverse to the owner of the easement, under a claim of right, open and notorious, exclusive and continuous for a period of 10 years."[3] As indicated in another New York Court of Appeals case, an "easement may be lost by adverse possession if the owner or possessor of the servient estate

1 Hinrichs v. Melton, 11 Cal. App. 5th 516, 526 (2017).
2 Matoush v. Lovingood, 177 P.3d 1262, 1265 n.2 (Colo. 2008).
3 Spiegel v. Ferraro, 73 N.Y.2d 622, 624–28 (1989).

claims to own it free from the private right of another, and excludes the owner of the easement, who acquiesces in the exclusion for [the prescriptive period]."[4] In Colorado, the elements are described as follows: "An easement is terminated by adverse possession upon a showing that use of the easement area was: (1) adverse to the easement holder's use of the easement; (2) open or notorious; and (3) continuous, without effective interruption, for the statutorily-mandated period of time for adverse possession."[5] In California, "a court may conclude that an easement has been extinguished where the owner of the servient tenement, under an adverse claim of right, with notice thereof to the owner of the dominant tenement, continuously during [the statutory period], uses the servient tenement in such a manner as to obstruct its use for easement purposes by the latter owner."[6]

One has to understand a critical difference between a traditional adverse possession case and that which terminates an easement. Merely showing actual possession would not be enough. "The owner of the servient estate claiming adverse possession of an easement already has the right to possess and use the land so long as that use is not inconsistent with the easement. Therefore, the owner of a servient estate must prove the use of the servient estate made during the period of adverse possession is sufficiently hostile and inconsistent with the use permitted by the easement."[7]

If a servient landowner wants to end an easement, he must take full and appropriate steps. For example, in one Montana case, an installation of metal, locked gate across access road did not extinguish easement rights by adverse possession, in part because access to the easement on foot, snowmobile, or motorcycle could be achieved by going around the gate.[8]

One extreme example of what should work to terminate an easement by adverse possession was described in a California case *Hinrichs v. Melton*.[9] In that case, the servient owner placed large boulders and a barbed wire fence that blocked an entrance to a trail that the dominant estate owner ultimately wanted to use. This was done for the full statutory period. The dominant owner complained that the servient owner had not shown hostility, because the servient owner had remained silent about whether the dominant owner could use

4 Woodruff v. Paddock, 130 N.Y. 618, 624 (1892).
5 177 P.3d at 1265.
6 Ross v. Lawrence, 219 Cal. App. 2d 229, 232 (1963).
7 Mueller v. Hoblyn, 887 P.2d 500, 507 (Wyo. 1994).
8 Shors v. Branch, 221 Mont. 390 (1986).
9 11 Cal. App. 5th 516 (Cal. Ct. App. 2017).

it. That argument did not work because "the boulders spoke louder than words."[10]

There is a special rule in the context of a right-of-way easement that exists on paper but has never actually been used. In that context, courts in certain states can only infer a hostile claim after the easement owner requests that the adverse user remove the obstruction and the adverse user refuses.[11] Another way this has been phrased, by a Montana court, is that "where an easement has been created but no occasion has arisen for its use, the owner of the servient tenement may fence the land and this will not be deemed adverse until such time as the need for the right-of-way arises and the owner of the dominant tenement demands that the easement be opened and the servient tenement owner refuses to do so."[12] In such a case, in theory, if the owner of the land leaves the obstruction or fence in place for 200 years, but the easement owner does not need access during that time, then the easement owner can either sit and wait it out, or alternatively file an action demanding access.

On the same subject, in one Arizona case, the court held that if the easement has never been used, and the servient estate owner wishes to claim termination of the easement by adverse possession, "there must be a clear, unequivocal message from the servient estate's owner, beyond mere fencing, prohibiting any future use of the easement for ingress/egress. The easement holder should not be left to speculate as to whether an easement may be partially extinguished or its scope of future use limited."[13] In that case, the servient owner claimed to have posted signs indicating how the space was to be used, but had little if any evidence showing it. The "documented plans to post signs, without more, did not constitute clear and convincing evidence of adverse possession."[14] What this means, conversely, is that if fencing is put in place along with clear posted signs indicating that the easement, in effect, is treated as no longer existing, that may be enough to terminate the easement.

The owner of the servient estate can also try another approach—to terminate just a part of an easement.[15] One example expressed by a court was that "if the servient owner of a parcel subject to an express roadway easement bars vehicles but allows pedestrians through, a fact finder

10 *Id.* at 527.

11 Will v. Gates, 254 A.D.2d 275, 276 (N.Y. App. Div. 1998), citing, among others, Castle Associates v. Schwartz, 63 A.D.2d 481 (N.Y. App. Div. 1978); *Spiegel*, 73 N.Y.2d at 626. *See also* Welsh v. Taylor, 134 N.Y. 450, 459 (1892) ("as long as there was no occasion for [easement owners] to use [the easement] the mere existence of a gate was not notice of any adverse claim").

12 Halverson v. Turner, 268 Mont. 168, 175 (1994).

13 Sabino Town Country Estates Ass'n v. Carr, 186 Ariz. 146, 150 (Ct. App. 1996).

14 *Id.* at 151.

15 *See* Glatts v. Henson 31 Cal. 2d 368, 371 (1948).

could find the easement partially extinguished or, if you like, the scope of the easement narrowed to use as a footpath."[16]

A somewhat unanswered question concerns whether a party can terminate an easement by necessity. As a refresher, "[a]n easement by way of necessity arises by operation of law when it is established that (1) there is a strict necessity for the right-of-way, as when the claimant's property is landlocked and (2) the dominant and servient tenements were under the same ownership at the time of the conveyance giving rise to the necessity."[17]

In a California case resolved in 2008, the servient owners claimed that if an easement by necessity had existed, they had terminated it by adverse possession.[18] The parties both agreed the servient owners had "erected a locked gate blocking the easement for longer than five years, and guarded the gate around the clock, preventing appellants from accessing the easement." But the alleged easement holder argued that this was irrelevant because, he claimed, terminating an easement by necessity is a legal impossibility. The court disagreed. It cited various cases, including one from 1949 in which that court held that "[t]he conceded facts deny the existence of a way of necessity. Assuming such right of way may have accrued when appellants or their predecessors acquired the parcels here involved, such easement was lost through the adverse possession of respondents . . . ."[19]

However, the same "boulder" case described above from 2017 in California seemed to see the situation otherwise, or at least partially. In *Hinrichs v. Melton*, the plaintiff owned two contiguous parcels of land and sold the southern parcel to the defendants in 1999.[20] This left the plaintiff's remaining parcel landlocked. Many years later, the plaintiff brought an action against the owners of three neighboring parcels, including defendants, in order to establish an easement to access plaintiff's parcel. The trial court granted the plaintiff an easement by necessity over a certain parcel, but not necessarily through the trail easement, which was terminated by adverse possession. The court held, "There is no doubt that [there was an extinguishment of] any easement over the trail by adverse possession. But that does not mean an easement by necessity over the . . . parcel has been extinguished by adverse possession. An easement by necessity cannot be extinguished as long as the necessity exists."[21]

---

16 Flanigan v. Gausewitz, No. G042991, 2011 WL 600442, at *1 n.6 (Cal. Ct. App. Feb. 22, 2011) (citation omitted).

17 Moores v. Walsh, 38 Cal. App. 4th 1046, 1049 (1995).

18 Kern v. Severe, No. A117151, at *1 (Cal. Ct. App. Apr. 21, 2008).

19 Miller v. Fowle, 92 Cal. App. 2d 409, 413 (1949).

20 11 Cal. App. 5th 516 (2017).

21 *Id.* at 530.

Chapter 24
A Former Tenant or Current Co-Owner Can Become an Adverse Possessor

"What's happened to me," he thought. It was no dream.
—*The Metamorphosis*, Franz Kafka

A FORMER TENANT CAN BECOME AN OWNER

If a landlord leases space to a tenant, and the tenant eventually wants to claim adverse possession, the tenant will have major difficulties. But many states, if not all of them, allow the tenant to succeed if the situation is right.

Alaska heard a case concerning this issue, providing a great deal of analysis on it. In that case, the claimant's predecessor was a former tenant of property, meaning it was originally a permissive occupant.[1] As we remember from Chapter 3, a party that occupies land with permission cannot claim the element of "hostility." These terms are polar opposites.

In any event, that claimant's predecessor eventually stopped paying rent, and argued that this fact meant "hostility" in and of itself. The Alaska Supreme Court rejected that argument. It indicated that at best, nonpayment of rent only terminates a lease, and thereafter makes the occupant a "tenant at sufferance."[2] That term is defined as one who wrongfully continues in possession without a claim of superior title. Moreover, the court held that "[a] tenancy at sufferance is a permissive interest and cannot be the basis for adverse possession." The court also indicated it did not want to "establish a rule that gives tenants an incentive to stop paying rent in the hope of establishing an adverse possession claim."[3]

Therefore, the court held that such a former tenant "must openly and explicitly disclaim and disavow any and all holding under his former

1 Glover v. Glover, 92 P.3d 387 (Alaska 2004).
2 *Id.* at 393.
3 *Id.*

landlord; and, furthermore, he must unreservedly and steadily assert that he himself is the owner of the true title."[4] It also held that such a claimant must provide even stronger evidence to prove adverse possession, in comparison to someone who simply had never had permission to enter. "[W]hen a claimant started out occupying land permissively, it is essential that his new, hostile interest in the property be made clear to the true owner. The behavior of a tenant and an owner will often be indistinguishable; if a tenant merely acts as he always did, the owner will not be on notice of his new, hostile claim. In almost every case, only a distinct and positive assertion of the new claim—or a repudiation of the owner's interest—will provide proper notice."[5] The court indicated that such a tenant would have to either (1) show a "distinct act, like an open announcement of his claim or a change in his use of the land," or (2) prove "overt and unambiguous" acts of ownership such as paying all taxes and insurance.[6]

The District of Columbia Court of Appeals (its highest court) heard an interesting case on this matter, which also provides guidance.[7] A residential building was held in the title of the estate of Wells. But Blanche Smith had allegedly occupied it as an adverse possessor. Mrs. Smith had originally been a tenant of the building from the 1950s, and then the owner, Mrs. Wells, died in 1960. Mrs. Smith paid no more rent after that, but she did make improvements to the house, and in 1968 she even leased out the space to new tenants. Finally, in 1985 Mrs. Smith filed a complaint to establish title by adverse possession to the property. The trial judge granted summary judgment to the estate of Mrs. Smith (Mrs. Smith died after she filed the case) on the grounds that Mrs. Wells's death in 1960 resulted in the destruction of what had been a tenancy at will and left Mrs. Smith in adverse possession. The judge relied on evidence of Mrs. Smith's control reflected by the payment of the real estate taxes, the improvements made, and the rent collected.

However, the high court reversed and did not grant adverse possession. It held that the lower court erred by not considering critical law. That included that Mrs. Smith entered the land with permission, and that "[a] permissive entry upon land does not ripen into adverse possession, no matter how long actual possession continues, until the holder disavows the ownership of the landowners by unequivocal conduct. There must be proof of a claim, act or declaration of hostility so manifest and notorious that actual notice will be presumed in order to

---

4 *Id.* (citation omitted).

5 *Id.* at 394.

6 *Id.* at 394–95.

7 Est. of Wells v. Est. of Smith, 576 A.2d 707 (D.C. 1990).

change a permissive or otherwise non-hostile possession into one that is hostile."[8] The court held that the claim of hostile possession based on the fact of the death of Mrs. Wells was not sufficient, because at best Mrs. Smith became a tenant at sufferance, with an implied continuation of all the terms of the previous agreement, including the covenants to maintain the premises in good condition.

It also held that the claims of paying the outstanding mortgage, taxes and utility expenses, making significant repairs and replacing the oil burner and porch, and leasing the property to other nonowners and collected rent, were not enough. This was in part because that the mortgage payments Mrs. Smith made were relatively minimal, and her other acts of alleged ownership could be seen as "consistent with the lease agreement."[9] In addition, the permits she obtained for work done on the property were taken out in Mrs. Wells's (or her deceased husband's) name. Moreover, the tax bills for the property were still in the name of the late Mrs. Wells and her deceased husband; apparently it would have worked in Mrs. Smith's favor if she had been able to convince the taxing authority to change the name on those bills. And finally, the court noted that "Mrs. Smith has never made any attempt to give actual notice to the true owners that she claimed the land adversely."[10]

In sum, an attorney representing a former tenant claiming to be an adverse possessor has his work cut out for him, especially in a state in which the court does not presume hostility. An attorney will have to obtain extremely strong evidence that the former tenant went through the metamorphosis.

In states in which hostility can be presumed in certain circumstances, a former tenant may have an easier time. New York is an example. New York also struggled with the issue about former tenants claiming to be owners. As indicated above, one of the reasons it is difficult for a former tenant to claim adverse possession status is that, if one originally enters land with permission from the owner, then it becomes difficult to prove when, if ever, the permission was denied, and that the true hostile possession began. As one New York court put it, "[I]f the first possession is by permission it is presumed to so continue until the contrary appears."[11]

New York's legislature eventually realized how difficult this was for courts to resolve. Its commission indicated that "[b]ecause it was uncertain whether specific acts were sufficient to constitute a clear repudiation

8 *Id.* at 710 (citation omitted).
9 *Id.* at 712.
10 *Id.* at 713.
11 Lewis v. New York Harlem R.R. Co., 162 N.Y. 202, 220 (1900) (italics omitted).

of permission or authority or sufficient to constitute an ouster, it was difficult to determine when, or if, adverse possession commenced. Many land titles were thus rendered unmarketable by the presumption of non-adverse possession even after many years of exclusive occupancy by a tenant or tenant in common."[12] Therefore, the New York legislature passed RPAPL section 531, which provides: "Where the relation of landlord and tenant has existed between any persons the possession of the tenant is deemed the possession of the landlord until the expiration of ten years after the termination of the tenancy; or, where there has been no written lease, until the expiration of ten years after the last payment of rent; notwithstanding that the tenant has acquired another title or has claimed to hold adversely to his landlord. But this presumption shall cease after the periods prescribed in this section and such tenant may then commence to hold adversely to his landlord."

That statute made a line in the sand: there is an automatic presumption that the tenant is holding the premises in a non-adverse context for ten years after the tenancy formally ends, but the period of non-adverse presumption is limited to that time period. And in New York, hostility is presumed so long as the other elements of adverse possession are met. This is great news for a former tenant, because a court might be willing to believe not only that the presumption of permission ends after ten years, but if the argument is convincing enough, that hostility is presumed to have started at the end of that ten years. However, the bad news is that tenants have to wait 20 years after the tenancy ends to claim adverse possession, whereas any other random person in the world would only have to wait ten years.

This statute affects former tenants in manners one might not expect. In one case,[13] the court was heavy-handed with that statute. The former tenant, and later adverse possession claimant, had occupied certain space, which was not technically included in the metes and bounds description of the lease at issue. The former tenant (unfortunately for its own interests) admitted that it had occupied that space under the mistaken belief that this particular space was indeed within the entirety of the premises described in the lease. The title holder then successfully argued that the claimant's occupancy of that particular space should be considered part of its tenancy, meaning the claimant would have to wait ten years after the lease terminated, and then another ten years after that to obtain a claim for that space. Since the former tenant could not hit those numbers, it lost its case. If however, the former tenant had simply alleged that it occupied that particular space without permission, and

12 1975 Report of N.Y. Law Rev. Comm'n, 1975 N.Y. Legis Doc. No. 65 (P) at 2–3.
13 Gallea v. Hess Realty Corp., 128 A.D.2d 274 (N.Y. App. Div. 1987).

that it had not believed it occupied that space as a tenant, it might have had better luck.

A CO-OWNER CAN BECOME A FULL OWNER

The only thing worse than losing one's recorded rights to property to a former tenant would be to lose those rights to a person who is a co-owner. Presumably there are few people who have to trust each other more than co-owners of real estate. At the very least, each would likely presume that they would keep those rights indefinitely. But even a co-owner can lose his rights to another co-owner through adverse possession.

There are various forms of co-ownership, and the primary ones that are litigated in adverse possession cases are tenancy-in-common cases. In a tenancy-in-common, each cotenant has an equal right to possess and enjoy all or any portion of the property as if he is the sole owner. And yet, "exclusive possession" is needed for an adverse possession case. How can one cotenant in common claim a special "exclusive possession," if the law indicates that he already had the right to exclusive possession? One cannot claim that simply because a tenant in common exercised the rights he already had, this had some deeper meaning. It would be like claiming that because I exercised my Fifth Amendment to remain silent during police questioning, I also have the right to avoid a trial or any potential conviction.

But there must be a way for one co-owner to establish adverse possession rights and defeat other co-owners' rights, if the situation is right. As an extreme, if one person has occupied real property not realizing it was co-owned by his never seen seventh cousin four times removed, and he spends 50 years building up the property, paying for all taxes and insurance, and takes all of the risks that belong to an owner, should he be denied full ownership simply because he never noticed that this distant relative living in the South Pole was listed in fine print on the deed? The solution to this puzzle is generally that one cotenant must "oust" the other cotenants in order to claim adverse possession. Then we have a new problem of trying to determine what ouster means in this context. But at least the attorney will know what word to use in his arguments.

New York is a good place to begin to understand how the courts resolve adverse possession cases between co-owners. In 1998, its high court was faced with a case[14] in which one cotenant in common had not "ousted" the other non-possessory tenant in common (at least not literally). The claimant had exclusive possession for approximately 13 years.

14 Myers v. Bartholomew, 91 N.Y.2d 630 (1998).

The court had to resolve a "perennial mind-buster" of whether the statute, RPAPL 541, required the plaintiff to have exclusive possession for ten years, or for 20 years, to acquire full title by adverse possession.

The court first described the right of non-possessory cotenants, and how the common law affected them. The court explained that since any cotenant has a right to possess the whole property, then "nonpossessory cotenants do not relinquish any of their rights as tenants-in-common when another cotenant assumes exclusive possession of the property."[15] The court indicated that it was best to set a law which avoids danger for a non-possessory tenant. Otherwise, the non-possessory tenant could face an adverse possession case even though he "would have had no reason even to protest the purportedly adverse possession."[16]

The court indicated that since courts must presume a cotenant's possession is possession by and for the benefit of all other cotenants, then under common law, "a tenant-in-common seeking to assert a successful claim of adverse possession is required to show more than mere possession; the co-tenant must also commit acts constituting ouster."[17] The court indicated that there could be actual ouster, such as an express communication to exclude cotenants, or implied ouster, "where the acts of the possessing co-tenant are so openly hostile that the non-possessing co-tenants can be presumed to know that the property is being adversely possessed against them."[18]

The court noted that these issues were difficult to resolve under common law, so the legislature eventually enacted a statute ultimately codified as RPAPL 541, which now states the presumption that one tenant is occupying with permission of the other cotenant "shall cease after the expiration of ten years of continuous exclusive occupancy by such tenant, personally or by his servant or by his tenant, or immediately upon an ouster by one tenant of the other and such occupying tenant may then commence to hold adversely to his cotenant."

This statute was meant to clarify matters, but actually it had the opposite effect. Commentators and courts could not agree about when the presumption of non-adverse possession ceases and the adverse possession period begins to run. Finally, the high priests decided that "[a]bsent ouster, a cotenant may begin to hold adversely only *after* 10 years of exclusive possession. RPAPL 541's statutory presumption, therefore, effectively requires 20 years—or two consecutive ten-year periods—of

15 *Id.* at 633.
16 *Id.*
17 *Id.*
18 *Id.*

exclusive possession before a co-tenant may be said to have adversely possessed a property owned by tenants-in-common."[19]

The proper way of examining this statute, as the high court decided, is that although ouster is a critical element in an adverse possession claim between cotenants in common, the ouster is presumed to have occurred after ten years of exclusive possession. Then the claimant with exclusive possession must wait for the statute of limitations to expire, which will not take place for another ten years. But if one tenant in common wants to obtain rights as an adverse possessor in a shorter period, he will have to immediately conduct either an explicit or implicit ouster, and then he can wait for merely ten years, instead of 20 years.[20] Therefore, if an attorney is representing an allegedly adverse possessor who was (1) a tenant in common and (2) only held the property exclusively for between ten and 20 years, he will have to search for a way to claim that this explicit or implicit ouster took place. The potential implicit ouster, of course, cannot just be the act of being in exclusive possession, because that is part of the original ten-year period.

Oregon has a somewhat similar history. Originally, if tenants in common owned property, hostile possession by one cotenant required more than mere occupation of the property.[21] The cotenant in possession was typically required to oust his tenants in common by providing them with actual notice that he "intend[ed] to occupy the property exclusively." The adverse possession period would not begin to run until after the possessing cotenant provided notice to the others of his intent to oust them.

But then things changed. The state amended a relevant statute, ORS 105.615, in 1989. "It did so because of the unique ouster and service issues that arise when a large number of people inherit property as tenants in common, but only one or more of them actually possess the property."[22] The current version of that statute provides a way for a tenant in common to acquire fee simple title to the property, by adverse possession, after possessing the property "for an uninterrupted period of 20 years or more" and paying "all taxes assessed against such property while in possession." One court held that this statute meant that once a cotenant takes those steps, the title vests as a matter of law to that cotenant, automatically.[23] No exceptions.

19 *Id.* at 634–35.
20 The older you get, the faster time flies. So, it would be better to do this when you are old like me.
21 Nedry v. Morgan, 284 Or. 65, 68 (1978).
22 Glenn v. Glenn, 310 Or. App. 661, 667 (Or. Ct. App. 2021).
23 *Id.*

In theory, this could lead to unfair results; what if two brothers owned a building together, and the "evil" brother lived in the premises alone, and in lieu of paying rent to the other brother, simply paid real estate taxes on it? Apparently, at least in Oregon, after 20 years, the "good" brother would no longer have a prayer of claiming ownership. The only way around it is described in the statute itself; it indicates that the "evil" brother does not obtain adverse possession rights if "otherwise agreed or provided in a granting document."[24] Therefore, as an extra precaution to a party seeking to avoid a claim of adverse possession, the "good" brother in that example could (1) make sure that the deed in his favor indicates that there could never be adverse possession, (2) enter into a written agreement with the "evil" brother concerning how exclusive possession by one is only intended as an accommodation, (3) make sure to sometimes pay taxes himself, or (4) periodically occupy the premises himself.

Other cases involving tenants in common and adverse possession include *Adams v. Johnson*, in which the Supreme Court of Minnesota held that a cotenant who occupied land undisturbed for 50 years as a sole owner, paid all taxes and insurance, and retained all of the profits from farming operations as well as made substantial improvements to the farm, overcame the presumption that one cotenant holds land with the implicit permission of others.[25] Similarly, in *Johnson v. James*, the Supreme Court of Arkansas held that where one cotenant has lived on and had sole and exclusive possession of the property in question for 36 years, exercising such acts of ownership as payment of taxes, enjoyment of rents, payment of insurance, and where the cotenants never asserted any claim to the property until it was acquired by eminent domain proceedings, and certain other factors were in the claimant's favor, the claimant asserted a valid claim of adverse possession.[26]

The Montana Supreme Court explained this concept as follows:

> When a cotenant . . . enters on the common land he is exercising a right which his title gives him; and his resulting possession is presumed to be consistent with his assumed title, and therefore to be the possession of his cotenants and himself . . . . But . . . where once it appears that the party occupying the premises holds not

24 Notably, the statute does not indicate if the "agreement" has to be contained in a "granting document." The placement of "or" in that statute leads to ambiguity.

25 271 Minn. 439 (1965).

26 237 Ark. 900 (1964).

> in recognition of, but in hostility to, the rights of his cotenants, his possession ceases to amount to constructive possession by them, becomes adverse, and, if maintained for the period provided for by the statute of limitations, will vest in the possessor a sole title by adverse possession to the premises.[27]

The concept of having one tenant in common jump from being a co-owner to being a full owner can be disturbing. That is revealed in a 1976 Hawaiian Supreme Court case called *City County of Honolulu v. Bennett*.[28] The issues in that case concerned matters that people from the continental United States would probably never imagine reading in an American law book. In that case, one piece of land at issue was known as "Parcel 9," and the court reached the issues by first hitting a crucial fact: "It is undisputed that Parcel 9 is a portion of the ancient ahupua'a of Hakipu'u, title to which was confirmed in Queen Kalama, widow of Kamehameha III, by Land Commission Award 4452, Apana 14."[29] After Queen Kalama died intestate in 1870 two sets of parties claimed to be the owners; one set claimed to be the sole owner, and the other claimed to be a tenant in common. The party claiming to be the sole owner alleged that even if that group were once a tenant in common, it had become an adverse possessor, and thus sole owner.

Hawaii's Supreme Court discussed how in the past when deciding how to handle adverse possession cases between tenants in common, it had one rule for nonrelated tenants in common, and another rule for blood-related tenants in common. In any event, it established a new universal rule. It held that there is a presumed "general fiduciary relationship between cotenants."[30] Therefore, it held that

> a tenant in common claiming by adverse possession must prove that he acted in good faith towards the cotenants during the statutory period. In most circumstances, this requirement of good faith will in turn mandate that the tenant claiming adversely must actually notify his cotenants that he is claiming against them. In the following exceptional circumstances, however, good faith is satisfied by less than actual notice: where the tenant in possession has no reason to suspect that a cotenancy exists; or where the tenant in possession makes a good faith, reasonable effort to notify the cotenants but is unable to locate them; or where the tenants out of possession

27 Fitschen Bros. Comm. Co. v. Noyes' Estate, 76 Mont. 175 (1926) (citation omitted).
28 57 Haw. 195 (1976).
29 *Id.* at 205.
30 *Id.* at 209.

> already have actual knowledge that the tenant in possession is claiming adversely to their interests. In these limited circumstances, the notice requirement will be satisfied by constructive notice and "open and notorious possession."[31]

Since the jury instructions had not contained those guidelines, the court held that a new trial was warranted.

There are other dangers a tenant in common must be aware of if he wishes to maintain ownership. For example, what if the property is owned by cotenants, but then some, but not all, of those cotenants execute a deed to a grantee, in which they purport to transfer the full ownership of that property to a new grantee, who was not previously a cotenant? If that grantee meets the other elements of adverse possession for the correct time period, then the cotenant not participating in the conveyance is deemed to be ousted, and on termination of the statutory period, title by adverse possession vests in the grantee.[32] No formal notice of ouster is necessary.

---

31 *Id.*

32 Kennedy v. Rinehart, 281 Or. 391, 394 (1978) (The court cited several other cases from other jurisdictions in which this was the law.).

Chapter 25
Mining Rights and Water Rights

Issues about adverse possession and related fields are difficult enough to grasp on their own. When one realizes that adverse possession in the context of mining rights and water rights have their own doctrines, it can be soul crushing. The area is complicated and too niche for a general book like this. Regardless, a lawyer trying to learn the subject should understand enough basics to sound knowledgeable, at least for the first meeting with the client. This chapter should provide a rudimentary background into these extremely complicated areas.

MINING RIGHTS AND RELATED CONCEPTS

To understand adverse possession of mining rights, one must first understand certain basics. Minerals in and under land are considered a part of the land—until the rights to those minerals are legally severed from the rights to the land. If there has been no severance, then adverse possession of the surface for the period fixed by statute will also generally give title to the minerals.[1] Vice versa is likely true as well.

A severance can be handled by deed—a deed would be executed that indicates one party has surface rights, and another has mining rights. Once there is a severance of the mineral interest from the surface estate, then there will be two separate and distinct estates (think of church and state). And once there is a severance, possession of the surface estate is not deemed possession of the severed mineral interest, and vice versa. To put it another way, once the severance has taken place, "possession of the surface by its owner is not adverse to the owner of the mineral below it. The mineral owner does not lose his possession by any length of nonuser, and the surface owner cannot acquire title to the minerals by adverse possession based on his exclusive and continued occupancy

1 Sachs v. Bd. of Trustees, 89 N.M. 712, 721 (1976); Broadhurst v. Am. Colloid Co., 85 S.D. 65, 73 (1970); Clay v. Mountain Valley Min. Ltd. P'ship, 351 P.3d 961, 968 (Wyo. 2015).

of the surface alone."[2] However, just to clarify, if there has been no severance, then, adverse possession of the surface for the period fixed by statute will also generally give title to the minerals.

If the minerals have been severed from the title to the surface, then those interests alone may be acquired by adverse possession, but this can take place only when the claimant meets the traditional elements of adverse possession. For example, it could not be done secretly; the exploration for minerals, as well as the mining operations in general, would have to meet the traditional elements of being open, notorious, continuous, and hostile—and even under color of title if it was required.[3] Also, case law indicates that once there has been severance of the minerals from the surface, "neither the owner of the surface nor the owner of the minerals can claim the other's estate merely by force of the possession of his own estate. Neither does the owner of the minerals lose his right by mere nonuse. His title can only be defeated by acts which actually take the minerals out of his possession."[4] As put by another court, "After severance, adverse possession of the minerals can only be acquired by actually producing the minerals and taking them from the ground."[5] In the case of oil and gas, a claimant must actually drill and produce oil or gas.[6] Some case law indicates that occasional taking of mineral by an alleged adverse possession is insufficient for an adverse possession claim.[7]

To get a feel of the various issues that can arise in a case concerning adverse possession of adverse rights, one may consult a Wyoming Supreme Court case entitled *Clay v. Mountain Valley Mineral Ltd. Partnership*.[8] In that case, the two main parties were the Clays and an entity known as "Mountain Valley." Mountain Valley's predecessor had filed a 1976 quiet title action based on adverse possession, and due in part to the default of the Clays' predecessors, Mountain Valley's predecessors were declared the owner of the real property in question. Therefore, the Clays' new case, in which they claimed title to mineral interests, failed due to res judicata. One of the arguments the Clays made was that Mountain Valley's predecessors would have only been entitled to claim the surface estate, because they had not produced minerals from

2 Deruy v. Noah, 199 Okla. 230, 232 (1947) (citation omitted).
3 McCoy v. Lowrie, 42 Wash. 2d 24, 26–27, 253 P.2d 415, 417 (1953).
4 Tomechko v. Garrett, 2021-Ohio-1377, ¶ 43, 172 N.E.3d 1087, 1098 (Ohio Ct. App. 2021) (citation omitted).
5 Barfield v. Holland, 844 S.W.2d 759, 767 (Tex. App. 1993).
6 Natural Gas Pipeline Co. v. Pool, 124 S.W.3d 188, 193 (Tex. 2003).
7 White v. McNabb, 140 Ky. 828, 131 S.W. 1021, 1023 (1910); Cent. Tr. Co. v. Harless, 108 W. Va. 618, 152 S.E. 209, 213 (1930).
8 351 P.3d 961 (Wyo. 2015).

the property. Therefore, according to the Clays, the previous judgment implicitly had only been for the surface. However, the court countered by explaining that prior to the severance of the minerals, the adverse possession of the surface would include the mineral estate.

The Utah Supreme Court heard a case involving adverse possession of mining rights on a rather obscure topic in *United Park City Mines Co. v. Estate of Clegg*.[9] In that case, there was a dispute over the ownership of mining claims. United Park City Mines Company (United Park) filed a lawsuit seeking to establish title to patented mining claims. The Cleggs, some of the defendants in the case, counterclaimed and argued that they had obtained the surface estate of the claims through adverse possession. The Cleggs had claimed that when they transferred certain deeds to others, they had mistakenly believed the deeds conveyed only the mineral estate. They claimed that this was irrelevant because the Cleggs had adversely possessed the surface area for decades afterward.

The Cleggs' problem, which led to them losing their adverse possession counterclaim, was that for an extended period of time, they failed to pay for taxes on the surface estate, despite it being common knowledge that property owners pay for property taxes. Their argument, that they did not have to pay the taxes, since the mining company was paying real estate taxes, and no separate taxes were assessed for the land, failed. In such a case, the court held, the Cleggs should have actively sought tax assessments on the value of the surface estate as used for other than mining purposes. This was especially the case because the relevant state statute required an adverse possession claimant to prove taxes had been paid for a seven-year period. Only one tax in that state is assessed if the surface and mineral estates of a mining claim are owned by the same person; therefore the Cleggs should have taken the extra step and pushed to find a way to pay the taxes on the surface much sooner. "If a party claims ownership of a piece of property, that claim can only be secured by seeking the obligations as well as the benefits of ownership. If that party waits for fifty years to meet those obligations, and then only in the face of imminent litigation, it can hardly be said that title was theretofore claimed."[10]

An interesting issue concerns timber rights. In an Arkansas Supreme Court quiet title action,[11] Smith originally owned the land and conveyed a timber deed to Carter, granting him the right to cut and remove timber from the land for 100 years. Later, Smith conveyed a warranty deed to Bonds, covering the same land but reserving to himself the oil, gas, and

9 737 P.2d 173 (Utah 1987).

10 *Id.* at 177.

11 Bonds v. Carter, 348 Ark. 591 (2002).

mineral interests. Bonds sued to quiet title, claiming that she acquired ownership (including timber rights) through adverse possession in part by paying taxes on the property for more than 15 years. The appellate court concluded that Bonds could not adversely possess the timber rights, because timber rights were separate and distinct from the land itself, in part by reviewing Arkansas taxation statutes. The court also analogized the matter to cases concerning adverse possession of mineral rights. Since Bonds had not actively asserted her interest in the timber until she filed the lawsuit, she could not claim an adverse interest in that aspect of the property.

WATER RIGHTS

In trying to understand the basics of obtaining water rights through adverse possession, the best way to get one's feet wet[12] is to review case law.

A state that seems to have a very basic black and white attitude is Wyoming. In one 1985 case, the plaintiffs claimed that they used water from certain tributaries, to the detriment of other parties that had properly obtained permits for those water rights. The plaintiffs claimed they had done so for decades, in an open, visible, notorious manner, and adverse to the proper appropriators. Therefore, they claimed adverse possession rights. However the appellate court held that the trial court properly dismissed the claim "for the simple reason that we here hold that water rights may not be acquired by adverse possession or prescription in this state."[13] The decision rested on various factors, including that the state's constitution indicates that natural sources of water are "the property of the state."[14] The court also noted that there could be no exception just because a party was taking over a water right that was initiated through the property permit process. To handle it in the plaintiffs' suggested matter, as the court saw it, "would cripple the permit procedure . . . [and] make impossible the efficient administration of water."[15] New Mexico also seems to bar adverse possession claims to water rights.[16]

In other states, such as Idaho, case law does allow a party to claim a prescriptive title to water. In 1976 it was held in *Gilbert v. Smith*[17]

12 Sorry about that.

13 Lewis v. State Bd. of Control, 699 P.2d 822 (Wyo. 1985).

14 *Id.* at 825, citing Wyo. Const. art. 8, § 1.

15 *Id.* at 826.

16 Turner v. Bassett, 134 N.M. 621, 627 (N.M. Ct. App. 2003), *rev'd on other grounds by* 137 N.M. 381 (2005).

17 97 Idaho 735 (1976).

that prescriptive title to water may be acquired by adverse use for five years where such use is open, hostile, exclusive, continuous, and under claim of right. The court indicated that the elements must be shown by clear and convincing evidence. However, Idaho courts recognize that the kind of proof necessary to establish adverse possession to water is not the same that is required for land. Although two parties generally cannot both use the same land at the same time without butting heads, taking water from the same source as a neighbor is a different issue. Therefore, the law is different. As one court put it:

> two parties may at the same time be in possession of water from a creek and neither hold adverse to the other; each may justly claim the right to use the water he is using, without affecting the rights of the other, and therefore, in order to constitute adverse possession of water, the burden is upon the claimant to show that his use of the water deprived the prior appropriators of water at times when such prior appropriators actually needed the water; the use does not become adverse until it interferes with the use thereof by the prior appropriators, and therefore proof merely that the claimant used water and claimed the right to use it is no proof whatever of adverse use.[18]

Other states also have looser laws, which are forgiving to an adverse possessor. For example, in one California case,[19] the plaintiffs had used a spring for their water source. The spring was on other parties' property, but the plaintiffs had the water transported by a pipe that ran from the spring. Plaintiffs ultimately sought to solidify those rights, prevent others from tapping into their pipe, and the right to maintain a water line across the defendants' property. They were successful at the trial level, but defendants appealed. On appeal, the court first held that water rights can indeed by obtained by prescription. The court noted that prescriptive rights cannot lie against the state, if the state seeks to enjoin unauthorized use, but that this case did not involve such issues. From there, the court noted that the elements of a prescriptive water rights were like a claim for a prescriptive easement, and that the plaintiff in such a case must prove use that is "(1) actual, (2) open and notorious, (3) hostile and adverse to the original owner, (4) continuous and uninterrupted, (5) under a claim of right, (6) for the statutory period

18 Vill. of Fairview v. Franklin, Maple Creek Pioneer Irr. Co., 59 Idaho 7, 17 (1938) (citation and emphasis omitted).

19 Brewer v. Murphy, 161 Cal. App. 4th 928 (Cal. Ct. App. 2008).

of five years."[20] The court had to examine such issues as whether the fact that the water line was partially underground mattered, with the "open and notorious" element, and in what manner the plaintiffs had recognized that the defendants did have certain rights, and what rights had been recognized. The court also had to review the parties' previous correspondence, and whether the plaintiffs were trying to negotiate an agreement, or whether the plaintiffs had made an admission against their interest in those letters. In the end, the court affirmed the judgment in plaintiffs' favor.

In Colorado, one must consider what type of water rights are at issue, and against whom adverse possession claims may be raised. For example, a critical statute provides that no adverse possession claim may be made against "any . . . water, water right . . . whatsoever dedicated to or owned by the state of Colorado, or any county, city and county, city, irrigation district, public, municipal, or quasi-municipal corporation, or any department or agency thereof."[21] This means, for instance, that no claimant may successfully argue adversely possessing unappropriated water that is part of a natural stream. A party also cannot adversely possess a water right that was abandoned by the prior owner. Apparently, the only kind of adverse possession of water rights are ones that originally belonged to another private owner, and were diverted, but which water rights were not abandoned. In Colorado, in order for claimants to adversely possess a water right they must show (1) that they diverted someone else's water right, and (2) that claimants beneficially used the water.[22] Moreover, nothing more than the specific amount of beneficial use could be claimed.

One Colorado Supreme Court case[23] shows the complexity of the law concerning adversely possessing water rights. An adverse possession claim arose between neighbors over legal interests in water and easement rights for three ditches diverting water from a certain river. The court held the elements for claiming an adverse possession right to water meant the claimant would have to "prove that his possession to the claimed amount of water was actual, adverse, hostile to the owner and under a claim of right, and open, notorious, exclusive, and continuous."[24] The court also noted that, "adverse possession is very difficult to establish. Our cases repeatedly reject such claims."[25] It pointed out that it had previously held that, "[i]t is not reasonable to

20 *Id.* at 938.
21 Colo. Rev. Stat. § 38-41-101(2).
22 Archuleta v. Gomez, 200 P.3d 333 (Colo. 2009).
23 *Id.*
24 *Id.* at 345.
25 *Id.* at 344.

suppose that priority of right to water, where water is scarce, or likely to become so, will be lightly sacrificed or surrendered by its owner. Nor should the owner of such a right be held to have surrendered it or merged it except upon reasonably clear and satisfactory evidence."[26] In a case concerning irrigation, the claimant would have to prove "the amount of water expressed in acre feet belonging to the deeded owner's water right that the adverse claimant has placed to beneficial consumptive use."[27]

Once that was established, the Colorado Supreme Court went on to discuss the particular case. It noted that the water court had awarded all of the title owner's interests in the adjudicated water rights to the adverse possession claimant. On appeal, the court held that certain of those rights may have been abandoned by the party with deeded interests, and should be deemed abandoned to the stream. The court noted that the claimant also had to prove that the amount which the claimant already had available to him was not sufficient for an actual beneficial use, and had to prove what portion the claimant had used of the deeded owner's water rights, to demonstrate the actual beneficial use. In reviewing the facts and law, the court noted how ditches were used to intercept water, how rotational agreements had been handled, how sub-irrigation matters were handled, and so on. The court remanded it because the claimant had not yet presented "evidence that he made actual beneficial consumptive use of all or any portion of the [title owner's] water rights."[28] The Supreme Court also noted that a court needed to review quantification of the use. It held that "[q]uantification is . . . necessary to prevent an unlawful enlargement of [title owner's] deeded irrigation water right interests. A water right decreed for irrigation purposes cannot lawfully be enlarged beyond the amount of historical beneficial consumptive use belonging to the perfected right."[29]

After the case was remanded, the Colorado Supreme Court heard the matter again.[30] It noted that the water court found that the claimant had adversely possessed his neighbor's deeded legal interests in two of the three ditches, but not the other ditch. That portion of the decision was affirmed. Some of the issues discussed in that final appeal included that the deeded owner had focused on irrigation efficiency and whether legal interests included the right to consume return flows. It also examined the evidence concerning how ditches had been operated

26 *Id.* at 345.
27 *Id.* at 346.
28 *Id.* at 348.
29 *Id.*
30 Archuleta v. Gomez, 290 P.3d 482 (Colo. 2012).

on rotation, and how the party that lost its rights had not exercised a turn in the rotation for more than the relevant statutory period. However, the water court had, according to the high court, improperly failed to issue an injunction against the claimant concerning the other ditch. The high court directed the water court to enter an injunction ordering the claimant to reconstruct the ditch, provide for an easement for the ditch across a portion of his parcel to the deed owner's adjoining parcel, and cease diverting any water that the deed owner's legal interest entitled him to divert to his that parcel.[31]

Of course, the purpose of this chapter again is not necessarily to teach anyone about adverse possession rights to water, but more to impress on litigators the difficulty and complexity of the matter, and that litigators must make sure that all elements a court might consider critical, are covered.

31 *Id.* at 491.

Part 6

Workarounds

> *[T]he history of evolution is that life escapes all barriers. Life breaks free. Life expands to new territories. Painfully, perhaps even dangerously. But life finds a way.*
>
> —*Jurassic Park,* Michael Crichton

In the nerdy world of magic, there is something called an "out." It means that if there is some reason the trick isn't working, the magician can try to find some other way to switch the direction of the trick halfway through, with the attitude of "This is what I intended all along."[1]

In potential adverse possession cases, there are "outs" as well, which are covered in this section of the book.

1 "I meant to do that." *Pee Wee's Big Adventure.*

Chapter 26
Easement by Prescription

One potential way of obtaining at least some relief for a client who does not have a valid adverse possession case is through easement by prescription. That is a quasi-adverse possession right, for limited purposes only. But it may be sufficient for your client's needs. This chapter gives its subject a little more attention than some others, in part because it is a rich field, and in part because a litigator only thinking about adverse possession might ignore the many possibilities this result can bring.

First, one has to understand that an easement is "a nonpossessory interest in another's land that entitles the holder of the easement to use the burdened property for some particular purpose."[1] If your client's claimed easement is not in writing, he may still have a chance to formalize those rights. "The equitable doctrine of prescriptive easements evolved to resolve conflicts between two competing interests: the interest of property owners in controlling the use of their property and the societal interest in protecting established patterns of land possession and use. However, the doctrine in essence allows a person to obtain a property interest without paying for it, and for that reason prescriptive easements are disfavored."[2]

Courts originally came up with the concept of a prescriptive easement as a fictional "lost grant"—"that long use must have originated in an early, but lost, lawful grant of the right—or to an analogy to statutes of limitations that apply to the related doctrine of adverse possession."[3] Regardless of the origins of the doctrine, the justification is that "established patterns of land possession and use should be protected and that a diligent occupant should be rewarded at the expense of a careless owner."[4]

---

1 Hisey v. Patrick, 309 Or. App. 625, 632 (Or. Ct. App. 2021).

2 *Id.* at 632–33 (internal quotation marks and citation omitted).

3 Wels v. Hippe, 360 Or. 569, 577 (2016).

4 *Id.* (citation omitted).

One typical description of the law can be found in a Connecticut Supreme Court case—a party claiming to have acquired an easement by prescription must demonstrate that the use of the property has been open, visible, continuous, and uninterrupted for a certain number of years as defined by the state, and made under a claim of right.[5] Other courts describe the law similarly. In Washington, to establish an easement by prescription, "a claimant must prove (1) use adverse to the title owner; (2) open, notorious, continuous, and uninterrupted use for a statutory period of time; and (3) that the owner knew of the adverse use when he was able to enforce his rights."[6] California is nearly identical: the party claiming a prescriptive easement must "show use of the property which has been open, notorious, continuous and adverse for an uninterrupted period of five years."[7] In this context, "adverse use" means that the claimant's use of the property was made without the explicit or implicit permission of the landowner.[8]

In Vermont, the elements necessary to establish a prescriptive easement on one hand, and adverse possession on the other, are essentially the same: an adverse use or possession that is open, notorious, hostile and continuous for a period of 15 years, and acquiescence in the use or possession by the person against whom the claim is asserted.[9] As one court put it, "The difference lies in the interest claimed."[10]

What about one of the traditional elements of adverse possession—exclusivity? "Unlike the establishment of title by adverse possession, exclusivity is not a necessary element for a valid claim to an easement by prescription."[11] Simply because one has an easement to certain space in a certain manner, does not mean it is an exclusive use of the entire property. "The elements for a prescriptive easement are the same as those for adverse possession, without the necessity of exclusivity."[12] When a party claims "exclusive easement by prescription," this is prohibited in Idaho, because it is "a type of easement that does not exist in [Idaho] law."[13] The more one claims "exclusivity," the more it sounds like a traditional

5 Westchester v. Greenwich, 227 Conn. 495, 501, 629 A.2d 1084 (1993).
6 Lee v. Lozier, 88 Wash. App. 176, 181 (1997).
7 Warsaw v. Chi. Metallic Ceilings, Inc. 35 Cal. 3d 564, 570 (1984).
8 Aaron v. Dunham, 137 Cal. App. 4th 1244, 1252 (2006).
9 Cmty. Feed Store, Inc. v. Ne. Culvert Corp., 151 Vt. 152, 155 (1989), citing Russell v. Pare, 132 Vt. 397, 401 (1974) (partially overruled by Lague, Inc. v. Royea, 152 Vt. 499 [1989]); VT. STAT. ANN. tit. 12, § 501.
10 *Cmty Feed Store*, 151 Vt. at 156.
11 Palisades Sales Corp. v. Walsh, 459 A.2d 933, 937 (R.I. 1983).
12 Xander Corp. v. Haberman, 2009 N.Y. Slip Op. 32900, 13 (N.Y. Sup. Ct. 2009). *See also* City of Tonawanda v. Ellicott Creek Homeowners Ass'n, Inc., 86 A.D.2d 118, 120 (N.Y. App. Div. 1982).
13 Luce v. Marble, 142 Idaho 264, 273 (2005).

adverse possession case, which means an easement would not be the end result.

Confusingly, not all states agree even with dispensing of the exclusivity element for a prescriptive easement case. For example, Montana requires exclusive use.[14] Maryland requires this as well. However, that state, and perhaps others as well, may distinguish between public and private prescriptive easements.[15] Kentucky also requires "exclusive" possession for the statutory period, among other elements.[16] In any event, perhaps the issue of what "exclusive" means in such states is the deciding factor.

The proof necessary to establish a prescriptive easement to use land is not the same as that to establish a claim of title by adverse possession in other ways. "[I]t is only the use to which the premises are put which must be shown to be adverse, open and notorious. To the extent that the use is established, it, of course, is hostile to the title of the servient estate."[17] Therefore, although plaintiffs seeking such an easement "must prove all the elements essential to title by prescription, their burden of proof must be measured in terms of the right to the use they claim, i.e. a very limited periodic use."[18]

Some courts hold that adversity is not required for a prescriptive easement. In Colorado, there is an exception to the general rule that permissive use cannot ripen into prescriptive use: "[A]dversity is not required when a grant [of an easement] has been imperfectly attempted."[19] In other words, if the landowner attempted to issue an easement, but did not do so properly, a party may still be able to claim a prescriptive easement. Other states may have similar laws.[20]

Regardless of some case law indicating the elements of a traditional adverse possession case are the same, this simply cannot be the case. One Kentucky court explained this well: using one of many potential examples.

> [T]he physical nature of the thing possessed must determine the character of the acts necessary to impart notice that the right to use

---

14 Public Lands v. Boone & Crockett, 259 Mont. 279, 283 (1993).

15 *See* Clickner v. Magothy River Ass'n, Inc., 424 Md. 253, 278 (2012).

16 Columbia Gas Transmission, v. Consol. of Kentucky, 15 S.W.3d 727, 730 (Ky. 2000).

17 Etz v. Mamerow, 72 Ariz. 228, 232 (1951).

18 United States *ex rel.* Zuni Tribe of New Mexico v. Platt, 730 F. Supp. 318, 321 (D. Ariz. 1990).

19 Lobato v. Taylor, 71 P.3d 938, 954 (Colo. 2002).

20 *Id.*, citing Nat'l Props. Corp. v. Polk Cnty., 386 N.W.2d 98, 105 (Iowa 1986) (noting that there may be a prescriptive easement even "where the original use was with a servant [sic] owner's consent"); Kirby v. Hook, 701 A.2d 397, 404 (Md. 1997) (applying an exception to the "general rule [that] permissive use can never ripen into a prescriptive easement . . . where there has been an attempt to grant an irrevocable easement which is void because of the statute of frauds").

> or possess is asserted and exercised without consent, continuously, and in open hostility to anyone's right to interfere. For example, it is impossible to continuously exercise the same acts of dominion over a river bank, sand bar and its accretions as an adverse possessor could exercise over pasture land or woodland, the area and usability of which are not affected by the rise and fall of a stream. A pipe conveying water is usually laid underground, and hence is not visible except at its inlet and outlet. Yet, if the owner of the land which it occupies throughout its length has notice of its existence, it could hardly be said that the right to maintain it was not adverse because the pipe was not visible or its use apparent.[21]

There seem to be unlimited examples of what kinds of prescriptive easements the court can consider issuing. Some examples include allowing the use of an area for purposes of loading and unloading vehicles;[22] allowing certain people to use a beach;[23] to use adjacent land as a "rough" in the context of golfing;[24] a right to leave a pipeline across land;,[25] the right to discharge irrigation wastewater;[26] the right to use a roadway only for certain purposes such as (1) hauling firewood onto certain property, (2) hauling stones away from a house, and (3) gaining access to a chicken house;[27] and to drive cattle across another's land.[28]

There are any number of reasons that one's client would not be able to prove an adverse possession right, but might be able to prove the slightly relaxed requirements for a prescriptive easement. For example, in Oregon, under ORS 105.620, in addition to the other elements of adverse possession, an adverse possession claimant must prove that that when he or his predecessor first entered into possession of the disputed area, he had an "honest belief" of actual ownership, "which belief continued for ten years, had an objective basis, and was reasonable under the particular circumstances."[29] It appears this "honest belief" requirement does not apply in that state for a prescription easement case.[30]

21 *Columbia Gas Transmission*, 15 S.W.3d at 730 (citation omitted).

22 Plymouth Canton Comm. Crier v. Prose, 242 Mich. App. 676, 678 (Mich. Ct. App. 2000).

23 Stone v. Green Hill Civic Ass'n, 786 A.2d 387, 388 (R.I. 2001).

24 MacDonald Properties, Inc. v. Bel-Air Country Club, 72 Cal. App. 3d 693 (2d Dist. 1977).

25 Riddock v. City of Helena, 212 Mont. 390, 391 (1984).

26 Merrill v. Penrod, 109 Idaho 46, 50 (Ct. App. 1985).

27 Dennis v. French, 135 Vt. 77, 79 (1977).

28 Crane v. Crane, 683 P.2d 1062, 1063 (Utah 1984).

29 *See* Wood v. Taylor, 307 Or. App. 688, 690 (Or. Ct. App. 2020).

30 *See* Bo & Lia Holdings LLC v. 2021 Morrison LLC. 315 Or. App. 372, 390 (Or. Ct. App. 2021) (dissent).

In California, one could also say it is more difficult to prove adverse possession than easement by prescription. In that state, adverse possession cannot be considered established unless at the very least, "the party or persons, their predecessors and grantors, have timely paid all state, county, or municipal taxes that have been levied and assessed upon the land for the period of five years during which the land has been occupied and claimed."[31] Conversely, a "prescriptive easement does not require payment of taxes."[32]

In some states, it could actually be more difficult to win a case for prescriptive easements in comparison to adverse possession cases. For example, in Washington, unlike adverse possession, which only requires proof by a preponderance of the evidence, all elements of a prescriptive easement must be proven by clear and convincing evidence.[33] This makes its law different from, for example, Connecticut. In that state, "[t]itle by adverse possession must be established by clear and positive proof. An easement by adverse use need only be established by a preponderance of the evidence."[34]

Other critical issues include presumptions. In Minnesota, "[w]here the claimant of an easement by prescription has shown open, visible, continuous, and unmolested use for the statutory period, inconsistent with the rights of the owner of the servient estate and under circumstances from which his knowledge and acquiescence may be inferred, the use will be presumed to be under claim of right and adverse, so as to place on the owner of the servient estate the burden of rebutting the presumption by evidence that the use was permissive."[35] (This is similar to law on adverse possession in many contexts too.)

Examples on technical issues are the best way to understand laws, including those concerning easements by prescription. In one Supreme Court of Oregon case,[36] the plaintiff sought a prescriptive easement to use a private dirt road owned by defendants, which allowed the plaintiff easy access to a highway. When the plaintiff wanted to build a cabin on his property, the county required him to obtain a written confirmation of his right to use that dirt road, but the defendants would not consent. The plaintiff therefore filed an action for a declaration that he had acquired a prescriptive easement to use the part of the dirt road that was on

31 Cal. Civ. Proc. Code § 325(b).

32 Mehdizadeh v. Mincer, 46 Cal. App. 4th 1296, 1305, 54 Cal. Rptr. 2d 284 (1996), *as modified on denial of reh'g* (July 24, 1996).

33 Maslonka v. Pub. Util. Dist. No. 1 of Pend Oreille Cnty., 23 Wn. App. 2d 1, 28 (2022); *reversed on other grounds*, 533 P.3d 400 (2023).

34 Sanford v. Dimes, 3 Conn. App. 639, 640 (Conn. App. Ct. 1985) (citations omitted).

35 Dozier v. Krmpotich, 227 Minn. 503, 507 (1949).

36 Wels v. Hippe, 360 Or. 569 (2016).

defendants' property. One of the critical issues in the case was whether his use of the road was presumptively by permission, or whether there was enough evidence to prove that his use had been adverse.

In that case, the court defined certain critical terms. "Open and notorious" meant the landowner would have to have "a reasonable opportunity to learn of its existence and nature."[37] And one definition of "adverse" use was "inconsistent with the owner's use of the property."[38] The court also indicated that the plaintiff would ordinarily have a relatively easy case to prove adverse use, because open and notorious use for the prescribed period normally gives rise to a rebuttable presumption of adverse use. However, in that case, because the road was preexisting before the plaintiff or defendant obtained title rights, the court held that "the claimant's use of the road—no matter how obvious—does not give rise to a presumption that it is adverse to the owner."[39] In such a case, the court held that it would be presumed that there was a friendly arrangement for the claimant to use the property. And that would especially be the case if other neighbors were using the road as well.

Therefore, the court held that the claimant would have had to prove that when he used the road, it interfered with actual owner's use of the road, or that the claimant had used the road under a claim of right. One example of the latter would be if the owner tried to block use of the road, but the claimant removed the blockade. In the case at issue, the best the claimant could do for "adverse" use was to prove that when he used the road, the noise and dust could be viewed from a distance. But that did not prove interference with the owner's use. The claimant also claimed that he "believed" he had the right to use the road without permission. But since he never communicated that belief, his own internal thoughts were meaningless. The Supreme Court ruled against the claimant.

A Colorado Supreme Court case, in which a prescriptive easement was granted, was resolved in 2021.[40] That case indicated one benefit of seeking that kind of relief instead of adverse possession. In that case, as indicated below, the claimant had sought to purchase the landowner's property at a certain point, which may be the death knell to an adverse possession claim. But the claimant still had the potential to succeed on its prescriptive easement case.

That case involved a piece of property that was approximately one-half acre. A large parcel had been conveyed to a condominium association,

37 *Id.* at 578.
38 *Id.*
39 *Id.* at 579.
40 Lo Viento Blanco, LLC v. Woodbridge Condo. Ass'n, 489 P.3d 735 (Colo. 2021).

but the disputed parcel had not been. Regardless, the condominium association maintained, used, and improved the disputed parcel in a number of ways. Parts were used for skiing to access a pedestrian bridge, parts had a gravel road, and the claimant installed electricity access, and installed a ground sprinkler system. Unfortunately for the condominium association, the association had also asked for permission to plant trees and shrubs in the space, and eventually even offered to purchase the disputed parcel in writing.

Eventually, another party acquired the disputed parcel, and when the association sought adverse possession rights, one appellate court held that its letter offering to purchase the disputed parcel was fatal to its adverse possession claim because that letter had interrupted the continuity of its adverse use prior to the vesting point. Luckily for the association, the appellate court remanded the case to the trial court to consider its prescriptive easement claim. On remand, the court held that the association had proved its right to a prescriptive easement, and the court subsequently determined the scope of that easement.

When the matter was appealed again, the Colorado Supreme Court noted that "[a]n easement by prescription is established when the prescriptive use is: 1) open or notorious, 2) continued without effective interruption for the prescriptive period, and 3) the use was either a) adverse or b) pursuant to an attempted, but ineffective grant." The court explained that "unlike a claim of title by adverse possession, a claim to a prescriptive easement does not require a showing of 'hostility' (i.e., a claim to exclusive ownership). Rather, in the context of prescriptive easements, an adverse use is a use made without the consent of the landowner, or holder of the property interest used, and without other authorization."[41] To put it another way, the court held that the "claimant seeking to establish a prescriptive easement need not show that it asserted exclusive ownership of the property during the prescriptive period. Rather, such a claimant must show that its use was without permission or otherwise unauthorized and that it interfered with the owner's property interests."[42] In Colorado, "[i]f the landowner does not overcome the presumption of adverse use and the claimant establishes all of the other elements for a prescriptive easement noted above, then the claimant will be deemed to have established the right to that prescriptive easement."[43]

The actual landowner then claimed that "it rebutted the presumption of adverse use by showing that, during the prescriptive period," the

41 *Id.* at 741 (citation omitted).
42 *Id.*
43 *Id.* at 742.

association did such things as (1) seeking permission to landscape the property, and (2) offering to purchase it.[44] With respect to the first issue, the court noted that even though it had sought permission, that permission was denied, but the association continued to use the property as if it were its own. And with respect to the second issue, the court seemed to believe that although this might implicitly prove the claimant admitted it did not own the property, when one is only seeking an easement, an admission of who owns the property is irrelevant. Therefore, the Colorado Supreme Court upheld the prescriptive easement awarded by the lower court.

Although attorneys familiar with adverse possession cases may realize that prescriptive easements have lesser standards, and may try to obtain success under that method, attorneys must be careful not to presume that they can seek precisely the same relief under both adverse possession claims and prescriptive easement cases.

In one California case,[45] the Hansens and Valov owned adjoining parcels. The Hansens had long used their parcel for farming, but it turned out they had also been farming on about ten acres of Valov's property. Eventually Valov sold his property to Sandridge Partners, L.P. Then the Hansens sued to quiet title to a "prescriptive easement for their continued use and occupation of the Subject Property."[46] The Hansens could not obtain full adverse possession rights because they failed to pay taxes for the property. So they sought a prescriptive easement. As part of the relief, they sought a ruling that Sandridge Partners, L.P. would have "no right to use or occupy any portion of the Subject Property."[47]

The trial court did not issue that relief, and the appellate court agreed that such relief would be inappropriate. The appellate court explained the difference between an estate in land, and an easement in land. It described an estate as "an ownership interest in land that is, or may become, possessory," and that "an easement is not a type of ownership, but rather an incorporeal interest in land which confers a right upon the owner thereof to *some* profit, benefit, dominion, or lawful use out of or over the *estate* of another."[48] It also indicated that "[a]n easement is, by definition, *less* than the right of ownership."[49] Since the Hansens requested a very broad form of relief, the court held that this was, in effect, a request for adverse possession relief. The court indicated that

---

44 *Id.*
45 Hansen v. Sandridge Partners, L.P., 22 Cal. App. 5th 1020 (2018).
46 *Id.* at 1027.
47 *Id.*
48 *Id.* at 1032 (citations omitted).
49 *Id.* (citation and internal quotations marks omitted).

simply calling it a prescriptive easement was not enough. The court had to examine the interest they sought, which would have divested Sandridge Partners, L.P. "of nearly all the rights that owners customarily have including access and usage."[50]

To put it another way, simply using labels such as "prescriptive easement" is not enough, because courts are required to see through those sorts of labels. It reminds one of the riddle that people claim Lincoln loved. He analogized a certain issue "to that of the boy who, when asked how many legs his calf would have if he called its tail a leg, replied, 'Five,' to which the prompt response was made that *calling* the tail a leg would not *make* it a leg."[51]

An Arizona federal court took on what has to be the oldest easement in American history, in *United States ex rel. Zuni Tribe of New Mexico v. Platt*.[52] The case concerned the Zuni Indians,[53] who as a part of their religion, make a regular periodic pilgrimage at the time of the summer solstice, from their reservation in northwest New Mexico to a certain mountain area in northeast Arizona, which they believed was their place of origin, the basis for their religious life, and the home of their dead. There was evidence that the Zuni pilgrimage occurred as early as the year 1540. Eventually, in 1985, one man declared that he would prevent the Zuni Indians from crossing his land on their pilgrimage. The United States on behalf of the Zuni Tribe instituted an action claiming a prescriptive easement by adverse possession across the Platt land. During the trial, there was evidence of the quadrennial pilgrimage both in testimony, and in motion picture documentation. One of the witnesses was 99 years old.

The court ruled that that there was actual possession of the route once every four years, and that the tribe did not recognize any other claim to the land at the time of the pilgrimage. The court also held it was used "continually" because it was used for every four years "at least since 1924 and very probably for a period of time spanning many hundreds of years prior to that year." The open and notorious aspect was met because they had not attempted to hide their pilgrimage or the route they were taking, It helped that "[t]he Zuni tribe also cut, tore down or placed gates in, fences on the property owned or leased by defendant and others."[54] The only issue left for the court

50 *Id.* at 1032 (Cal. Ct. App. 2018).

51 Reminiscences of Abraham Lincoln by Distinguished Men of His Time 242 (Allen Thorndike Rice ed. & collected, 1853–1889) (1909). My father told me this riddle when I was a boy, but at the time I couldn't understand it for the life of me.

52 730 F. Supp. 318 (D. Ariz. 1990).

53 That is the term of art used in the opinion.

54 730 F. Supp. at 323.

was to determine the scope of the easement. The court noted that the scope of a prescriptive easement is determined by the use through which it is acquired. So, the court ultimately granted an easement of a certain route established by the court, which was limited to a "2 day period (one day each direction), during the summer solstice, once every four years to commence in 1993 and to continue on at 4 year intervals."[55]

55 *Id.* at 324.

Chapter 27
Deed Reformation

A number of cases are ones in which a party attempts to claim a portion of land not only pursuant to adverse possession but also through the doctrine of deed reformation. That is, the claimant argues that the deed itself is mistaken, and should be deemed rewritten.

An example of such a case in which both doctrines might apply would be if a seller had owned a large space, and entered into an agreement to transfer a portion of it to a buyer. Then the seller drafts the deed in a way that (on paper) accidentally gave more land to the buyer than was agreed. If the seller maintained control over the space he believed he still owned, then if he met the elements, he could try to claim adverse possession over it. But if he could not meet all of the elements for adverse possession, because (for example) he did not occupy the space for the statutory time period after the sale, the seller would have to resort to a claim for deed reformation.

Unfortunately, as difficult as it is to succeed on an adverse possession case, succeeding on a deed reformation case may be even more difficult. Generally, deeds are presumed to be carefully written and prepared, and presumed to reflect the intentions of the parties. Therefore, if the either the purchaser or seller seeks to reform such a deed, and claim a different portion of land, more land, or less land, was being transferred, he would need to prove one of the following: "(1) a mistake on the part of both parties; or (2) a mistake on the part of one party with fraud or inequitable conduct on the part of the other party; or (3) an error on the part of the scrivener."[1] It is considered an "extreme equitable remedy."[2] The proponent of reformation generally must prove his case by clear and convincing evidence—at the very least.[3] In some states, like Mississippi, the burden of proof is the ultimate—beyond a reasonable doubt.[4]

1 *In re* Est. of Summerlin, 989 So. 2d 466, 480 (Miss. Ct. App. 2008).
2 Meyer v. Marine Builders, Inc., 797 N.E.2d 760, 772 (Ind. Ct. App. 2003).
3 *See* Jacobson v. Jacobson, 557 P.2d 156, 158 (Utah 1976).
4 McCoy v. McCoy, 611 So. 2d 957, 961 (Miss. 1992).

If one is going to allege fraud, one must do so with particularity, pleading each element in detail to the degree possible. A typical list of elements for fraud, in the context of reformation is that there was "(1) a material misrepresentation of past or existing fact which (2) was untrue, (3) was made with knowledge of or in reckless ignorance of its falsity, (4) was made with the intent to deceive, (5) was rightfully relied upon by the complaining party, and (6) which proximately caused the injury or damage of which the plaintiff complains."[5] Depending on the context or the state, it may also be possible to claim deed reformation if the mistake was just in the way the deed was written, even if just one party prepared it.[6]

In a typical case in which one is seeking adverse possession rights, a number of years must have elapsed from the claimant's original use. Therefore, if one is already filing an adverse possession case, that claimant might believe that his deadline to seek to reform a deed would have already elapsed, and therefore the reformation claim would be pointless. In New York, for instance, an action to reform a deed based upon a mistake must generally be commenced within six years after the mistake is committed.[7]

However, it is still worth a try, even if years have elapsed. In New York, for deed reformation based upon mistake or fraud, there is an exception to the time limitation in favor of the claimant. That is "as to one who is in possession of real property under an instrument of title, the statute never begins to run against his right to reform that instrument until he has notice of a claim adverse to his under the instrument, or until his possession is otherwise disturbed."[8] The same (or a version of the same) is true in some other states as well.[9]

5 Angel v. Powelson, 977 N.E.2d 434, 444–45 (Ind. Ct. App. 2012).
6 Hart v. Blabey, 287 N.Y. 257, 262 (1942).
7 N.Y. C.P.L.R. 213.
8 Hart v. Blabey, 287 N.Y. 257, 262 (1942).
9 *See* Klepper v. Stover, 193 Kan. 219, 221–22 (1964); Strode v. Spoden, 284 S.W.2d 663 (Ky. 1955).

Chapter 28
Obtaining the Value of Improvements

If one represents an adverse possession claimant who spent money improving the property or the like but ultimately loses the adverse possession portion of the case, can he at least receive compensation for his investments? This issue is not set in stone. But at the very least, an attorney should give it a try.

Georgia has a statute partially addressing the matter. In that state, if a party is successful in an ejectment against another (such as an alleged adverse possessor), then the defendant, who is in "bona fide possession of the land under adverse claim of title may set off the value of all permanent improvements placed on the land in good faith," and that "if the value of such improvements at the time of the trial exceeds the mesne profits [that is, the damages the plaintiff would have obtained for the rental value of the land], the jury may render a verdict in favor of the plaintiff for the land and in favor of the defendant for the amount of the excess of the value of the improvements over the mesne profits."[1]

Case law reveals how various courts tackle this issue. One case[2] addressing the right to compensation for improvements conducted during a time in which property has allegedly been adversely possessed took place in Georgia. In that case, a man named Hollifield owned certain land, and he built some improvements on neighboring land. He erected a brick and iron-work fence, paved a driveway, and began an addition to the structure on his lot, even though he knew that it encroached on plaintiffs' lands. He had claimed that he had intended to buy that adjacent land. When the plaintiffs sued for ejectment, they were successful and defeated his counterclaim for adverse possession in part because he had not occupied the land for a long enough period of time. The court also dismissed his counterclaim for unjust enrichment, and that was a primary issue for appeal.

---

1 Ga. Code Ann. § 44-11-9(a).

2 Hollifield v. Monte Vista Biblical Gardens, Inc., 251 Ga. App. 124 (Ga. Ct. App. 2001).

In that case, the appellate court also ruled against Hollifield for several reasons. First, he had bad faith, because he knew the property did not belong to him. Second, he claimed to have done the renovations because "it was one of the most ugly pieces of property in the state of Georgia, number one. It was an eyesore to the entire community and it didn't represent me because what I was living next door to I just didn't want that next door to me. That was my number one reason to clean it up, to make it look decent because wouldn't nobody come to see me with that over there, water, trees and everything all in the place. It was a mess."[3] In other words, he admitted that he did the work as a volunteer, without desiring compensation for it. This meant he could not meet all of the critical elements of quantum meruit: "(1) the provider performed as agent services valuable to the recipient; (2) either at the request of the recipient or knowingly accepted by the recipient; (3) the recipient's receipt of which without compensating the provider would be unjust; and (4) provider's expectation of compensation at the time of rendition of services."[4] If that were not enough, he also failed to prove that the plaintiffs obtained a benefit from his services.

In one North Dakota case, the claimant had insufficient evidence to support the adverse possession claim. Yet he had allegedly made improvements valued at $12,000, and the court therefore granted the claimant a $12,000 lien against the lot at issue. On appeal, the court asked an important question: "[M]ay an owner be forced to pay for improvements made on his property by a third party when the improvements were made without his knowledge or consent?" A statute addressed the issue: "[I]n all cases where the plaintiff has made permanent improvements on the property in good faith, while in possession under color of title, he may recover the reasonable value thereof as against the defendant recovering the property when the reply shall allege the facts, stating particularly the value of the improvements and the value of the property, and shall demand appropriate relief."[5] Therefore, the lien was approved on appeal.[6]

If an adverse possession claimant never had color of title, but did improvements on property anyway, there are other reasons he may have a difficult time in claiming unjust enrichment. In a nearly 100-year-old case from North Carolina,[7] the plaintiff purchased a lot of land from Engle Land Company in 1909, but neglected to record the deed.

3 *Id.* at 128.
4 *Id.* at 128–29.
5 N.D. CENT. CODE § 32-17-09.
6 Benson v. Taralseth, 382 N.W.2d 649, 654–55 (N.D. 1986).
7 Eaton v. Doub, 190 N.C. 14 (1925).

Regardless, he occupied it as adverse possessor. Later, the defendants, who were judgment creditors of Eagle Land Company, obtained judgments and/or liens against plaintiff's property. The value of the land, without the improvements, was less than the judgment, but the value of the property with the improvements was substantially in excess of the judgment sum. In that state, an unregistered deed did not constitute color of title, as against the creditors, under the factual scenario in the case.

Since the plaintiff had no valid adverse possession case, he had tried to claim that so long as he paid the value of the land without the improvements to the creditors, the land should be released from the liens. The court struggled with the idea. It cited Shakespeare, indicating that "[w]e should be glad to emulate the wisdom of Portia, who in rendering judgment in the action pending before her, gave to plaintiff who 'craved the law' his 'pound of flesh,' but no more."[8] Unfortunately for the plaintiff, the court ultimately held he was not entitled to this kind of equitable relief because the defendants did not induce plaintiff to make the improvements. The court cited a legal encyclopedia, which indicated that "[a]s a general rule, in order that one may recover compensation for improvements made on another's land, even in a court of equity it is necessary that he shall have made such improvements in good faith while in bona fide adverse possession of the land under color of title."[9] However, since technically plaintiff's possession as against defendant was not under color of title, he had no right to recover. At the end the court held that they wished to express "regret," which probably did not comfort the plaintiff much.

If one's client has built a house in the wrong place, but cannot prove adverse possession, he still may be able to pull off the ultimate hat trick: a verdict that allows the client to keep the premises regardless. In an unusual, if not unique, case in Georgia,[10] a father had divided up his property equally among his five children, and showed one of his sons, Richard, which portion he intended to give him. Then Richard built a house in the space his father had showed him; his siblings even helped build it. Unfortunately, Murphy's Law was in effect, and it turned out there was a mistake. Richard had built the house on the wrong lot, or perhaps his father had made a mistake concerning which child received which property. Regardless, Richard's cruel siblings decided to seek relief against him.

8 *Id.* at 20.

9 *Id.* at 24.

10 Mitchell v. Mitchell, 274 Ga. 633 (2001).

Richard and his wife counterclaimed for adverse possession, but as the dissent pointed out, that argument could not have worked in part because he did not meet the time requirements. The dissent also indicated that equitable estoppel (a concept described in Chapter 30) would not have worked in part because in that state, estoppel only worked defensively. Nor would deed reformation (a concept described in Chapter 27) have worked, as the partially dissenting judge saw it, because Richard received the deed as a gift.[11] Regardless, the jury awarded Richard and his wife title. The Supreme Court of Georgia affirmed without explicitly indicating what category the relief fell under. It held that "[u]nder the peculiar circumstances of this case, it cannot be said the court erred in awarding defendants the property upon which the house was built and now stands."[12] The court also held that "[g]iven plaintiffs' failure to act in an appropriate and timely manner when they knew, or should have known, that Richard's house was built on the wrong lot, we believe that the trial court, in the exercise of its inherent equity power . . . chose the most equitable solution to this conflict."[13]

11 *Id.* at 635.
12 *Id.* at 634.
13 *Id.*

Chapter 29
Boundary by Acquiescence, Agreement, and Practical Location

Mr. A and Mr. B are neighbors. At some point, someone had placed a fence that encroached on Mr. B's land, at least as a surveyor might view the situation, or perhaps as the deeds might reveal. If Mr. A and Mr. B implicitly or explicitly agreed that the fence represented what they considered their mutual boundary line, then under certain circumstances, the fence is the official boundary line. Objective reality no longer matters; a perfect survey, and possibly even the language on the deeds, become irrelevant. "A fence, by acquiescence,[1] may become the accepted boundary even though it is contrary to the survey line."[2] The Dude from *The Big Lebowski* said, "That's just, like, your opinion, man," but in this kind of case, an opinion can become fact.

Just as the Devil is known by many names, this concept is known by many names, depending on the state: boundary by acquiescence, boundary by practical location, boundary by agreement, title by acquiescence, or the agreed boundary doctrine. But some courts might distinguish between some of these doctrines, to some degree, even if on first review they all seem the same.

One typical description of the elements is from Utah: "(i) occupation up to a visible line marked by monuments, fences, or buildings, (ii) mutual acquiescence in the line as a boundary, (iii) for a long period of time, (iv) by adjoining land owners."[3] That concerns the very basics, but the deeper one delves, the more complicated and unclear it becomes, especially because there is no universality on the matter.

Certain states handle the cases with a more complicated analysis, including separate elements for subcategories. For example, in Wisconsin, one obtains relief either by "(1) Acquiescence for the period of time

1 This has to be the most difficult word to spell in the English language; if I spelled it correctly throughout this book, it's a miracle.

2 Reynolds v. GFM, LLC, 429 S.W.3d 336, 339 (Ark. Ct. App. 2013).

3 Essential Botanical Farms, LC v. Kay, 270 P.3d 430, 432–33 (Utah 2011) (citation and emphasis omitted).

equal to the statute of limitations[,] (2) Express agreement between the parties when a boundary is established pursuant to a dispute and long acquiescence even if such period falls short of the statutory [limitation period,] (3) Both parties taking from a common grantor with reference to a marked boundary which was shown to them [, or] (4) Building a fence in reliance on a survey and acquiesced in for a period of years where there is no competent evidence showing the true boundary line to be different from the fence line."[4]

In any event, the basic doctrine could be extremely useful to a litigator who has a client that cannot meet the traditional elements of an adverse possession case. In such a case, then depending on the state, a claimant may not need to prove hostility or a claim of right, continuous use, actual occupation, or even the requirement to keep the fence in place for a particular number of years.

Various courts have explained the basis for the doctrine. One court indicated that "[t]he doctrine of acquiescence was created to allow a person to acquire property when occupying part of a neighbor's land due to an honest mistake as to the location of the true boundary, because the adverse intent requirement of the related doctrine of adverse possession could not be met under those circumstances."[5] As another court put it, "The purpose of the agreed-boundary doctrine is to secure repose and prevent litigation. The doctrine promotes the stability of agreements adjusting a disputed boundary as a method adopted in good faith by the parties to settle a controversy. It arose as a way to settle disputes over boundaries in an earlier time, when surveys were notoriously inaccurate and the monuments and landmarks they described could not be located."[6] Another court similarly indicated that "[t]he doctrine of boundary by acquiescence appears to be a relic from the days when, perhaps due to insufficient surveying or recording methods, the actual legal boundary between two adjacent properties was often unknown or unknowable."[7] The doctrine "derives from [the] realization, ancient in our law, that peace and good order of society [are] best served by leaving at rest possible disputes over long established boundaries."[8] The same court held that it "fills an important gap in the law left unaddressed by other doctrines."[9]

4 Production Credit Ass'n of Mandan v. Terra Vallee, Inc., 303 N.W.2d 79, 85 (N.D. 1981), citing Beasley v. Konczal, 87 Wis. 2d 233 (1979).
5 James v. Griffin, 626 N.W.2d 704, 707–08 (N.D. 2001) (citation omitted).
6 Mehdizadeh v. Mincer, 46 Cal. App. 4th 1296, 1304 (Cal. Ct. App. 1996) (citation omitted).
7 Fischer v. First Am. Title Ins. Co., 388 S.W.3d 181, 190 n.7 (Mo. Ct. App. 2013).
8 Staker v. Ainsworth, 785 P.2d 417, 423 (Utah 1990) (citation omitted).
9 *Id.*

Many courts indicate that the issues in this chapter are slightly different from those in most adverse possession cases, which concern what party actually has title to land. The boundary by acquiescence doctrine, instead, concerns the boundaries of the title one already has. As a North Dakota court put it, "acquiescence establishes a *boundary,* not *title* to land."[10]

If one's state courts put this doctrine in the category of establishing a boundary, and not title to land, it may affect how one files the case. "A dispute in which each owner admits the title of the other but disagrees as to the physical location of the boundary is not a title controversy."[11] The Supreme Court of Nebraska held that when a case concerns a simple boundary dispute, and not a title dispute, the case must be brought as an action in ejectment, or pursuant to its statute that addresses the issue, Neb. Rev. Stat. section 34-301.[12] Luckily for the claimant in that particular action, since the parties had pursued the boundary dispute as a quiet title action without objection, the court did not dismiss it on that ground, and treated it as a boundary dispute case.

The general law may be understandable, but nearly every state has its own way of handling such cases.[13] As one court put it, "A review of the doctrine of acquiescence reveals that there is little uniformity among the states in its application and requirements."[14] That is an understatement. Sometimes it seems that the exceptions exceed the rules.

A good litigator will have to look through all of the details of state law concerning what it takes to prove boundary by acquiescence or the like. In some states, the law is in flux. One court even described the concept as "somewhat murky."[15]

A litigator's first consideration is whether the doctrines of adverse possession on the one hand and boundary by acquiescence (or a similar doctrine) on the other, are truly separate. If they are one and the same, a claimant will have to find a way to prove that all of the traditional elements, including hostility, actual occupancy, claims of right, and the statutory period, are met. If they are different, a claimant may have a much more relaxed standard to meet.

Alaska's Supreme Court eloquently explained that there is a difference between adverse possession cases and the acquiescence cases, and what the difference is (at least within the confines of its state): "Boundary by acquiescence arises from some of the same policy considerations

10 *Fischer*, 388 S.W.3d at 189.
11 Hall v. Allen, 771 S.W.2d 50, 52 (Mo. 1989) (citation omitted).
12 The Rush Creek Land Live Stock v. Chain, 255 Neb. 347, 353–54 (1998).
13 "Yes, we're all individuals!" *Life of Brian* (1979).
14 Production Credit, Etc. v. Terra Vallee, 303 N.W.2d 79, 83–86 (N.D. 1981).
15 Conduff v. Stone, 968 S.W.2d 200, 204–05 (Mo. Ct. App. 1998).

as adverse possession, but rather than creating a means whereby a party can acquire title to land without the other owner's consent, it allows parties to establish the location of a boundary by consent, but without written agreement."[16] The court went on to indicate that "boundary by acquiescence does not require possession to be adverse; it requires the opposite: mutual acquiescence to possession."[17] An Arkansas court similarly explained the difference, noting that "establishment of a boundary line by acquiescence does not require adverse possession of the land by one party. When the adjoining landowners occupy their respective premises up to the line they acquiesce in as the boundary for a long period of time, they and their grantees are precluded from claiming that the boundary thus acquiesced in is not the true boundary, although it may not be."[18] One California court simply indicated the doctrine is different from adverse possession "in that it is based upon consent."[19]

The benefit to a claimant, if the doctrine is not considered under the umbrella of adverse possession, is that less elements need be proved. For example, a claim of acquiescence does not require that adverse possessor prove hostility or that his possession was without permission.[20]

Not all states consider the boundary by acquiescence doctrine separately from adverse possession. In one South Dakota case[21] the city of Deadwood[22] sought to claim certain property from a private party. Because of the history of ownership, there was no acquiescence in a rock wall boundary by adjoining landowners until 12 years before the action was filed, and in that state, one needs 20 years to meet the statutory requirement of adverse possession. The city claimed that the doctrine was "distinguishable and independent from the doctrine of adverse possession."[23] It also claimed that the court could "presume" that the 20-year statutory requirement had been met just by "the acquiescence by all parties to such boundary."[24] The private owner argued, conversely, that "the doctrine of acquiescence in boundaries is merely a potential component of adverse possession—not an independent legal doctrine."[25] The Supreme Court of South Dakota agreed with the pri-

16 Lee v. Konrad, 337 P.3d 510, 520 n.34 (Alaska 2014) (citation omitted).
17 *Id.*
18 Jennings v. Burford, 60 Ark. App. 27, 32 (1997) (citations omitted).
19 Eimon v. Severson, 2d Civil No. B249662, at *5–6 (Cal. Ct. App. Oct. 14, 2014).
20 Houston v. Mint Grp. LLC, 335 Mich. App. 545, 568 (2021).
21 City of Deadwood v. Summit, Inc., 607 N.W.2d 22 (S.D. 2000).
22 Yes—the same city in the HBO series of the same name, with more swearing than a Richard Pryor routine.
23 *Deadwood*, 607 N.W.2d at 27.
24 *Id.*
25 *Id.*

vate owner. This case also indicated that the "acquiescence" part of the claim is actually a different way describing "hostility." In any event, since the 20 years had not elapsed, there was no valid adverse possession case.

Wisconsin is an example of a state that seems to be unable to make up its mind on this issue. In 1970 its Supreme Court indicated how the idea of acquiescence came to be a supplement to the original rules of adverse possession.[26] As the court indicated, originally, "adverse intent was the first prerequisite of adverse possession. This meant that in order for the adverse possessor to start the twenty-year period running, he must commence his possession with knowledge that the land he was encroaching upon was not his and with an intent to dispossess the true owner. This meant that one who occupied part of his neighbor's land, due to an honest mistake as to the location of his boundary, could never start the statute running because he never formed the requisite adverse intent."[27] Therefore, as its Supreme Court explained, eventually courts developed the doctrine of acquiescence, which substitutes mutual acquiescence for adverse or hostile intent. Other older Wisconsin cases also treated the acquiescence doctrine as a distinct from adverse possession.[28]

Yet at least one modern Wisconsin case seemed to consider boundary by acquiescence as just another form of adverse possession.[29] In that case, a party had built a fence mistakenly not on the survey line, but in a place he believed was the actual boundary. He claimed his neighbor acquiesced to that line. The court held there is a concept it described as "adverse possession by acquiescence," which occurs when neighboring property owners treat a common marker as their joint property line for the statutory 20-year period. And in the case at issue, for the statutory period, the parties treated the fence line as the boundary between their properties. The adverse claimant's neighbor believed the claimant owned the land to the east of the fence line, and, as a result, he acquiesced in the claimant's use of that property. Under these circumstances, the appellate court held that the lower court properly reviewed the existence of the fence line in its adverse possession analysis. It held that acquiescence "is simply another form of adverse possession."[30]

26 Buza v. Wojtalewicz, 48 Wis. 2d 557 (1970).

27 *Id.* at 562–63.

28 *See* Peter H. & Barbara J. Steuck Living Tr. v. Easley, 2010 WI App 74, ¶ 37 (Wis. Ct. App.), citing Grell v. Ganser, 255 Wis. 381, 383–84 (1949); Seybold v. Burke, 14 Wis. 2d 397, 403–06 (1961).

29 Fabry v. Jagiello, 2019 WI App 21, 386 Wis. 2d 630 (Wis. Ct. App. 2019). *See also* Menzner v. Tracy, 247 Wis. 245, 251–52 (1945).

30 *Id.* ¶ 21.

Just to further prove that confusion sometimes reigns, one can review a footnote from the Supreme Court of Wisconsin, which indicates that "[a] boundary line different from that described in the respective deeds of adjoining landowners may be established under the respective principles of adverse possession, prescription, agreement, practical location, acquiescence or estoppel. Each of these has a different factual background though too often they are confused by the courts."[31]

This kind of confusion can be a potential boon to a litigator, who can attempt to pigeonhole the case into a category that works best for his client. The Wisconsin example also serves as a reminder that no matter how black and white one's state's law may seem on the issue, if one delves deep enough, one may find gray.

If adverse possession is considered separate from the boundary by acquiescence doctrine, one must review what elements are not necessary from a traditional adverse possession case, and need not be proven. One must also determine what elements do need to be proven for this doctrine, that might not be relevant in an adverse possession case.

A litigator also has to determine whether a non-adverse possession case to establish boundaries is just one category, or several. For example, Utah at once point conflated boundary by agreement, and boundary by acquiescence. Now it does not; it considers them separately.[32] Arkansas similarly has at least two different doctrines. In the case of a boundary by oral agreement, "four factors must be present: (1) there must be an uncertainty or dispute about the boundary line; (2) the agreement must be between the adjoining landowners; (3) the line fixed by the agreement must be definite and certain; and (4) there must be possession following the agreement."[33] Conversely, a boundary by acquiescence arises from actions and not words, and has somewhat different elements, in that state.[34] Such a boundary comes from implied agreement, which is presumed to exist by the long acquiescence of adjoining landowners who apparently consented to a dividing line between their properties.[35]

Other courts seem to consider certain doctrines as the same or nearly the same. In Idaho, "[a] boundary by agreement is also sometimes called a boundary by acquiescence . . . . [A]cquiescence is merely regarded as competent evidence of the agreement, and alone is not enough to establish a boundary by agreement."[36] Nonetheless, "[a] long period of

31 Northrop v. Opperman, 331 Wis. 2d 287, 298 n.10 (Wis. 2011), citing 6 John S. Grimes, Thompson on Real Property § 3034, at 506 (1962).

32 Anderson v. Fautin, 379 P.3d 1186, 1191 *et seq.* (2016).

33 Nunley v. Orsburn, 312 Ark. 147 (1993).

34 Jennings v. Burford, 60 Ark. App. 27 (1997).

35 Raborn v. Buffalo, 260 Ark. 531 (1976).

36 Huskinson v. Nelson, 152 Idaho 547, 550 (2012).

acquiescence . . . provides a factual basis from which an agreement can be inferred."[37] Its Supreme Court explained that "'boundary by acquiescence' is simply another name attached to the doctrine of boundary by agreement; it is not a separate legal theory."[38]

Yet further confusing the matter is a description from a Michigan court, which indicates that there are three separate doctrines of acquiescence: "(1) acquiescence for the statutory period; (2) acquiescence following a dispute and agreement; and (3) acquiescence arising from intention to deed to a marked boundary."[39]

Another issue is the claimant's burden. In Maine, the "party claiming title by acquiescence bears the burden of proof by clear and convincing evidence."[40] The Utah Supreme Court agreed with that, indicating that courts "generally require clear and convincing evidence to deprive an individual of an interest in real property. Because boundary by acquiescence also alters fee simple ownership of real property, we hold that a claim of boundary by acquiescence must be proven by clear and convincing evidence."[41] A Minnesota court similarly held that the evidence of practical location of a boundary must be clear, positive, and unequivocal.[42]

In Arkansas, however, the burden for boundary line by acquiescence is merely preponderance of the evidence.[43] A Michigan court similarly held that "[t]he claimant need only establish acquiescence by a preponderance of the evidence, rather than by the stricter clear-and-cogent-evidence standard."[44] On the fence is Alaska—its Supreme Court made a point to indicate that it has never resolved whether preponderance, or clear and convincing, is the standard that applies.[45]

As indicated previously in Chapter 13, a traditional adverse possession claimant must consider real estate taxes; that may not apply here. Therefore, if the state requires a claimant to pay taxes in order to obtain adverse possession rights, then a party who seeks a portion of his neighbor's property and did not pay taxes on that portion, he will likely have to resort to the doctrine described in this chapter. For

37 Griffel v. Reynolds,136 Idaho 397, 400 (2001).

38 Downey v. Vavold, 144 Idaho 592, 595–96 (2007) (citation and internal quotation marks omitted).

39 Houston v. Mint Grp., LLC, 335 Mich. App. 545, 567 (2021) (quotation marks and citation omitted).

40 Gammon v. Verrill, 651 A.2d 831, 832 (Me. 1994).

41 Essential Botanical Farms, LC v. Kay, 270 P.3d 430, 436–37 (Utah 2011).

42 Allred v. Reed, 362 N.W.2d 374, 376 (Minn. Ct. App. 1985).

43 Myers v. Yingling, 372 Ark. 523, 527 (2008).

44 Edinger-Fowler v. Kezelian, No. 339164, 2018 WL 5276457, at *9–10 (Mich. Ct. App. Oct. 23, 2018), citing Walters v. Snyder, 239 Mich. App. 453, 458 (2000).

45 Collins v. Hall, 453 P.3d 178, 191 n.37 (Alaska 2019).

example, in California, although the tax obligation normally is a major impediment to adverse possession cases, "[o]nce it is found that the parties agreed upon a boundary, the payment of taxes according to deed descriptions amounts to payment of taxes on the area up to the agreed-upon boundary."[46] In that state, instead of paying taxes beyond the official borderline, the only elements under the "agreed-boundary doctrine," are that the party claiming the land bears the burden to prove that there is "[1] an uncertainty as to the true boundary line, [2] an agreement between the coterminous owners fixing the line, and [3] acceptance and acquiescence in the line so fixed for a period equal to the statute of limitations or under such circumstances that substantial loss would be caused by a change of its position."[47]

Some states, such as Minnesota, have a statute specifically addressing taxes in boundary acquiescence cases, and the difference in how cases are handled if the claimant paid real estate taxes. In that state, its relevant statute[48] provides that a title holder seeking to reclaim property from an adverse possessor must do so within 15 years, which is further reduced in certain contexts to only five years if the party claiming title by adverse possession had paid taxes for at least five consecutive years. But the statute further clarifies that this particular provision does "not apply to actions relating to the boundary line of lands, which boundary lines are established by adverse possession."

Another element a litigator must consider is the time period that has elapsed after the alleged agreement or acquiescence. In a state in which acquiescence is just a form of adverse possession, then the statutory time period will be easily determined. If it is considered a separate doctrine, there are several ways the state could handle it. Some states have statutes specifically setting the minimum necessary time of occupancy in the context of boundary by acquiescence.[49] Other states require the same period as the statute of limitations for adverse possession.[50] Again, this can be true even when the courts explicitly recognize the doctrines of adverse possession and acquiescence as distinct legal doctrines.[51]

---

46 Caballero v. Balamotis, 144 Cal. App. 2d 58, 61 (1956) (citation omitted).

47 Mehdizadeh v. Mincer, 46 Cal. App. 4th 1296, 1302–03 (Cal. Ct. App. 1996) (citation and internal quotation marks omitted).

48 MINN. STAT. § 541.02.

49 *See* City of Deadwood v. Summit, Inc., 607 N.W.2d 22, 28, n.5 (S.D. 2000), citing, for example, IOWA CODE ANN § 650.14; NEB. REV. STAT. § 34–301.

50 *Id.*, citing Sackett v. Atyeo, 217 Mich. App. 676 (1996) (citing MICH. COMP. LAWS § 600.5801[4]); Lakeview Farm, Inc. v. Enman, 166 Vt. 158 (1997) (citing VA. CODE ANN. tit. 12, § 501).

51 607 N.W.2d at 28, n.6, citing inter alia Engquist v. Wirtjes, 68 N.W.2d 412, 416 (Minn. 1955); Shoemaker v. Houchen, 994 S.W.2d 40, 45 (Mo. App. 1999).

Some courts, like those in Maine, describe the time period ambiguously: a "long period of years."[52] An Arkansas court similarly indicated that "[t]he period of acquiescence need not last for a specific length of time, but it must be for 'many years' or 'a long period of time' sufficient to sustain the inference that there has been an agreement concerning the location of the boundary line."[53] In such a state, if there has not been a "long period of time," a good litigator will have to attempt to claim there is some other basis for the court to infer acquiescence.

The best result for a claimant is if the court does not require any amount of time to have passed after the agreement was entered. Oregon described the idea of requiring evidence of time passing to be the "minority view and has been criticized as a failure to recognize the different bases for adverse possession and boundary by agreement."[54] Utah similarly repudiated any requirement to show passage of any particular time because "[o]nce such agreement is proven, it may form the basis for an enforceable boundary—without respect to the length of time in which the parties have embraced it."[55] Therefore, if one is in a state which has not conclusively addressed this particular issue, and one represents a claimant who only allegedly made the "agreement" within a short time before the action was filed, one can try these arguments about the reduced time period from other states.

On yet another issue, in some states, like Michigan, a "precise line" is not necessary as long as the parties share a general understanding of the location of the fictional boundary line for the time period.[56] This is not universal. In at least one state, Arizona, the courts require that the boundary in question must be "visible, definite, and clearly marked."[57] Washington similarly indicates that the line "must be certain, well defined, and in some fashion physically designated upon the ground, *e.g.*, by monuments, roadways, fence lines, etc."[58] Notably, this shows a major difference between boundary line by recognition and acquiescence cases on the one hand, and adverse possession cases on the other, in that state. In Washington, "an adverse possessor does not have to prove possession along a straight, well-defined boundary line."[59]

New York as well has this tough standard—it indicated that "application of the [practical location] doctrine requires a clear demarcation

52 607 N.W.2d at 28, n.5, citing Davis v. Mitchell, 628 A.2d 657, 660 (Me. 1993).
53 Mealey v. Arndt, 206 Ariz. 218, 222 (Ct. App. 2003).
54 Blaisdell v. Nelsen, 66 Or. App. 511, 515 n.2 (Or. Ct. App. 1984).
55 Bahr v. Imus, 250 P.3d 56, 67 (Utah 2011).
56 Walters v. Snyder, 239 Mich. App. 453, 458 (2000).
57 Mealey v. Arndt, 206 Ariz. 218, 222 (Ct. App. 2003).
58 Lamm v. McTighe, 72 Wash. 2d 587, 592–93 (1967).
59 Reinertsen v. Rygg, 161 Wash. App. 1037 (Wash. Ct. App. 2011).

of a boundary line and proof that there is mutual acquiescence to the boundary by the parties such that it is definitely and equally known, understood and settled."[60] One Maine court held that an elements of acquiescence was "possession up to a visible line marked clearly by monuments, fences or the like."[61] In that state, an old roadway could be a "visible line" establishing a boundary,[62] and a remains of a hedge between properties could also be a "visible line" establishing a boundary.[63] But in that state, an edge of a hayfield would not rise to that level.[64]

A litigator handling real property cases and hearing the idea of an "oral agreement" about real property might consider the claim unenforceable. One might believe the statute of frauds prevents that relief. (For more on the statute of frauds, see Chapter 17.) However, as one Utah court put it, an oral agreement "between adjoining owners as to the location of a boundary line" does not violate the statute of frauds, "provided the agreement is followed by actual . . . possession by each of the owners up to the line so agreed upon, and provided further, that the proper location of the line is uncertain or in dispute . . . . [I]f the location of the true boundary is not known to the adjoining owners, a parol agreement between them fixing its location is not regarded as transferring an interest in land but merely determining the location of existing estates."[65] Many other jurisdictions use the same rationale to justify the doctrine of boundary by agreement, without allowing the statute of frauds to be used as a defense.[66] As one court put it, if the proper elements are present, "the agreement is not considered an exchange of land and is not within the statute of frauds."[67] Therefore, a litigator representing a party making a claim to extend his boundary has to make sure that his client describes the agreement like this: "We were not sure where the true line was, and we argued about it, but eventually we agreed to set up the line in this location." If your client, as a claimant, instead describes the agreement as being something along the lines of "I will give you that portion of my land in exchange for that portion of your land," the agreement is much more likely to be deemed unenforceable.

60 Jakubowicz v. Solomon, 107 A.D.3d 852, 853 (N.Y. App. Div. 2013) (internal quotation marks and citations omitted).
61 Calthorpe v. Abrahamson, 441 A.2d 284, 289–90 (Me. 1982).
62 Marja Corp. v. Allain, 622 A.2d 1182, 1184 (Me. 1993).
63 Davis v. Mitchell, 628 A.2d 653, 657 (Me. 1993).
64 Crosby v. Baizley, 642 A.2d 150, 153–54 (Me. 1994) (partially superseded by statute).
65 Bahr v. Imus, 250 P.3d 56, 66–67 (Utah 2011) (citations omitted).
66 *Id.* at 67, n.9.
67 Faulkner v. Lloyd, 253 S.W.2d 972, 974 (Ky. Ct. App. 1953).

Another issue special to the acquiescence doctrine is whether the parties must have had an original disagreement about where the boundary existed. (This is tied into whether the statute of frauds would bar evidence of such an agreement.) In Missouri, "[a]cquiescence in the existence of a fence as a barrier, for convenience or for any reason other than as boundary will not constitute an agreement that it is a boundary or establish it as the true line."[68] Therefore, in that state, the courts determined that "[t]he doctrine of boundary by acquiescence appears to be applicable only to uncertain or disputed boundaries, as opposed to cases where the location of the true boundary is known."[69] In order to have a prima facie case for boundary by agreement, one must prove that "the adjoining property owners dispute the true location of the property line, and subsequently acquiesce to a barrier established as a boundary."[70] Oklahoma seconded this idea that a boundary by agreement or boundary by acquiescence only applies if the boundaries were originally disputed or uncertain.[71] In fact, the court held that to apply the doctrine of boundary by acquiescence or boundary by agreement when there would be objectively no dispute as to where the boundary is, would violate the statute of frauds.[72] In Florida, the courts have also held that the uncertainty or dispute must be mutual as to both property owners.[73]

A state like Arkansas, on the other hand, has clarified that an enforceable boundary line by acquiescence may exist without the necessity of a prior dispute.[74] The elements described by New Hampshire courts also do not require that there was an original dispute or disagreement about the location of the boundary.[75] In New Mexico, the elements of uncertainty and dispute are not essential conditions to establish boundary lines by acquiescence.[76] New York has similarly held that neither an unknown or disputed boundary line, nor even an agreement between adjoining owners, are required elements of the doctrine of practical location.[77]

68 Conduff v. Stone, 968 S.W.2d 200, 204 (Mo. Ct. App. 1998).
69 *Id.* at 205.
70 *Id.*
71 McGlothlin v. Livingston, 276 P.3d 1042, 1047, 1048 n.12 (Okla. Civ. App. 2012).
72 *Id.* at 1047–48.
73 DuBois v. Amestoy, 652 So. 2d 919, 920 (Fla. 4th Dist. Ct. App. 1995), citing Evans v. Forte, 510 So. 2d 327 (Fla. 2d Dist. Ct. App.), *rev. denied*, 518 So. 2d 1274 (Fla. 1987).
74 Myers v. Yingling, 372 Ark. 523, 530 n.3 (2008); Harris v. Robertson, 306 Ark. 258, 261 (1991).
75 O'Hearne v. McClammer, 163 N.H. 430, 435–36 (2012) (citation omitted).
76 Woodburn v. Grimes, 58 N.M. 717, 720 (1954).
77 Jakubowicz v. Solomon, 107 A.D.3d 852, 853 (N.Y. App. Div. 2013).

A state like Michigan, on yet another hand, and as indicated further above, has three theories of acquiescence for a new property boundary line. One of them depends on acquiescence following a dispute and agreement, but others do not.[78]

There always seems to be an outlier, if one searches hard enough. For example, it would seem to be only logical that boundary by acquiescence, as the Supreme Court of North Dakota put it, "allows a property owner to acquire neighboring property due to an honest mistake over the location of the boundary line."[79] But even that law is not universal. Maine seems to have a very different attitude about this. It held in one case that both parties' predecessors-in-title had been mistaken as to the boundary line, and therefore "any actions indicating acquiescence were the result of a mistake, which cannot form the basis of title by acquiescence."[80]

Another issue is whether the claimant must have actually occupied the lot up to the new alleged boundary. In New Hampshire, this is one of the critical elements.[81] But in a state like Kentucky, under the doctrine of agreed boundaries, so long as certain elements are present, "it is immaterial whether there has been any possession as to the agreed line."[82] The same is true in Arkansas; there is no "requirement of adverse usage up to a boundary fence to establish a boundary by acquiescence."[83]

A litigator representing the claimant should not solely focus on the existence of a fence or whatever monument denotes the alleged lot line. At least some courts indicate that there must be evidence about the intent behind building it. "An owner of property does not acquiesce in a fence as a boundary merely because he builds the fence upon his own property and not upon the property line."[84] The litigator should also consider what the intent of the fence builder was, or at least what the intent of the property owners was. As an example of what is insufficient, the Oklahoma Supreme Court considered it critical to note that "[i]t clearly appears that the fence was not erected as a boundary fence, but simply for the purpose of enabling the builders of the fence to serve their own purposes."[85] As another example, if a row of hedges is deemed put

78 Houston v. Mint Grp., 335 Mich. App. 545, 567 (2021) (citation omitted).

79 McCarvel v. Perhus, 952 N.W.2d 86, 89 (N.D. 2020) (citation omitted).

80 Hamlin v. Niedner, 955 A.2d 251, 253–54 (Me. 2008), citing Anchorage Realty Trust v. Donovan, 2004 ME 137, ¶¶ 11–12, 880 A.2d 1110, 1112.

81 O'Hearne v. McClammer, 163 N.H. 430, 435–36 (N.H. 2012) (citation omitted).

82 House v. Hodges, No. 2016-CA-001912-MR, 2019 WL 5681192, at *5 (Ky. Ct. App. Nov. 1, 2019), citing Howard v. Howard, 271 Ky. 773 (1938).

83 Myers v. Yingling, 372 Ark. 523, 527 (2008).

84 Production Credit, Etc. v. Terra Vallee, 303 N.W.2d 79, 85 (N.D. 1981) (citation omitted).

85 Kinkade v. Simpson, 200 Okla. 507, 508 (1948).

in place "purely for aesthetic purposes," that would be insufficient for an acquiescence case.[86]

Yet another issue is whether one must prove that, if the parties did not have an express agreement on the topic, that at the very least the parties "in good faith manifested, by their acts, occupancy, and improvements with respect to their respective properties, a mutual recognition and acceptance of the designated line as the true boundary line."[87] This is required in the state of Washington.

Another issue is how to prove acquiescence. This can be done in various manners, including from a party's silence, or inferring from that party's conduct.[88] The Supreme Court of North Dakota held that "[i]n order to establish a boundary by acquiescence, it is not necessary that the acquiescence should be manifested by a conventional agreement, but recognition and acquiescence must be mutual, and both parties must have knowledge of the existence of a line as a boundary line."[89] The Supreme Court of Missouri indicated that instead of being required to provide direct evidence of an agreement fixing a boundary line, such an agreement "may be inferred from the acts, conduct, and . . . from the long acquiescence of the parties."[90] The same court held that when abutting landowners use and occupy "up to a common boundary for a long time without disturbance, . . . [s]uch possession and use are evidence that there was an agreement to establish the line,—not only to corroborate other evidence of such an agreement, but even if there be no other such evidence."[91]

In certain cases, nearly no evidence at all may be necessary to prove acquiescence: case law has held that acquiescence is established when a preponderance of the evidence "establishes that the parties *treated* a particular boundary line as the property line."[92]

In case anyone believed the doctrine described in this chapter was simple and easy to decipher, one should review New York law. In that state, there are many unexplored issues due to a statute passed in 2008. New York cases seem to indicate that the practical location/acquiescence doctrine is separate from adverse possession, but that if the parties acquiesced to a practical location of a boundary line for more than the

86 Clark v. Buttonwoods Beach Ass'n, C.A. No. KC-2014–0271, at *1 (R.I. Super. Aug. 30, 2017).

87 Lamm v. McTighe, 72 Wash. 2d 587, 592–93 (1967).

88 Ward v. Shipp, 340 N.W.2d 14, 16 (N.D. 1983).

89 Hausner v. Melia, 212 Neb. 764, 771 (1982), quoting 11 C.J.S. Boundaries § 79 (1938).

90 Tillman v. Hutcherson, 348 Mo. 473, 478 (1941).

91 *Id.* (citation and internal quotation marks omitted).

92 Mason v. City of Menominee, 282 Mich. App 525, 530 (Mich. Ct. App. 2009) (citation omitted) superseded by amendment to statute.

statutory period governing adverse possession, that that would be "conclusive of the location of the boundary line."[93] Since New York courts describe the doctrine as requiring the use of "adverse possession" statutes of limitation, implicitly one would assume that means the doctrine is separate, and it just borrows a limitation period.

However, the New York legislature in 2008 enacted RPAPL 543, which specifically defines what actions across boundary lines may constitute "adverse" occupancy. RPAPL 543(1) now provides: "Notwithstanding any other provision of this article, the existence of de [minimis] non-structural encroachments including, but not limited to, fences, hedges, shrubbery, plantings, sheds and non-structural walls, shall be deemed to be permissive and non-adverse." Since there is now a specific statute in New York that indicates that fences over a boundary line are not a basis to claim adverse possession, one might come to the conclusion that fences over lot lines are now not a basis to make any claims of landownership over a lot line, whether through adverse possession or any other method like acquiescence. Since many cases about acquiescence, nationwide, involve fences, it is unclear if the legislature was suggesting boundary acquiescence claims based on fences are no longer permissible in New York. On the other hand, RPAPL 543 does not specifically indicate that a boundary by acquiescence claim is now forbidden in New York. So perhaps the statute just means that a party claiming he controls portions of the property over the true borderline as indicated by a fence, must specifically label the claim in the lawsuit as boundary by acquiescence rather than adverse possession. In one case, a party seeking to claim adverse possession of a portion of his neighbor's property pursuant to a rock wall, was barred from that relief due to RPAPL 543. Notably, in a footnote, the court pointed out that "[p]laintiffs did not raise the 'boundary line by acquiescence' theory in their complaint or submissions in opposition to defendants' motion and, thus, we decline to address its applicability here."[94]

The point here is not of course simply to point out gaps in one state's law, but to indicate that there are many other potential gaps in the doctrine throughout the United States. An attorney facing a potential losing case cannot simply accept the standard, without trying to find some exception to a rule.

93 Kaneb v. Lamay, 58 A.D.3d 1097, 1098 (N.Y. App. Div. 2009).
94 Sawyer v. Prusky, 71 A.D.3d 1325, 1328 n.4 (N.Y. App. Div. 2010).

Chapter 30
Boundary by Estoppel and Easement by Estoppel

Another way of avoiding the difficulty of proving adverse possession (or even the difficulty of proving boundary by acquiescence) would be to prove estoppel. This chapter addresses the law of boundary by estoppel and easement by estoppel.

If a boundary by estoppel argument works, this would avoid needing to prove certain elements in a traditional adverse possession case, such as the length of time one's client has occupied the space. But there are other elements involved that do not appear in traditional claims based on adverse possession or boundary by acquiescence.

The boundary by estoppel concept could work in the following example. Mr. A and Mr. B are neighbors, and Mr. A shows Mr. B where Mr. A intends to construct a building. As it turns out, if Mr. A does the construction, it would be over the lot line, onto Mr. B's space. But Mr. B informs Mr. A that this proposed construction would be perfectly fine because, as Mr. B sees it, the proposed construction would be within Mr. A's property. (The concept would especially work if Mr. A believed Mr. B was telling the truth, and if Mr. B's claim seemed believable at the time.) If Mr. A constructs the building, and then Mr. B finds out he had been mistaken, and tries to compel Mr. A to remove the building, the court will likely rule against Mr. B, and hold that Mr. A can keep that building intact. In this way the situation may be different from a boundary by acquiescence case, because in those cases the claimants need to prove there was a certain amount of time that neighbors used the false lot line as the true lot line. But in this Mr. A versus Mr. B estoppel scenario, likely the court would not need the building to have been maintained for any particular amount of time.

The Supreme Court of Minnesota indicated this concept applies when "[t]he party whose rights are to be barred must have silently looked on with knowledge of the true line while the other party encroached thereon or subjected himself to expense which he would not have incurred had the line been in dispute."[1] Another way of phrasing it is that boundary

1 Wojahn v. Johnson, 297 N.W.2d 298, 304 (Minn. 1980).

by estoppel "arises when one owner erroneously represents to the other that their common boundary is along a certain line, and the second owner in reliance takes detrimental action. The boundary by estoppel doctrine estops the first owner from denying that the common boundary line is not where he acquiesced or represented it to be located."[2] At least one court has held that the burden is clear and convincing evidence.[3]

A Kentucky court set forth the necessary elements to invoke the doctrine of boundary by estoppel:

> (1) Conduct which amounts to a false representation or concealment of material facts, or, at least, which is calculated to convey the impression that the facts are otherwise than, and inconsistent with, those which the party subsequently attempts to assert; (2) intention, or at least expectation, that such conduct shall be acted upon by the other party; (3) knowledge, actual or constructive, of the real facts. As related to the party claiming the estoppel, they are: (1) Lack of knowledge and of the means of knowledge of the truth as to the facts in question; (2) reliance upon the conduct of the party estopped; and (3) action based thereon of such a character as to change his position prejudicially.[4]

Utah's Supreme Court held that there are three elements to establish a property boundary through equitable estoppel. First, the claimant "must establish an affirmative statement by a neighboring landowner regarding the location of a shared boundary." Second, the claimant "must show that it has engaged in some act in reasonable reliance on the representation of the neighboring property." Notably, "reasonable" here means, at the very least, that the claimant must not have known of the true boundary line. And third, there must be "proof of injury."[5] If someone spent a few hundred dollars building a fence in the wrong place, that alone would probably not be of sufficient gravity to sustain an estoppel case.

It is helpful to review an example to understand the concept and its limits. In one Oklahoma case, the defendants, who claimed title to portions of the plaintiff's property laying on defendants' side of a fence argued the plaintiff was estopped from denying title to the defendants for the reason that the defendants had mowed the lawn, trimmed the

2 Lee v. Tipton, No. 2010-CA-002189-MR, at *18–19 (Ky. Ct. App. May 18, 2012) (citation and internal quotation marks omitted).
3 Roy v. Cunningham, 46 Wn. App. 409, 415 (1986).
4 Embry v. Turner, 185 S.W.3d 209, 215 (Ky. Ct. App. 2006).
5 Bahr v. Imus, 250 P.3d 56, 63–64 (Utah 2011).

shrubs, and planted grass on their side of the fence. The court rejected this argument, stating the plaintiff's failure to object to such activity did not operate as an estoppel.[6]

Another situation in which the doctrine would not work was described in a Kentucky case.[7] In that case, the plaintiffs argued that the construction of a garage and "other improvements" aptly demonstrated their detrimental reliance. However, they failed to particularly specify these "other improvements," the date such improvements were constructed, or the location of such improvements upon the property. Moreover, the evidence showed that the defendant was unaware of the garage before or during its construction. Therefore, the court held there could not have been acquiescence in the construction of the garage at its present location.

Another case in which there was no boundary by estoppel took place when the claimant's action consisted of tearing down an old fence, and building a new one. The problem was that she admitted that she located the new fence in a new location because she could "more easily trim growth coming through it and because it would keep her dog in her yard." The court held that this meant her decision to relocate was not based on where she believed the property line was.[8]

A case of when the doctrine would work is where a seller represents a particular line to be the boundary between the property that he is selling and the property that he is retaining, and he induces a buyer to buy up to the purported boundary. In such a case, the seller is estopped from later denying the accuracy of his representation of the boundary. In one Oregon Supreme Court case,[9] the plaintiff had bought land from her father, who identified a particular line as the boundary between her property and his remaining property. He even built a fence on that line. The plaintiff daughter paid to have a house built on a site that was selected by her father, who supervised the construction of the house, which turned out to encroach over the boundary described in the deed. Because the father, in ignorance of his ownership of the land, had encouraged the plaintiff daughter to incur expenses to build her house, he and his wife were estopped from asserting their title to the degree it injured the plaintiff.

The same rule was applied in another Oregon case called *Riesland v. Schick*.[10] There, when the defendants bought their land and house,

6 Kinkade v. Simpson, 200 Okla. 507, 197 P.2d 968 (1948).
7 Lee v. Tipton, No. 2010-CA-002189-MR, at *20 (Ky. Ct. App. May 18, 2012).
8 Stevenson v. Brodt, No. A09–2222, 2010 WL 4068727, at *14 (Minn. Ct. App. Oct. 19, 2010).
9 Clark v. Hindman, 46 Or. 67 (1905).
10 111 Or. 42 (1924).

the plaintiff acted as the grantor's agent in the sale. There was a line between the lot that the defendants bought and the neighboring lot, which appeared to be the boundary. The plaintiff showed the defendants that line, and explained that a survey was unnecessary because he "knew" that this was the real boundary line. The defendants bought their lot, intending to live in the house. The plaintiff later bought the neighboring lot from the same grantor. As it turned out, the line between the lots, which defendants had counted on, was more than 22 feet away from the true boundary—in plaintiff's favor. To make matters worse for defendants, the line ran through the house that the defendants had purchased. Luckily for defendants, the court held that the plaintiff was equitably estopped from asserting where the true boundary was.

Leaving boundaries aside, one can also seek an easement by estoppel. Once we are in the world of easements, we have to remember terms such as "easement," which means a right to cross or otherwise use someone else's land for a particular purpose; "servient tenement," which means the property subject to the easement; and "dominant tenement," which means the property whose owner has a right to an easement over the title holder's property.[11]

In California, a court indicated that "[t]he decisions that have created an easement based on estoppel involve varying circumstances, but they all involve reliance by the owner of the dominant tenement on the representations and conduct of the owner of the servient tenement of such a character that equity establishes an easement in order to prevent an injustice."[12] The court also described this as the creation of an "irrevocable license to a particular use of property."[13]

The Texas Supreme Court held that "[t]he owner of land may create an easement by a parol agreement or representation which has been so acted on by others as to create an estoppel *en pais* [i.e. equitable estoppel]. As where he has by parol agreement granted a right of such easement in his land, upon the faith of which the other party has expended moneys which will be lost and valueless if the right to enjoy such easement is revoked, equity has enjoined the owner of the first estate from preventing the use of it."[14] In that state, there are three elements necessary to create an easement by estoppel: "1) a representation communicated, either

11 These terms of art are easy to forget; I included the definitions to remind myself if I reread this book.

12 Rozanova v. Uribe, No. H044161, 2018 WL 5000022, at *6–7 (Cal. Ct. App. Oct. 16, 2018) (citation omitted) (This is a "non-citable" case.).

13 *Id.*

14 Harrison Co. v. Boring, 44 Tex. 255 (1875) (citations and internal quotation marks omitted).

by word or action, to the promisee; 2) the communication was believed; and 3) the promisee relied on the communication."[15]

In one Texas case, the court held that there was sufficient evidence of an easement by estoppel.[16] This was due in part to the fact that the property at issue was bought with the understanding that the road was the means of access, and there was reliance on the belief that they could use it. The parties seeking to use that road, or their predecessors, had built a house in a location near the road, and had spent significant amounts of labor and money in improving that property. There was also testimony that the claimants had contributed to the maintenance of the road.

In Michigan, a court also handled a case concerning a potential easement by estoppel, but ruled it did not exist.[17] There had been a trail road that defendants used, but eventually after many years, the plaintiff built a new access road into its property and no longer needed the trail road. The plaintiff then filed an action seeking to enjoin the defendants from further using the trail road. The defendants raised various claims, including that they had an easement by necessity, and that there was an easement by estoppel. The trial court held that there was both, but the appellate court held that there was only an easement by necessity, and not one by estoppel.

In that case, there had been an agreement concerning the mutual use of a road. The parties had verbally agreed to use the trail road over their properties for their joint benefit. But the party seeking an easement by estoppel had not relied upon this agreement to his detriment. In fact, he thought his rights were based upon the fact that the trail road was a public road "instead of the correct position that he had an easement over the road by necessity."[18] The party seeking the easement had also not taken steps to, for example, maintain the road.

The appellate court held that there was no easement by estoppel because "there was no fraud present, or misrepresentations made by plaintiff to defendants concerning the agreement, that the expenditures upon and maintenance of the trail road by defendants after their arrangement with plaintiff did not differ from those accomplished before the agreement."[19] The court also noted that the expenditures on the trail road in recent history "were not substantial." To put it another way, since the defendants had treated the road as an easement by necessity, they could not suddenly switch gears and claim to have an easement

15 Stallman v. Newman, 9 S.W.3d 243, 246 (Tex. App. 1999) (citations omitted).
16 Holden v. Weidenfeller, 929 S.W.2d 124 (Tex. App. 1996).
17 Birch Forest Club v. Rose, 23 Mich. App. 492, 498–501 (Mich. Ct. App. 1970).
18 *Id.* at 499.
19 *Id.* at 500.

by estoppel. One might wonder why the court addressed the easement by estoppel claim, if it had decided there was an easement by necessity. Presumably this is because if, in the future, the defendants were provided another new road or means of access, then the old trail road would no longer be an easement by necessity, and the defendants could not claim it under the easement by estoppel method.

Chapter 31
Presumed Grant

The presumed grant theory works in many states. It is yet another way of claiming land that has been used by the possessor for an extended period. Many cases indicate it is primarily useful for a claim against the state; many courts bar adverse possession claims against a state (as was discussed in Chapter 21.) In fact, at least one court has held that the doctrine has "little or no relevancy" if a party is permitted to seek adverse possession against the state.[1] But it also has relevancy in other contexts, as indicated below, such as where an adverse possession claim requires color of title and/or tax payments, and the claimant cannot prove either of those elements. It also may have relevancy if the state law does not allow for certain kinds of tacking claims in the context of adverse possession, but would allow it in the context of a presumed grant.

The concept is that, in certain circumstances, if one has occupied property for a long enough time, in the correct manner, the court will presume that the named title owner had actually deeded the property to that claimant (or his predecessor), and for some unknown reason, the deed never got recorded. It is just that if there is a reason that an adverse possession would fail, the presumed grant theory can possibly come to the rescue. "Where adverse possession can be shown, the doctrine of presumption of grant has no application."[2]

The Supreme Court of Texas observed that "[t]he rule is essential to the ascertainment of the very truth of ancient transactions. Without it, numberless valid land titles could not be upheld."[3] A Massachusetts court discussed the concept as follows: "The slippery slope of inferring the existence of a lost, unrecorded deed may well be perilous, but the refusal to infer the existence of such a deed could also have grave consequences, and our courts have long found the practice proper . . . . The

1 State v. Philips, 400 A.2d 299, 306 (Del. Ch. 1979).
2 Bd. of Trustees v. Rye, 521 So. 2d 900, 906 (Miss. 1988).
3 Magee v. Paul, 110 Tex. 470, 478 (1920).

Supreme Judicial Court [its high court] has treated a claim of an actual lost deed as distinct from one claiming adverse possession."[4]

One treatise explained the doctrine in part in this manner, also indicating that it is different from adverse possession: "The doctrine . . . that the long continued possession of land by one claiming as owner gives rise to the presumption of a valid conveyance to him or to the person under whom he claims, though ordinarily similar in its practical results [to a claim of adverse possession], is entirely independent [from a claim of adverse possession]. It involves a presumption of the rightfulness of one's possession, while [adverse possession is] applicable only when the possession is . . . wrongful."[5]

On the other hand, some states seem to meld the two concepts. For example, one Texas court held that the doctrine is "a common law form of adverse possession."[6] The Supreme Court of Vermont held that adverse possession "is sometimes described as based on a presumed grant that becomes incontestable after the passage of the statutory time."[7] A Utah court held that there was essentially no difference between the idea of a presumed grant and adverse possession. "To say [adverse possession] rights are founded upon presumed grants is simply another illustration that 'the voice is Jacob's voice, but the hand is the hand of Esau.' I think therefore that in this day in our law, prescriptive rights are founded upon adverse possession and not upon presumed grants."[8]

If a court does distinguish between the two concepts, then to make the matter even more confusing, some courts do not presume a grant, at least in certain cases: "One asserting title to [land lying between the usual high water mark and the usual low water mark on a tidal navigable watercourse] must be prove a specific grant from the sovereign[,] which is strictly construed against the grantee."[9]

The U.S. Supreme Court has addressed the presumed grant concept in several cases. In what is described as the "seminal" case on the topic, *Fletcher v. Fuller*,[10] the Court was faced with a situation as follows. The Fletchers, whose family had been in possession of land for almost 100 years, could not produce a missing deed—the deed conveying title to the Fletchers' vendor, who was the grandson of the original

---

4 Poor v. Lombard, 72 Mass. App. Ct. 719, 721 (Mass. App. Ct. 2008) (citations omitted).

5 4 Tiffany, Real Property § 1136 (3d ed. 1939). *See also* Phillips v. State, *ex rel.* Dep't of Nat. Res. & Env't Control, 449 A.2d 250, 256 (Del. 1982), citing that portion of the treatise.

6 Fair v. Arp Club Lake, Inc., 437 S.W.3d 619, 626 (Tex. App.-Tyler 2014, no pet.)

7 Clark v. Aqua Terra Corp., 133 Vt. 54, 57 (1974).

8 Big Cottonwood Tanner Ditch Co. v. Moyle, 109 Utah 213, 242 (1946).

9 Coburg Dairy, Inc. v. Lesser, 318 S.C. 510, 512 (1995) (partially abrogated by Est. of Tenney v. S.C. Dep't of Health & Env't Control, 393 S.C. 100 [2011]).

10 120 U.S. 534, 551 (1887).

owner. In the trial, the Fletchers asked for a jury instruction—the presumption of a lost grant. The Supreme Court held that the trial court judge improperly denied that request, ruling that the "presumption of a deed is one that may be rebutted by proof of facts inconsistent with its supposed existence, yet where no such facts are shown, and the things done, and the things omitted, with regard to the property in controversy, by the respective parties, for long periods of time after the execution of the supposed conveyance, can be explained satisfactorily only upon the hypothesis of its existence, then the jury may be instructed that it is their duty to presume such a conveyance, and thus quiet the possession."[11] It also held that "the doctrine . . . is that the presumption of a grant is indulged merely to quiet a long possession which might otherwise be disturbed by reason of the inability of the possessor to produce the muniments of title which were actually given at the time of the acquisition of the property by him or those under whom he claims, but have been lost, or which he or they were entitled to have at that time, but had neglected to obtain, and of which the witnesses have passed away, or their recollection of the transaction has become dimmed and imperfect . . . ."[12]

The U.S. Supreme Court later restated the rule in *U.S. v. Fullard-Leo*: "[I]t is the general rule of American law that a grant will be presumed upon proof of an adverse, exclusive, and uninterrupted possession for 20 years, and that such rule will be applied as a presumptio juris et de jure [that is, a presumption of law], wherever, by possibility, a right may be acquired in any manner known to the law."[13]

A Delaware case from 1979 called *State v. Phillips*[14] provides another good introduction for understanding the subject, including when the presumption exists, and under what circumstances it can be overcome. In that case, the State sought to claim title to 13 acres of oceanfront property, which it claimed it had obtained since it obtained independence from Great Britain in 1776. The defendants and/or their predecessors had claimed sole and exclusive possession of the property from 1912.

The court first noted that although a party could not obtain title against the state by adverse possession when the decision was written, from 1843 until 1953 it had been possible to obtain title against the state by adverse possession. Therefore, it ruled that the defendants could attempt an adverse possession argument at trial for certain portions of the claimed land.

---

11 *Id.* at 550.
12 *Id.* at 551.
13 331 U.S. 256, 271 (1947) (citation omitted).
14 400 A.2d 299 (Del. Ch. 1979).

Leaving that to the side, the defendants had also asserted the doctrine of presumed or lost grant. The court first described how there was no dispute that Delaware recognized the legal concept of the doctrine or presumed or lost grant—it had done so (as of 1979) for at least 130 years. However, it noted that to the degree the presumption existed, it would only be a presumption of fact, and that it would not be a presumption of law. Therefore, the presumption could be overcome.

After that decision was issued, there was a trial. After trial, the Delaware Supreme Court heard certain issues in the case. It held that the State had indeed rebutted the presumption of a grant. That was in part because "the grants among the [claimants'] predecessors in title excluding the area in dispute are inconsistent with a claim of ownership."[15] In other words, the claimants' predecessors had effectively admitted that they had never been granted title, when they omitted that property from their own grants.

In another case, from Mississippi,[16] its Supreme Court concluded that under the unusual set of facts, the presumption of grant against the state never even arose, despite how long the property had been occupied. In that case, the court first explained that "[t]his doctrine of presumption of grant is not precisely synonymous with adverse possession, though the two are 'indissolubly linked.' Where adverse possession can be shown, the doctrine of presumption of grant has no application . . . . The greatest practical difference between adverse possession and the doctrine of presumption of grant is that the latter allows assertions of claims against the sovereign, despite statutes barring adverse possession against the State."[17]

In that case, some of the land at issue was called "Sixteenth Section Land." That land is owned by the State of Mississippi, which is intended to remain in trust for the support of public education. The local school board has control and management of such lands.

The court held that the only means by which the Sixteenth Section Land could have been sold by the State, was if there had been an election held to approve the sale of such lands. The claimant argued that the court was required to make certain presumptions, including that the election had taken place. However, the court held that the presumption of lost grant would not apply "due to the extensive chain of inferences required."[18] Those inferences were (1) that the missing deeds existed; (2) that the deeds in question actually transferred full fee simply

15 Phillips v. State *ex rel.* Dep't of Nat. Res. & Env't Control, 449 A.2d 250, 256 (Del. 1982).
16 Board of Ed. of Calhoun C. v. Warner, 853 So. 2d 1159 (Miss. 2003).
17 *Id.* at 1166–67 (citations and emphasis omitted).
18 *Id.* at 1168.

title, instead of simply a leasehold interest; and (3) that the deeds were authorized by the election. The court concluded that despite how the common law normally applies, that presumption "should not be used to defeat a constitutional and statutory interest in, and duty towards, the lands held in trust for the schoolchildren of Mississippi."[19] It therefore reversed the lower court that had applied the presumed grant.

Texas courts also address presumed grant cases. In one very recent case, its Supreme Court described the doctrine as both a "common law form of adverse possession" and "title by circumstantial evidence."[20] To establish title by this doctrine in that state, the evidence must show "(1) a long-asserted and open claim, adverse to that of the apparent owner; (2) nonclaim by the apparent owner; and (3) acquiescence by the apparent owner in the adverse claim."[21] In Texas, the Court of Appeals had added an additional fourth element—a gap in the title. When the matter went higher, the Supreme Court seemed to indicate that this was an error, and that there was no basis for such a fourth element.[22] Notably, the wording of that case does not explicitly indicate certain traditional adverse possession elements are necessary.

In an earlier Texas Supreme Court case called *Howland v. Hough*,[23] the plaintiff's chain of title showed a continuous chain of conveyances, except that there was a gap in the chain of title from the 1845 patent to Irvine to an 1878 deed from Hill to Meissner. The plaintiff could not produce direct evidence of possession for the right time period, which would prevent a successful adverse possession case. However, luckily for the plaintiff, the defendant did not suggest that any purported heir or grantee of Irvine had asserted a claim to the property. The Supreme Court held that "[a]lthough the presumption of a lost grant or conveyance is usually one of fact, it has been sufficiently established in this case to presume it as a matter of law because the deeds are so ancient and the evidence is undisputed."[24]

New Mexico also recognizes the doctrine; it can be an especially useful tool in that case, because in that state, in order to prove adverse possession, one must also prove color of title, as well as payment of taxes during the period of possession. Neither of those requirements are required for a presumption of a grant.[25]

19 *Id.* at 1168–69.
20 Van Dyke v. Navigator Grp., 668 S.W.3d 353, 366 (Tex. 2023).
21 *Id.*
22 *Id.*
23 570 S.W.2d 876 (Tex. 1978).
24 *Id.* at 879.
25 El Paso Prod. Co. v. PWG P'ship, 116 N.M. 583, 590 (1994).

Two other issues for a litigator to consider are (1) the length of time one must be in possession to make the claim of a presumption of a grant, and (2) whether one can prove the tacking requirements for an adverse possession case. For example, in South Carolina, adverse possession may be established by the relatively short ten-year statute of limitation.[26] However, for such a claim, tacking is allowed only between an ancestor and an heir; tacking between successive occupants would not be sufficient.[27] Therefore, if one's client cannot meet the tacking requirements, he could consider South Carolina's common law, which recognizes the 20-year presumption of a grant.[28] The good news for a claimant who cannot meet the strict tacking rules between ancestors and heirs, but can meet the 20-year period between parties in privity, is that he may have a valid presumed grant case.[29]

A Supreme Court of Hawaii case, *United Congregational Evangelical Churches v. Kamamalu*,[30] has a great analysis of the presumed grant doctrine. It also reveals that even if it cannot be applied literally, the court may find a way to provide a solid result for a claimant. The case involved a dispute between the United Churches of Moku'aikaua and Helani and the State of Hawaii over the ownership of two church lots, and concerned some history in Hawaii—some history being more than 100 years before it became a state.

In that case, the lots were originally allotted to Victoria Kamamalu, Hawaii's crown princess, in 1848. The lots were later surveyed and described as "School lot" and "School and Church lot." The trial court determined that the United Churches and their predecessors had continuously occupied and used the lots for over a hundred years, primarily for church and graveyard activities. Therefore, the trial court ruled in favor of the United Churches based on two grounds: (1) the government's title to the lots was lost by operation of a reverter statute when school uses ceased in 1888, and (2) the United Churches acquired title through adverse possession from the heirs of Victoria Kamamalu.

On appeal, the State argued that it retained ownership of the lots since 1850, which is when the School Lands Act provided that school and church lots would be "reserved" as government property. The State also contended that the reverter statutes, which in theory could have allowed for a return of such property to the original owners, had been repealed

---

26 *See* S.C. Code §§ 15-3-340, 15-67-210, 15-67-220.

27 Getsinger v. Midlands Orthopaedic Profit Sharing Plan, 327 S.C. 424, 429–30 (Ct. App. 1997), citing Terwilliger v. White, 222 S.C. 176 (1952); Terwilliger v. Marion, 222 S.C. 185 (1952).

28 *Id.* at 430, citing Terwilliger v. Daniels, 222 S.C. 191 (1952).

29 *Id.* citing White, 222 S.C. 176.

30 59 Haw. 334 (1978).

before the triggering actions took place. The Hawaiian Supreme Court agreed with those arguments.

With respect to the adverse possession case, the court noted that "it is well established that adverse possession may not run against the sovereign."[31] So that claim had no basis either.

Then it addressed the United Churches' alternate argument of presumed grant. The court first explained that "[i]n contrast to the doctrine of adverse possession, the doctrine of a presumed lost grant, arising out of adverse, exclusive, and uninterrupted possession for a substantial number of years, may be applied against the sovereign."[32] Unfortunately for the churches, any presumption of a lost grant of title had been rebutted by evidence such as the churches' predecessor in title requesting a grant of one lot (and implicitly admitting a lack of title), and other written statements of the officers of the churches' parent organization, admitting that title belonged to the government. If that were not enough, since the School Lands Act of 1850 indicated the lots were vested in the government, that alone was a partial rebuttal of a presumed grant.

If one reads the preceding, one would assume all was lost for the United Churches. However, there was good news for the United Churches after all. Although there had been a rebuttal of the presumption of a grant of title, the government had not rebutted "a presumption of a lost grant of lesser rights." The court held that "[i]n furtherance of basic considerations of justice and equity, and by analogy with the law regarding presumed lost grants of easements, we hold that the United Churches possess equitable rights in the lots which entitle the churches to continue to use the lots for religious and educational purposes, including burial purposes, until such uses are abandoned."[33] Whether a practitioner can use that unique case to argue for analogous easement claims not involving church or school property is highly questionable. But it may be worth a try.

31 *Id.* at 341–42.
32 *Id.* at 342.
33 *Id.* at 343.

Part 7

Miscellaneous Matters

Chapter 32
Bench Trial versus Jury Trial

Although presumably a great deal could be said about the pros and cons of trying an adverse possession case before a jury, the critical issue in this chapter is whether one's state even gives litigants the option. The right to a jury trial in a civil action is sometimes described as fundamental; in the context of federal cases, the Seventh Amendment of the Constitution guarantees it. Many other states have similar language. And many states provide the right to a jury trial on adverse possession cases apparently without debate. But the matter is not cut and dried. Just as is true for many technical aspects of adverse possession litigation, there is no uniformity among the states on this particular topic. Although this chapter is not intended to cover all 50 states' law, the following is a short background on some of the states' methods of analysis.

One way of handling the matter is the Georgia method. Its high court ruled that "[a]dverse possession is usually a mixed question of law and fact. The judge decides whether, as a matter of law, the facts alleged by the claimant are sufficient to constitute a claim of adverse possession. The jury decides whether the claimant has presented sufficient evidence to establish the elements of adverse possession."[1]

Alabama has another method of analysis. In one case,[2] the high court held that the lower court had correctly cited the law—that there is no right to a jury trial in an equity suit involving adverse possession. However, in that case, the court held that the true dispute in the case was an action at law in the nature of ejectment, and that since ejectment existed in the common law, the right to trial was preserved for that cause of action, under its constitution.

Another state, Washington, distinguishes between whether the plaintiff claiming title possesses the disputed land, or whether the plaintiff is simultaneously seeking to eject the defendants. In one case,[3] the court

1 Proctor v. Heirs of Jernigan, 273 Ga. 29, 29 (2000) (footnote omitted).
2 Pugh v. Calloway, 295 Ala. 139 (1976).
3 Durrah v. Wright, 115 Wash. App. 634 (2003).

went into depth with its history, noting that its constitution guaranteed a right to a trial by jury, which existed at the time of the adoption. The court then had to go back in time, before 1889, when the constitution was ratified. It noted that its code at the time granted the right to a jury trial for a common law action, but not an equitable action. And an action for ejectment was described as "common law," but adverse possession cases were not listed in that manner. Then the court noted that in the complaint, the plaintiffs alleged that they were in possession, and did not allege or seek ejectment. Therefore, the court affirmed the lower court's decision which denied plaintiffs a jury trial. Minnesota follows this method as well.[4]

West Virginia's high court addressed this issue as well. It first noted that although its rules of civil procedure had abolished the distinction between law and equity, it still had to analyze case law passed before those rules took effect, in order to determine whether a party had a right to a jury trial. The court noted, somewhat confusingly, that a court of equity would be the proper forum for reformation of a deed on the ground of mutual mistake, but that adverse possession "normally involved questions for the jury."[5]

Missouri has a different way of handling such cases. In one case,[6] its high court was faced with a party who sought to quiet title pursuant to claims of adverse possession and boundary by acquiescence. The court held that if these were legal claims, the claimant would be entitled to a jury trial, but not if they were equitable claims. The court then determined that its statute that governed actions to quiet title "authorizes relief under both legal and equitable principles." But it ultimately decided that in Missouri, adverse possession claims are classified as legal, and not equitable. So, a jury trial was appropriate.

The high court of Alaska came up with an apparently unique method of analysis on a related issue. In *McGill v. Wahl*,[7] property owners brought an action against adjoining property owners seeking a prescriptive easement to prevent the adjoining owners from obstructing a certain roadway. The Supreme Court held that the lower court properly ruled that the defendants, the adjoining owners, were not entitled to a jury trial. The court first explained that the Alaska Constitution only provided a jury trial for causes of action that are legal, and not equitable. It held that a claim for a prescriptive easement is like a claim for adverse possession—that it is an equitable claim and was historically tried in courts of equity. The defendants had argued that the action was like

4 Denman v. Gans, 607 N.W.2d 788, 793 (Minn. Ct. App. 2000).
5 Warner v. Kittle, 167 W. Va. 719, 726 (1981).
6 State *ex rel.* Barker v. Tobben, 311 S.W.3d 798 (Mo. 2010).
7 839 P.2d 393 (Alaska 1992).

an ejectment, and implicitly that an ejectment action could be heard by a jury. The high court rejected that argument, holding that "[o]ur rule prevents the awkward situation where a party who takes the aggressive stance of seizing possession of disputed property is awarded the right to a jury trial."[8]

An appellate court in Massachusetts, unlike other courts, appeared not to consider the difference between law and equity as relevant. It simply held that "[i]ssues arising out of a claim to title by adverse possession present questions of fact . . . and such questions are triable by jury."[9]

One may also consider whether a relevant statute is on point. For example, if one is seeking to be awarded title in New York to a disputed portion of property, one can (or perhaps must) do so under its statutory Real Property Actions and Proceedings Law (RPAPL) article 15. Its statute CPLR 4101 indicates that "issues of fact" in the context of a "determination of a claim to real property under article fifteen of the real property actions and proceedings law" shall be tried by a jury, unless some exception fits. However, even under that statute, "equitable defenses" and "equitable counterclaims" would be tried by the court.

In sum, an attorney attempting to resolve whether the case may, or may not, be heard by a jury must do some research on the critical considerations that apply in that state. An attorney may also need to consider how to phrase causes of action or defenses to a cause of action, or what causes of action or defenses should be included, depending on whether the attorney is seeking a jury trial or a bench trial.

8 *Id.* at 397.

9 Hutchins v. Maloomian, 32 Mass. App. Ct. 950, 950 (1992) (citations omitted).

Chapter 33
Burdens and Presumptions

Critical issues for a litigator handling an adverse possession case are presumptions and burdens.

One infamous case in Boulder, Colorado, is a good place to begin. In *McLean v. DK Trust*,[1] the plaintiffs sought a claim for adverse possession of a portion of one of their neighbors' lots. (Not coincidentally, the plaintiffs, a married couple, were both attorneys.) The trial court granted relief in the plaintiffs' favor, in part by addressing the law of presumptions. The court held that "the initial presumption is in favor of the record title holder," but that "a presumption that the possession is adverse arises after the claimant has demonstrated that he has been in actual and exclusive possession of the property for the statutory period." The court then noted that "[a]ssuming that a presumption of adversity arises, the burden then falls upon the challenging party to overcome the presumption." Finally, the court held that plaintiffs had proven their case "by a preponderance of the evidence."

One defendant told reporters that they had lost one-third of one lot, making it too small to sell or build a home on. According to one reporter, "more than 200 people flocked to the property, where they hoisted signs with slogans such as 'Thou shall not steal' and shouted 'shame' and 'thief' at the McLean/Stevens home." The wife of the losing party posted a sign on her own property facing the plaintiffs: "You will never enjoy a stolen view."[2]

Within a matter of months, Colorado's legislature responded to people's outrage, and amended its adverse possession statute in various manners. The current statute is within CRS section 38-41-101. It is now much more difficult for an adverse possession claimant to succeed. Claimants now must prove *each* element of adverse possession

---

1 Case Number 06 CV 982, District Court, Boulder County.

2 *Judge, Lawyer Take Land in Squatters' Rights Case*, The Columbus Dispatch, Dec. 9, 2007. The parties ultimately settled the case rather than having it handled by an appellate court.

by clear and convincing evidence. The amended statute also indicated that there would no longer be a presumption of adverse possession just because of actual and exclusive possession. The amendment also made it less palatable for Colorado residents to seek adverse possession, because the court may compensate the party who loses his property, including for the taxes he paid during the time it was adversely possessed.

Of course, not all states follow Colorado's example. But regardless of the state, any attorney will need to focus on presumptions, shifting burdens, how to rebut burdens, and what elements, if any, may be presumed to exist in an adverse possession case.

Most states, and the District of Columbia, require adverse possession to be proven by clear and convincing evidence or some alternative phrasing of the same concept.[3] As one New York court put it, "Since adverse possession [is] a means of cutting off legal claims to title, it has historically been strictly applied in the sense that all constituent elements must be proved, with the burden resting on the adverse claimant, with the adverse possessor's acts construed against him, and every inference in favor of a possession that is subordinate to the title of the true owner."[4]

A minority of the states, but at least ten, require adverse possession only to be proven by the preponderance of the evidence or a variant thereof.[5]

In some states, the law is not crystal clear concerning what burden applies. For example, the Supreme Court of Texas indicated in 1954 that proof of all the elements of adverse possession must be clear and satisfactory.[6] But 36 years later, in 1990, in a footnote, the same court held that this "clear and satisfactory" language was just an admonition to exercise great caution in weighing the evidence, and that it does not supplant the usual preponderance of the evidence standard of proof.[7] This seemed to match what one Texas appellate court held in an adverse possession case resolved in 1979: "Appellants had the burden to plead and prove each of the statutory requirements by a preponderance of the

3 Grace v. Koch, 81 Ohio St. 3d 577, 581 n.2 (1998) (citing numerous cases; the court at the time indicated that 33 states and Washington DC required the clear and convincing standard).

4 Joseph v. Whitcombe, 279 A.D.2d 122, 125 (N.Y. App. Div. 2001).

5 Grace v. Koch, 81 Ohio St. 3d 577, 581 n.2 (1998) (The court cited numerous cases and indicated that as of 1998, 14 states required a preponderance standard or a variant of preponderance.).

6 Orsborn v. Deep Rock Oil Corp., 153 Tex. 281, 290 (1954).

7 Rhodes v. Cahill, 802 S.W.2d 643, 645 n.2 (Tex. 1990).

evidence in order to prevail on their adverse possession claims. Such proof must be clear and satisfactory."[8]

In an appellate case heard in Texas in 2022, the parties opposing the adverse possession claim requested the court instruct the jury on the burden of proof by adding, "[t]he proof must be 'clear and satisfactory,' which means you must exercise great caution in weighing the evidence." The trial court refused to do so, and this was one basis for appeal. The intermediate appellate court agreed with the trial court, holding that "[a]dding to the preponderance-of-the-evidence instruction the . . . requested language would have yielded nothing more than juror confusion, and would potentially misstate the law regarding the proper burden of proof as articulated by our Supreme Court."[9]

The concepts that a burden of proof could be a "preponderance" standard, but that the burden could also be deemed as a "clear and satisfactory" standard, but then yet again a jury instruction should not use the "clear and satisfactory" standard, are difficult concepts to explain. But the bigger lesson from the case is that in some states, one can at least attempt to use creative ways to suggest one phrasing of a standard over another.

Other cases seem to indicate that what one needs to do to obtain a presumption of adverse possession is much more restricted. The Supreme Court of Wyoming held that "[w]here there is no clear showing to the contrary, a person who has occupied the land for the statutory period, in a manner plainly indicating that he has acted as the owner thereof, is entitled to a presumption of adverse possession; and the burden shifts to the opposing party to explain such possession."[10] One way of defeating such a case once that presumption is shown, is for the title holder to prove that the "claimant's use of the property is shown to be permissive."[11]

One Mississippi appellate court held that "the majority of jurisdictions recognize a presumption of adverse use once evidence has shown use of the property for the prescriptive period."[12] The same court held that "[r]equiring a litigant who is attempting to establish adverse possession . . . to prove that there was no permission for use would be unreasonable. The law typically frowns upon requiring a party to prove a negative averment."[13] The U.S. Supreme Court has spoken to this general issue as well; that if the subject matter of a negative claim lies peculiarly within

---

8 Ramirez v. Wood, 577 S.W.2d 278, 287 (Tex. Civ. App. 1979).

9 McDuff v. Brumley, No. 07–17–00248-CV, 2022 WL 3154818, at *8 (Tex. App. Aug. 8, 2022).

10 Kimball v. Turner, 993 P.2d 303, 305 (Wyo. 1999) (citations omitted).

11 *Id.* at 306 (citations omitted).

12 Morris v. W.R. Fairchild Constr. Co., 792 So. 2d 282, 285 (Miss. Ct. App. 2001).

13 *Id.* at 284.

one party, then the burden of proof is on the party averring the negative.[14] That law can be helpful to a litigator who wishes to try to shift burdens. One must do his best to claim that his adversary is the one trying to prove a negative, rather than that the claimant is trying to prove a positive.

One Wisconsin case addressed presumptions and how to rebut them. In that state, one statute concerning adverse possession requires the party to have a "claim of title."[15] However, that element is "presumed when all other elements of adverse possession are established."[16] In one case, a party claimed that presumption would be irrebuttable, but the court disagreed, citing an early 20th-century case that held that "upon unexplained, exclusive, continuous occupancy of land under a chain of title, by one not the true owner, for the statutory period . . . there arises . . . the presumption that, during all such period, the possession had all the requisites of an adverse holding, *subject to be rebutted by proof that it was in fact subordinate to the right of the true owner*, but conclusive in the absence of such rebuttal."[17] A modern court held that this must be a rebuttable item, because "[i]f the requirement that the disputed land be occupied 'under claim of title' were irrebuttable, its presence in the statute would be meaningless."[18]

Another critical issue, somewhat addressed in Chapter 3, is when or if hostility may be presumed to exist. In other words, even if the burden looks oppressive, a claimant may at least avoid the burden for that one particular element. If the presumption about hostility would exist normally, the title holder may use various methods to attempt to rebut the presumption or claim it does not exist, which is a matter further described in Chapter 16.

Although this chapter concerns adverse possession cases and not easements, one should check if there is a difference in burdens. In Delaware, for instance, proof of an easement by prescription is by clear and convincing evidence, but adverse possession cases are handled using the preponderance method. One court noted that although this "might seem incongruous to require proof of a prescriptive easement by clear and convincing evidence while only requiring proof by a preponderance of the evidence to work a forfeiture of title," this was indeed the law in that state.[19] This is also addressed in Chapter 26.

---

14 United States v. Denver Rio Grande R.R. Co., 191 U.S. 84, 92 (1903).

15 Wis. Stat. § 893.25.

16 Wilcox v. Est. of Hines, 355 Wis. 2d 1, 18 (2014).

17 Ovig v. Morrison, 142 Wis. 243, 249–50 (1910) (emphasis added).

18 355 Wis. 2d at 21.

19 Ayers v. Pave It, LLC, Civil Action No. 01812-S, 2006 WL 2052377, at *2 (Del. Ch. July 11, 2006).

Chapter 34
Potential Objections to Testimony

Every adverse possession case, to one degree or another, will likely depend in part on testimony, whether in the form of an affidavit or in court. This book is not designed to cover all potential issues or potential objections to testimony, but there are a few matters that seem to come up more often than others in the context of adverse possession.

PAROL EVIDENCE

Generally, parol evidence is not admissible. Parol evidence is that which contradicts, modifies, or varies the terms of a written, complete, and final agreement. This would not normally seem to be an issue in a typical adverse possession case. However, the parol evidence rule does raise its head sometimes in adverse possession cases.

The primary example is if the claimant is basing his adverse possession case on color of title, and the document at issue does not clearly identify the property at issue. Some cases will then prevent the claimant from introducing evidence concerning what the deed truly means. In one Supreme Court of Washington case, it was held that an instrument, in order to operate as color of title, must describe and purport to convey the land in controversy, but that "it cannot be aided by parol evidence."[1] In that state, the case law seems to be that if one is claiming color of title, and a description of the land at issue is not specifically in the document, then one cannot claim property under color of title by using parol evidence.[2]

However, the Supreme Court of Vermont once held that in an action to prove adverse possession by color of title, parol evidence of the contents of a lost deed was admissible to show the extent and character of the possession of the grantees and those claiming

1 Scramlin v. Warner, 69 Wash. 2d 6, 10 (1966) (emphasis added).
2 Campbell v. Reed, 134 Wash. App. 349, 358 (Wash. Ct. App. 2006).

under them.[3] In New York, at least one old case indicates that title by adverse possession can be upheld on satisfactory undisputed parol evidence.[4]

HEARSAY

Many attorneys who hear their adversary's witness testify about what someone else said, will instantly yell "Objection—hearsay!" But the laws on hearsay are subtle, especially in the context of adverse possession cases. Each case seems to be unique, but reviewing various cases can help one to come up with decent arguments on either end in the context of adverse possession. Just as a refresher, a typical definition of hearsay is a statement, other than one made by the declarant while testifying at the trial or hearing, offered in evidence to prove the truth of the matter asserted.

One example of a potential hearsay issue would be if a claimant testifies that others told him that a certain portion of land was the portion he was purchasing. That would only be hearsay in certain contexts. The response to a hearsay objection on such an issue would be that one is trying to prove the claimant's state of mind at the time of the purchase, and not necessarily whether those people were telling the truth. If the claimant believed those people, it might help to prove that he had a claim of right.[5] This cuts both ways of course. If the title holder wants to claim that he heard people tell the claimant, before the purchase, that a certain portion of land was not part of the parcel he was purchasing, this could also theoretically be admissible.

Some states have very particular rules about hearsay concerning boundaries, which rules tie in with adverse possession cases. If one's adverse possession case concerns where ancient boundaries are located, at least in one state declarations about that topic would be deemed hearsay, but potentially admissible regardless. In order to have such declarations admitted in Connecticut, one must prove "(1) that the declarant is dead, (2) that he would be qualified as a witness to testify if present, and especially that he had peculiar means of knowing the boundary, (3) that the statement was made before the controversy in suit arose, and (4) that he had no interest to misrepresent the truth in making the declaration."[6]

3 Oatman v. Barney, 46 Vt. 594, 598 (1874). *See also* Lawrence v. Pelletier, 154 Vt. 29, 32 (1990).

4 *See* Freedman v. Oppenheim, 187 N.Y. 101 (1907).

5 *See* Air Stream Corp. v. 3300 Lawson Corp., 24 Misc. 3d 1208(A), 2009 WL 1857340, at *5 (N.Y. Sup. Ct. 2009), *judgment rev'd on other grounds*, 84 A.D.3d 987 (2d Dep't 2011), *order rev'd on other grounds*, 18 N.Y.3d 972 (2012).

6 Wildwood Associates, Ltd. v. Esposito, 211 Conn. 36, 43–45 (1989), citing inter alia Mentz v. Greenwich, 118 Conn. 137, 144 (1934).

There are some specific statutes indicating that certain kinds of relevant evidence in a typical adverse possession case would be admissible, regardless of hearsay claims. For example, under the Federal Rules of Evidence, Rule 803(20) indicates that the following evidence is not excluded by the hearsay rule: "A reputation in a community—arising before the controversy—concerning boundaries of land in the community or customs that affect the land . . . ." Many states have similar laws, which follow that one. In a North Carolina case, which had a statute following that one, witnesses were permitted to testify regarding the use of local roadways before their lifetimes.[7] In Mississippi Supreme Court case, evidence that property had been known as one party's camp house for years was admissible under its version of the same rule.[8] Although these were not adverse possession cases, the concepts may work in an adverse possession case; both cases were cited in an Indiana case concerning adverse possession.[9]

Regardless of the above, that exception applies only to reputation or general consensus evidence; it does not allow for a party to admit specific statements or assertions made by the predecessor in interest regarding a boundary.[10]

In Georgia, ordinarily, title to land "cannot be proved by hearsay testimony."[11] Conversely, in that same state, a statute indicates that "[d]eclarations by a person in favor of his own title shall be admissible to prove his adverse possession."[12] Notably, an adverse possession claimant is not necessarily trying to prove "title to land," but this is an issue both sides could attempt to raise arguments about.

Another basis to introduce potential hearsay evidence would be to prove that the claimant was using the property in an open and notorious manner. Therefore, if the testimony is something along the lines of "Everyone in town told me that the claimant owns property X," then that could avoid the hearsay issue. One is not trying to prove necessarily that the town gossips are telling the "truth" about who owns it. Rather, one is trying to prove that there is a general reputation in the neighborhood. This is a part of the reputation or notoriety of ownership, which is an element of adverse possession (see Chapter 7), so it should be admissible.[13]

---

7 Broyhill v. Coppage, 79 N.C. App. 221, 224 (1986).
8 Williams v. State, 595 So. 2d 1299, 1306 (Miss. 1992).
9 Roser v. Silvers, 698 N.E.2d 860, 864 (Ind. Ct. App. 1998).
10 *Id.*
11 Smith v. Stacey, 281 Ga. 601 (2007).
12 GA. CODE ANN. § 24-3-7(b).
13 *See* Walker v. Town of Fruithurst, 272 Ala. 141, 144 (1961).

A Maryland case from 1966 also addressed hearsay issues—in that case, concerning boundaries. A party sought to introduce a statement made by a predecessor in title to real property, concerning where the boundary was located. The people who had allegedly discussed this had died before the trial took place. The court held that "the declarations of a deceased former owner of land are admissible as an exception to the hearsay rule to prove the boundaries thereof provided there was no controversy as to the boundaries at the time the declarations were made."[14] Since in that case, there was an argument that no controversy existed at the time, it was deemed admissible.

One South Carolina case[15] resolved in 1990, concerning hearsay, reveals how far back the claims of a title can be based on. A man named Frank Johnson, Jr., as agent for the heirs of William F. Pritchard, instituted an action against certain defendants including ones with the last name of Henry. Johnson claimed that William F. Pritchard, his heirs, and devisees, owned by adverse possession the subject property for a period in excess of 70 years. The Henrys answered and, by way of counterclaim, alleged title based on a document issued by the U.S. government shortly after the Civil War. The court held in favor of the adverse possession claimants.

On appeal, the Henrys argued that the trial judge should not have allowed the heirs to introduce a critical letter and enclosures from an attorney, dated 1937. That date was 53 years before the appeal was decided. In that letter there was also a certificate of title and an affidavit from the 1930s tending to prove the Pritchards had a valid adverse possession claim.

The appellate court had to go through two steps to determine that these records were proper for admission. First, it addressed the issue of authenticity. The court held that "[t]he general rule is that documents and writings of all kinds purporting to be 30 or more years old, if they are relevant to the inquiry and produced from proper custody and are on their face free from suspicion, are said to prove themselves and are admissible into evidence without the ordinary requirement as to proof of execution and authenticity."[16] Then it turned to whether the statements within the letter were hearsay. The court held that "[a] careful examination of authorities reveals a growing majority of the courts of this nation are in favor of the admission of recitals in ancient documents as an exception to the hearsay rule. Rule 803(16) of the Uniform Rules of

14 Wilt v. Wilt, 242 Md. 129, 134 (Md. 1966).

15 Johnson v. Pritchard, 302 S.C. 437 (S.C. Ct. App. 1990).

16 *Id.* at 443.

Evidence is in accord with this trend."[17] Even though that state had not adopted those rules, it held that such evidence was admissible.

In an Indiana case concerning an adverse possessor who successfully obtained title, the original title holder argued on appeal that the adverse possessor did not have the right to introduce hearsay. He argued the hearsay was a statement made to the claimant that a particular fence was the southern boundary of the parcel claimant was buying. The court held that "whenever it is competent to prove an act or transaction, the declaration of the actor, accompanying the act, in relation thereto or explanatory thereof, may also be proved."[18] The court held that since the agent of the seller had walked the boundaries of the parcel that the adverse possession claimant was purchasing, and while doing so, that agent described the dilapidated fence line as being the southern boundary of the parcel, then the statement was properly admitted.[19]

In a Nebraska case, a party tried to introduce hearsay evidence to prove that the adverse possession claimants had used the disputed property with permission, so that they had no valid adverse possession claim. The trial court had failed to allow her to introduce those statements at trial. On appeal, the court noted that there are statutory "residual hearsay exceptions," and that its Supreme Court had "stated that in determining whether a statement is admissible under the residual exception to the hearsay rule, a court considers five factors; (1) the statement's trustworthiness, (2) materiality of the statement, (3) probative importance of the statement, (4) interests of justice, and (5) whether notice was given to an opponent."[20] In that case, for various reasons, including that the alleged statements were oral and not made under oath, and may have been elicited by the use of leading questions, and also that the notice of intent did not identify specific statements, the appellate court held that the district court did not abuse its discretion in determining that those conversations were not admissible. Federal Rules of Evidence Section 807 also contains details about hearsay being permitted under similar qualifications, and some states have adopted the same rule.

Even if testimony might be considered hearsay, one has to see if there is an exception. For example, in one Louisiana case, defendants sought adverse possession based on the location of a fence, but the plaintiff

17 *Id.*

18 Clark v. Aukerman, 654 N.E.2d 1183, 88 (Ind. Ct. App. 1995) (citation and brackets omitted).

19 *Id.*

20 Stamm v. Fisher, No. A-14–592, 2015 WL 3484497, at *5 (Neb. Ct. App. June 2, 2015).

produced testimony from a person who had heard the ancestors in title admit that the fence was not on the boundary line. The court deemed this hearsay but admissible under the declaration against interest theory, including because the statement was made by a person unavailable (due to death).[21]

Other case law also indicates that exceptions to hearsay rules are critical. For example, in one Tennessee case, a party who had once owned the property at issue had allegedly made statements about the width of the right of way. One party testified about what that former owner had said on that matter, and the court held that this was admissible: "Declarations of former owners which took place during ownership and especially accompanied with possession are admissible to establish boundary lines. It is not necessary that the former owner testify to the declarations. They may be testified to by third parties who heard the declarations."[22]

Even if one's state indicates that there is no specific exception to the hearsay rule, one may be able to find another way around it. For example, the Federal Rules of Evidence section 807(a) provides in relevant part that even if there are no explicit and applicable exceptions to the hearsay rule, the hearsay statement may still be admissible if "(1) the statement is supported by sufficient guarantees of trustworthiness—after considering the totality of circumstances under which it was made and evidence, if any, corroborating the statement; and (2) it is more probative on the point for which it is offered than any other evidence that the proponent can obtain through reasonable efforts." Many states have similar, if not identical language, in their rules of evidence.

DEAD MAN'S STATUTE

Many adverse possession cases concern transactions with dead people. That can cause a problem in terms of evidence.

A dead man's statute, which is also sometimes known as a dead man's rule, generally prohibits a witness, who is an interested person, from testifying about his communications or transactions with a deceased person. Well over half of the states have expressly rejected such a rule.[23] In fact, the Supreme Court of Hawaii called it "archaic" when noting that its state had not adopted it.[24] Criticism of the rule is hardly new.

21 Briggs v. Pellerin, 428 So. 2d 1087, 1090 (La. Ct. App. 1983).

22 England v. England, No. E2011–02094-COA-R3-CV, 2012 WL 4503434, at *4 (Tenn. Ct. App. Oct. 2, 2012), citing Norman v. Hoyt, 667 S.W.2d 88, 90 (Tenn. 1983).

23 Ed Wallis, *Outdated Form of Evidentiary Law: A Survey of Dead Man's Statutes and a Proposal for Change*, 53 Clev. St. L. Rev. 75, 76 n.2 (2005).

24 Hew v. Aruda, 462 P.2d 476, 479 (Haw. 1969).

The English philosopher Jeremy Bentham in the 1700s described the exclusion of survivor's testimony a "blind and brainless" technique.[25]

But a number of states still have statutes concerning the issue, in which there are at least some restrictions from introducing such evidence, in certain contexts. Some examples are Arizona, Colorado, Indiana, Louisiana, Maryland, Michigan, New York, Pennsylvania, South Carolina, Tennessee, Virginia, Washington, and West Virginia. Conversely, at least one state defines the concepts in "Dead Man's Statute" differently; in Connecticut, C.G.S. 52–172 admits certain statements of deceased persons in evidence as an *exception* to the hearsay rule.[26]

If one is litigating in a state applying the traditional rule under the dead man's statute, there may be several exceptions or variations. For example, a Michigan statute permits an interested witness to testify as to any communications he had with the deceased if the living person's testimony "is supported by some other evidence tending to corroborate his claim."[27] In West Virginia, Rule of Evidence 804(b)(5) indicates that in cases by or against a representative of a deceased person, a statement by a deceased person is not excluded as hearsay if the statement was (1) made by the decedent at issue, (2) in good faith and on the decedent's personal knowledge, and (3) under circumstances that indicate it was trustworthy. A similar rule exists in South Dakota.[28]

One also needs to be familiar with the case law concerning the statute, whether in the context of adverse possession or otherwise. For example, in Arizona, the application of that statute "is discretionary with the trial judge, and he can permit testimony regarding conversations and transactions with the deceased whenever he feels justice will be served."[29]

To the degree the dead man's statute exists in one's state and might apply, there may be various ways around it in an adverse possession case. In one New York case,[30] plaintiffs, as adverse possession claimants, had sought to produce evidence of a dead person's transactions and communications with a dead person. The plaintiffs claimed they had entered a rent to buy agreement with the late person. The court held that to the degree plaintiffs were claiming ownership based on any such document, the dead man's statute prevented such evidence.

---

25 Cavanah v. Martin, 590 P.2d 41, 42 n.9 (Alaska 1979) (citation omitted).

26 O'Brien v. Coburn, 46 Conn. App. 620, 632 (1997).

27 Mich. Comp. Laws Ann. § 600.2166(1).

28 S.D. Codified Laws § 19-19-804(5).

29 Condos v. Felder, 92 Ariz. 366, 371–72 (1962).

30 Edwards v. All Star Recovery Corp, 63 N.Y.S.3d 305, 2017 WL 3026216 (N.Y. Sup. Ct. 2017).

However, the court held that for an adverse possession case, a claim of right was also critical, and that "[t]he Dead Man's Statute does not bar evidence of the transaction offered as evidence of Plaintiffs' state of mind and belief they had claim of right."[31] In addition, the court held it critical that the defendant title holder, who derived title indirectly from the deceased person, had testified about the same transaction. In such a case, the plaintiffs were permitted to testify despite the Dead Man's Statute, since it concerned the same subject that defendant was offering testimony about.

31 *Id.* at *5.

Chapter 35
De Minimis Issues, Nonstructural Encroachments, and Lawn Mowing

One issue that has received de minimis attention is resolving the issue of a claimant who has adversely possessed a de minimis portion of his neighbor's property. There are many sub-issues, including (1) how to define "de minimis" space, (2) whether the encroachments themselves can be described as "de minimis," (3) whether it makes a difference if the encroachment is structural or nonstructural (if it is nonstructural, the de minimis encroachment might not be a potential basis for an adverse possession case), and (4) how to define what is structural versus non-structural. Some of these questions are unanswered or have only been answered in broad strokes.

One might consider that a minimal intrusion into another's property would be a quintessential adverse possession case. If one accidentally has encroached on his neighbor's land by a small amount, then presumably if that encroachment remains in place long enough without objection, the claimant should be able to claim that land as his own, and not risk the danger of being forced to remove the encroachment. Dicta from at least one case would indicate that this is logical.[1]

But in New York, a statute partially resolves part of this issue against the adverse possession claimant: "Notwithstanding any other provision of this article, the existence of de minimus [sic] non-structural encroachments including, but not limited to, fences, hedges, shrubbery, plantings, sheds and non-structural walls, shall be deemed to be permissive and non-adverse."[2] To put it another way, this appears to mean that if one has placed a nonstructural encroachment on someone else's property, but it only intrudes or encroaches by a small amount, then regardless of hostility, a claim of right, or any other factor, that particular nonstructural encroachment cannot be used as a basis for an adverse possession.

---

1 Prentiss v. Cadenazzi, C.A. No. NC 03–0265, 2006 WL 1314262, at *13 (R.I. Super. May 8, 2006).

2 N.Y. Real Prop. Acts. Law § 543. The Latin term is normally spelled in most texts as "de minimis."

(In theory, the statute might mean that all such nonstructural encroachments themselves are deemed "de minimis" as a matter of law, without regard to where they are located; this is an issue that may not be fully resolved. The statute is oddly and ambiguously phrased.)

One examining that statute might be able to claim that implicitly, the converse is true. That is, if the structure is permanent or "structural" then the person placing that structure could indeed claim adverse possession concerning that space, no matter how "de minimis" the space was.

Other issues remain elusive, such as whether the law concerns a one-dimensional analysis of "de minimis" or two dimensions. At least one case indicates that a fence that only encroached by a depth of 3.75 inches could not the basis for an adverse possession claim.[3] What if the fence intruded by a depth of "only" six inches, but the fence had a length of ten miles—a total square footage of five square miles? Would a court consider this "de minimis"? (In one case on a slightly different issue, a Texas court held that a 21.6-inch encroachment on property that is 67 feet wide is not de minimis. But that was in part because the fence was "constructed in blatant violation" of a judgment in a prior litigation.[4]) And would it make a difference if the intrusion were accomplished through shrubbery, instead of a fence?

A careful litigator will also need to note that even if one's client is complaining about his neighbor's de minimis intrusion onto the client's property, then simply proving that the neighbor never adversely possessed it may not be enough to obtain relief in the title holder's favor. Regardless of whether it is a "structure," the court may determine that equity would not compel removal of a small intrusion. If that were not bad enough, in certain cases, your client, the title holder, may not even be entitled to anything more than token damages. For instance, where the encroachment of the wall of a building on the adjoining property was from one-half to five-eighths of an inch, the court in one California case[5] sustained a judgment denying a mandatory injunction and instead awarded damages of $10 where there was no direct evidence that the less-than-an-inch encroachment caused any actual damage to the plaintiff. The court stated that where the injury was so slight as to bring it within the maxim of "de minimis," a mandatory injunction should not be issued.

However, if the party built the structure intending to trespass, it is possible that a court would rule that the de minimis defense would fail.

3 Meckler v. Schnell, 950 N.Y.S.2d 724 (Sup. Ct. 2010).
4 Green v. Parrack, 974 S.W.2d 200, 206 (Tex. App. 1998).
5 McKean v. Alliance Land Co., 200 Cal. 396 (1927).

In a New York case entitled *Goodfarb v. Freedman*, "where the wrong was unwarranted or where defendant acted with full knowledge and planned his violation of the plaintiff's rights, his position does not appeal to the equitable conscience and an injunction should issue."[6] In that case, the court held that neighboring property owners were entitled to a mandatory injunction requiring demolition of a studio that violated a restrictive covenant. Equitable defenses were not permissible in that case.

Of course, New York represents just one point of view concerning structural encroachments and whether they are necessary. There are other points of view. In Wisconsin, for example, "[t]he placement of structural encroachments on the land is not a requirement of adverse possession. Rather, any actual visible means which give notice of exclusion from the property to the record owner or to the public and of the defendant's domination over it, is sufficient."[7] How Wisconsin, or other states, would handle a nonstructural encroachment, which was only "de minimis," would be a separate issue.

Other than eating apple pie, what could be more American than mowing lawns? Of course, something this critical has to wind up in adverse possession cases. The Sisyphean goal of a well-manicured lawn occupies a great deal of space in Americans' heads, as pointed out in Thorstein Veblen's book *The Theory of the Leisure Class*. One author of a book on litigating adverse possession cases, as a boy, mowed the lawn in the suburbs, and promised himself, based on the drudgery of this one chore alone, never to live in a suburb as an adult. And if you have a conversation with someone who has a lawn, and you ask the right questions, you can always get a story about some war concerning how the neighbor is taking care of his lawn the "wrong" way. A ten-second internet search found two murders (one in Tennessee, and one in Missouri) in the past few years between neighbors over lawn-mowing issues. The subject even winds up in literature. In *Rabbit, Run*, by John Updike, there is the story of how the previous neighbor used to cut the entirety of a strip of grass between two houses, but the new "Methodist" neighbor refused, and had his own way: he "cut exactly his half, one swath of a lawnmower, and then pushed his lawnmower back inverted on his own walk, when it would have been just as easy to push it back along the other half of the strip and not leave such a ridiculous job." The main character's father says, "When I hear that old fool's wheels rattle along his walk so self-righteously, my blood pressure goes up so I hear my ears

6 76 A.D.2d 565, 574 (N.Y. App. Div. 1980).

7 Meyer v. Palmquist, 2001 Wis. App. 254 ¶ 11, 248 Wis. 2d 526 (Wis. Ct. App. 2001) (internal quotation marks, ellipses, and brackets omitted).

pop."[8] But perhaps the Methodist neighbor was simply trying to avoid making it seem that he was preparing an adverse possession claim.

In New York, lawn mowing could be a way of proving one had a decent adverse possession case.[9] The good old days ended in 2008. Now, for cases affected by the new statute, "the acts of lawn mowing or similar maintenance across the boundary line of an adjoining landowner's property shall be deemed permissive and non-adverse."[10]

But the rest of America is not New York. There are many states that address, and have not conclusively decided, the issue of whether lawn mowing can be used as part of one's case to prove ownership of land beyond the actual boundary line. For some cases, lawn mowing is one of a number of uses that may be sufficient to grant adverse possession.[11] Although mowing the grass may be some evidence of a claim of right, lawn mowing can also be seen as "an act of neighborly accommodation."[12] In one case, a court held that "[i]t is a well-known fact that many thousands of homeowners have no boundary fences and that adjoining owners occasionally trespass on their neighbors' lands in cutting grass . . . . Such harmless trespasses are committed upon the well-founded assumption that ordinarily a neighbor will acquiesce in and consent to them."[13] Therefore, many courts hold "maintaining a lawn is not, by itself, sufficient to establish that use is open and notorious in a developed neighborhood."[14]

---

8 Italics omitted.

9 *See* Franza v. Olin, 73 A.D.3d 44, 47 (N.Y. App. Div. 2010).

10 N.Y. R.P.A.P.L. 543.

11 See cases cited by First Congregational Church of Enosburg v. Manley, 183 Vt. 574, 578 (2008), including Dombkowski v. Ferland, 2006 ME 24, 893 A.2d 599 (mowing, clearing, driving, fencing, and drilling a well); Collins v. Cabral, 348 Mass. 797 (1965) (mowing, clearing land, using land for recreational activities, seeding ground, and constructing septic tank on disputed land); Brennan v. Manchester Crossings, Inc., 708 A.2d 815, 821–22 (Pa. Super. Ct. 1998) (mowing, raking leaves, planting seed, and using land for storage and recreational activities).

12 Mesher v. Connolly, 633 Wash. 2d 552, 556 (1964).

13 Romans v. Nadler, 217 Minn. 174, 180–81 (1944).

14 First Congregational Church of Enosburg v. Manley, 183 Vt. 574, 578 (2008).

Chapter 36
Champerty

If anyone picked up this book hoping to learn about medieval France, and how some tenants and/or partial owners paid their "rent," and how that relates to adverse possession, he is in luck.

The word "champerty" comes from a kind of French feudal tenure in land: a "champart." The tenant-by-champart partially owned the land, which it had purchased from a grantor. The tenant-by-champart then had to pay sums to the grantor, based on a portion of the income from the purchased land. But the grantor took the risk that the crops might fail, which would mean it would not receive anything.[1]

The modern term "champerty," in English, generally concerns when one party purchases an interest in a claim under litigation. The idea is that the new party would bear the expenses of the litigation, but also would share benefits if the lawsuit succeeded. In the context of landownership and other matters, some felt this tainted the judicial process. This is because a person could buy an interest in land for a relatively small sum, and push litigation forward that might have otherwise been deemed pointless or irrelevant. And, believe it or not, many of the evil people engaging in such transactions were lawyers themselves. In New York, the early prohibition of champerty was limited—only against attorneys.[2] The champerty statutes, in New York, are now directed at preventing the "strife, discord and harassment" that would be likely to ensue "from permitting attorneys and corporations to purchase claims for the purpose of bringing actions thereon."[3] As the Supreme Court of Kentucky put it, the policy and purpose of champerty statutes is to "discourage litigation."[4]

At one point, a number of states had champerty laws existing in the context of land and adverse possession cases. However, it appears that

1 *See generally* Bluebird Partners, L.P. v. First Fid. Bank, N.A., 94 N.Y.2d 726, 733–34 (2000).

2 *Id.*

3 Fairchild Hiller Corp. v. McDonnell Douglas Corp., 28 N.Y.2d 325, 329 (1971).

4 *See* Great W. Land Mgmt., Inc. v. Slusher, 939 S.W.2d 865, 869 (Ky. 1996).

Kentucky, Tennessee, and Oklahoma[5] may be the only ones left with such laws.

One critical Kentucky statute provides that "[a]ny sale or conveyance, including those made under execution, of any land, or the pretended right or title thereto, of which any other person has adverse possession at the time of the sale or conveyance, is void; but this section does not render void any devise of land in adverse possession."[6] In other words (so it appears) if the title holder to property has a potential argument that the adverse possessor claimant who is on his property is without rights, then the transfer is void. To put it another way, this statute operates to void a conveyance of land by a grantor to a grantee when such land is being held adversely by a third party.[7] In such a case, the title would remain, in effect, with the grantor, and the alleged grantee would have no standing to seek relief against the adverse possession claimant. At least, that is the way it appears. A claim of champerty may only be used, however, as a shield to or in defense of a claim from the person who obtained that evil champertous deed. An adverse possession claimant who simply alleged that his adversary has a champertous deed would not, in and of itself, let that alleged adverse possessor properly claim title to land.[8]

In Kentucky, the person claiming adverse possession and trying to take advantage of the champerty statute must still meet the various traditional elements of adverse possession.[9] However, under that statute, "possession by a third party need not be for any specific length of time. To render the conveyance champertous, and therefore void, it is sufficient if the adverse character of the possession is such as would ripen into a fee simple title under the limitation adverse possession rule had it continued uninterruptedly for the period prescribed."[10]

Under Tennessee's law of champerty, an agreement to sell land "shall be utterly void where the seller has not personally, or by the seller's agent or tenant, or the seller's ancestor, been in actual possession of the lands or tenements, or of the reversion or remainder, or taken the rents or profits for one (1) whole year next before the sale."[11] This presumably means that if a title owner has been out of possession for a year or more, and he is worried about the status of his land, including because it has been adversely possessed by a third party, and he attempts to sell the

5 OKLA. STAT. ANN. tit. 21, § 548.
6 KY. REV. STAT. § 372.070(1).
7 *See* Cowherd v. Brooks, 456 S.W.2d 827, 830 (Ky. 1970).
8 Ballard v. Moss, 268 S.W.2d 35, 38 (Ky. 1954).
9 *Cowherd*, 456 S.W.2d at 830.
10 Wells v. Wells, 346 S.W.2d 33, 36 (Ky. 1961) (citation omitted).
11 TENN. CODE ANN. § 66-4-202.

land, so that the new title owner will have to deal with the adverse possession claimant, the agreement would be void. A related statute goes on to provide that any suit brought for the recovery of real property "shall be forthwith dismissed, with costs, by the court in which such suit may be pending," upon a finding by the court that the deed conveying the property to the plaintiff was champertous.[12] But that statute does not indicate that the adverse possessor will automatically have a claim on the property. Notably, in that state, if the alleged adverse possessor seeks to render a deed void as champertous, that adverse possessor need only be in possession of the disputed property at the time the allegedly void deed was transferred to that party who had purchased it.[13]

In any event, champerty is an interesting potential partial defense for an adverse possession claimant, but it has serious restrictions on its use and where it can be used.

12 *Id.* § 66-4-203.

13 Robinson v. Harris, 37 Tenn. App. 105, 118 (1952).

Chapter 37
Adverse Possession in the Wake of a Tax Lien Foreclosure

Even nonlawyers may understand the devastation that can occur to a homeowner who does not pay real estate taxes. Anyone who knows the plot of *House of Sand and Fog* would understand.

When one does not pay real estate taxes, those taxes, and other costs, become a lien on the real estate. The taxing authority can then foreclose on the lien to collect the sums. To take one example of state law, in New York, in order to foreclose on the lien, the lienholder must file a petition and serve it on the real estate owner. If the owner has no valid defense, either the tax district would get possession of the property directly, or an auction is held to sell the property to the highest bidder.[1] If it is sold, part of the proceeds are used to pay the lienholder, and voila, the new owner's rights are fresh as a daisy, without that nasty lien clouding things over.

That is the theory, in any event. But an alleged adverse possessor may throw a wrench in the works. The law on this issue is not completely consistent.

Many, if not most, cases disfavor an adverse possessor in this situation. For example, in a North Carolina case,[2] the plaintiffs sought title to a tract of property under the doctrine of adverse possession. More than three years before the plaintiffs filed their quiet title action, title to the property in dispute had been conveyed to the defendant through a tax foreclosure sale. The defendant argued the plaintiffs' quiet title claim was barred by the one-year statute of limitation for challenging tax foreclosure deeds and the trial court granted summary judgment for the defendant. The lower court and appellate court both held that the defendant was entitled to summary judgment as a matter of law for those reasons. But the court went on to address the alleged adverse possessors' rights. It held that "the effect of a judgment foreclosing a tax lien on real property is to extinguish all rights, title and interests in the real property

1 N.Y. Real Prop. Tax Law §§ 1120, 1136.
2 Overstreet v. City of Raleigh, 75 N.C. App. 351 (1985).

subject to foreclosure, including a claim based on adverse possession. The interest in the disputed property acquired by purchasers at a tax foreclosure sale is fee simple and the purchaser's title defeats claims of ownership based on adverse possession."[3]

The same court, nearly 30 years later, confirmed that this was the law.[4] In that case, the plaintiff claimed he and his predecessors had adversely possessed a certain disputed area for more than 50 years. But the disputed area had been deeded by the tax commissioner to defendant's predecessor in 1997, and the plaintiff filed the case in 2009, meaning he filed it beyond without waiting for 20 years after that deed, as is normally required, in that state, for adverse claims with no color of title. Therefore, he could not claim adverse possession. Since he could not be deemed an owner, he could not claim trespass. His backup argument, that he did not get notice of the tax foreclosure sale personally, was pointless, because the court held that personal notice of a foreclosure sale need not be given to a purported adverse possessor whose alleged interest in the land is not recorded.

The Wisconsin Supreme Court held similarly in *Leciejewski v. Sedlak*.[5] In that case, certain property had been transferred in a tax lien foreclosure sale to a certain county, which then transferred that same property to a certain family called the Leciejewskis. The family was infamous; anyone trying to pronounce their name would suffer a tongue injury. In any event, Mr. Leciejewski later noticed that his neighbors, the Sedlaks, had an already existing shed, boathouse, and cabin on the property. The Leciejewskis sought to have those buildings removed, but the Sedlaks claimed ownership by adverse possession.

The court held that the Sedlaks had no viable case of adverse possession, by citing the relevant statutes at issue to infer that the intent was to rule out any claims to the foreclosed property, including adverse possession. The court held that "[t]he interest in the disputed property that the Leciejewskis acquired from the county is a fee simple interest, and their title defeats the Sedlaks' claim of ownership based on adverse possession."[6]

In reaching that conclusion, the court cited a Washington case[7] in which the court held that the tax foreclosure vested in the purchaser of a tax deed, or in his assignee, a new title superior to any prior possessory rights, no matter how exclusive or adverse. It also cited a Colorado

3 *Id.* at 353.
4 Dixon v. Gifford, 225 N.C. App. 264 (2013).
5 116 Wis. 2d 629 (1984).
6 *Id.* at 640.
7 Label v. Cleasby, 13 Wash. App. 789 (1975).

case[8] in which the court held that a valid tax deed erases all former interests in the land, including those arising from adverse possession.

If your client is the adverse possession claimant though, the dissent to that Wisconsin case provides some ideas on how to argue the matter. The dissenting judge believed that the defendants had already obtained adverse possession rights before the foreclosure sale. Therefore, the dissenting judge believed that the Sedlaks, the "actual owners," should have been given proper notice of the tax sale. Without such direct notice, the dissenter believed they were deprived of that property without due process.[9]

In various states, a critical issue seems to be how a court describes a tax foreclosure proceeding. If it is deemed in rem, meaning a case concerning property itself, and not concerning people's rights, then an alleged adverse possessor may be in trouble. There are states that hold that a tax foreclosure proceeding is an in rem action, and that this fact means it erases all former interests in the land.[10] However, the dissent in the Wisconsin case indicated that simply because a foreclosure proceeding is deemed "in rem" should not serve as a whitewash, to prevent an adverse possessor from obtaining notice of the sale.

In New York, a relevant case addressed the issue, and held against plaintiffs who claimed that they had adverse possession prior to the tax foreclosure sale.[11] In that case, the court noted in part that "the title conveyed in a tax sale is not simply the title of the delinquent property owner. Rather, as the [highest court] has noted, '[t]he purchaser of property at a tax sale . . . acquires a new and complete title to the land under an independent grant from the sovereign, a title free of any prior claims to the property or interests in it.'"[12]

One lengthy Maryland case also held that a tax sale extinguished an adverse possession claim, especially because in that case, the adverse possessor had not occupied the space for the full statutory time by the time the tax lien sale took place.[13] In that case, the court considered issues such as that the government agency had the right to levy taxes, and, therefore, it needed a method that would allow sale to the highest bidder not only to ensure it receives the taxes, but also that enough

8 Whiteman v. Mattson, 167 Colo. 183 (1968).

9 116 Wis. 2d at 644.

10 *See* Graham v. Lambeth, 22 Kan. App. 2d 805, 807 (1996), citing inter alia Harrison v. Everett, 135 Colo. 55, 60 (1957); *In re* Foreclosure of Tax Liens, 106 Wis. 2d 244, 251 (1982).

11 Borisenok v. Hug, 212 A.D.2d 282, 283–84 (N.Y. App. Div. 1995) (citation omitted).

12 *Id.* at 283 (citation omitted).

13 Lippert v. Jung, 366 Md. 221 (2001).

bidders be available to protect the purchaser's title. If potential purchasers are not assured that they would obtain title free from claims of adverse possessors, then this may reduce what kinds of bids the non-taxpaying owner would receive. The court also gave a history lesson about land titles in Maryland, including how "the Lord Proprietors, the original grantees of the English kings, were granted and seized of title to land in the new world."[14] The case cites ancient grants of land, including ones that have spellings such as "discoverey," "confirme," "authoritie," and "thinke." Since, as the court saw it, the Lord Proprietors received their title from the English kings, along with the right to, in turn, grant the lands to others, the state also obtained those same rights. Implicitly, therefore, since landownership is subject to taxes, then if the taxes are not paid, the title goes back to the state, which again has the right to grant land to others. To put it another way, "If the taxes are not paid, the title to the land through the tax sale process is granted and titled anew to the tax sale purchaser."[15] The court also indicated that modern legislation tends to strengthen tax titles, again in order to encourage people to invest in them. This Maryland case indicated that its view was the majority view.

There are several cases that, in one respect or another, appear to hold that a tax sale does not affect the rights of an adverse possessor. In one Kansas case,[16] the plaintiff (named Graham) had originally owned a tract of land known as Tract B, which he paid taxes on. Someone else owned Tract A, but did not pay taxes, so a new party named Lambeth bought Tract A at a lien foreclosure sale. When Lambeth saw that Graham's barbed wire fence encroached on his new property—a ten-foot strip of land, Graham proved that he had been in open, exclusive, and continuous possession of the disputed property for more than 15 years under a good faith belief of ownership. The question was whether Graham's claim was superior to any grant contained in a subsequent sheriff's deed.

Lambeth argued that the relevant statute should be interpreted to mean that the filing of a sheriff's deed conveys a clear title. But the court held that the sheriff's deed did not and could not convey the ten-foot strip of land, because by then it was already adversely possessed by Graham. It held that under its interpretation of its statute, one who buys at a tax sale (1) only buys the interest of the previous owner, and (2) is bound by the rule of caveat emptor. The court also cited cases from other states, in which the courts held that (1) a deed subsequent to a

14 *Id.* at 237.
15 *Id.* at 240.
16 Graham v. Lambeth, 22 Kan. App. 2d 805 (1996).

tax foreclosure sale can only convey what the prior owner had, and (2) if adverse possession created an interest prior to judgment, it was not conveyed through the new title.

Another interesting argument Lambeth made was that since Graham claimed ownership of the strip, he should have paid the property taxes and thereby protected his interest. The court disagreed, because Graham had believed this strip of land was part of the lot he was paying taxes for. The court also held that an adverse possessor is not required to pay taxes to succeed in a claim of ownership, and therefore "it would appear contradictory to be able to defeat the interest through tax foreclosure."[17] Finally, the court noted that the deed from the sheriff "contains no wording indicating it to be a warranty deed."[18] There are several other cases that seem to hold that a tax sale does not affect a claim of adverse possession. For example, in *Tanner v. Michigan Trust Co.*,[19] the Supreme Court of Michigan held that tax sales did not interrupt the continuity of a 15-year adverse possession period.

Additionally, there are cases that cannot be put in a neat category. One example is *Picerne v. Sylvestre*,[20] where the Rhode Island Supreme Court held that the alleged adverse possessor should at least have been able to present a claim of adverse possession, in opposition to the tax sale redemption procedure. But even that court noted, "Under our law, the collector's deed is in the nature of an independent grant from the sovereign which bars or extinguishes all former titles, interests, and liens not specifically excepted. The title conveyed is absolute . . . ."[21]

In any event, an attorney handling a case concerning a dispute between an alleged adverse possessor and one that has obtained title through a tax lien foreclosure, has many issues to consider. This is especially if one lives in a state in which the law is unclear. Some issues are whether the adverse possessor occupied a portion of a lot, or the entire lot. If it is just a portion, it is more reasonable that he did not pay full taxes on it, and would not have known if they were unpaid. Other issues are whether the adverse possessor had already occupied the premises for the entire statutory period, before it was sold in a foreclosure sale. If so, one can claim that this adverse possessor's rights have already vested, and to deprive him of those rights without notice would deprive him of his due process rights. Another

---

17 *Id.* at 808.

18 *Id.*

19 220 Mich. 260 (1922).

20 113 R.I. 598 (1974), *overruled on other grounds*, 122 R.I. 85 (1979).

21 *Id.* at 600.

issue is the exact text of the statutes at issue that allow the government authority to foreclose on a tax lien. One must also review the exact wording of the deed that transfers title as a result of the unpaid taxes. Is it a warranty deed that guarantees clear title, or is it some lesser form of a deed? In addition, one must examine in what contexts the state law requires the adverse possessor to pay taxes in order to claim adverse possession status.

Chapter 38
Attorneys' Fees

Here in America, surprisingly enough, we use the American Rule. That is, generally the successful party in a litigation must pay his own attorneys' fees, unless there is a specific statute or contractual clause that indicates otherwise.

In certain adverse possession cases, there are a number of statutes that permit the successful party to collect attorneys' fees. So one should either plead such a statute, or at the very least remind the court at the conclusion of the case about such a statute. An attorney has to do his homework to see if any statute applies.

Texas is one example of a state that provides successful parties with a potential means of obtaining attorneys' fees. Its Practice and Remedies Code section 16.034 provides in relevant part that, "In a suit for the possession of real property between a person claiming under record title to the property and one claiming by adverse possession, if the prevailing party recovers possession of the property from a person unlawfully in actual possession, the court . . . may award costs and reasonable attorney's fees to the prevailing party."

In the state of Washington, a relevant statute provides, "The prevailing party in an action asserting title to real property by adverse possession may request the court to award costs and reasonable attorneys' fees. The court may award all or a portion of costs and reasonable attorneys' fees to the prevailing party if, after considering all the facts, the court determines such an award is equitable and just."[1] In some respects, the meaning of this language is debatable. For example, does it apply to easements? The case law seems to indicate that it does not.[2]

In that state, the losing side can fight the potential attorneys' fees award, or the potential award, by claiming that it would be either inequitable, or unjust, to award such fees. Another ground for challenging an award of fees would be to claim that certain work performed by one's adversary

1 Wash. Rev. Code § 7.28.083(3).

2 Sw. Suburban Sewer Dist. v. Fish, 17 Wash. App. 2d 833, 843 (2021).

was not necessary, or that (for example) if one's adversary's previous motion within the context of the litigation had been unsuccessful, it would be inequitable to award fees for that motion. Yet another basis for challenging such an award would be to claim that one's adversary was not truly the "prevailing" party, because certain claims were denied.

Arizona has an unusual statute concerning attorneys' fees. A prevailing party in an action to quiet title may recover costs and attorneys' fees if that party (1) first served a quitclaim deed on the other party 20 days before bringing the action to quiet title, (2) asked the other party to execute the deed, and (3) tendered consideration of five dollars along with the request (and the other party refused to execute the deed).[3] One would want to make sure there was solid evidence that the five dollars was actually tendered; it would be dreadful to lose tens of thousands of dollars in potential attorneys' fees just because there was a question about a five dollar bill.

Oklahoma has passed the Nonjudicial Marketable Title Procedures Act,[4] which indicates that where there is an instrument filed that clouds or casts an "apparent cloud" on one's title to real property, then one can request that the party remove it, and if the other party does not, then the first party can file a quiet title action. If the first party's action is successful, the first party may seek attorneys' fees. But if the case is against an adverse possessor who had no instrument filed in the first place, case law indicates that this is not a basis for the true owner to obtain attorneys' fees.[5]

Another way of making a claim for attorneys' fees is to claim that punitive damages are proper. In one Mississippi case, the court granted attorneys' fees in favor of an adverse possession claimant, when the title holder had taken improper steps such as removing boundary markers, and constructing gates and a fence in derogation of the adverse possessors' rights. In that state, attorneys' fees can be awarded if punitive damages are also proper. And in that state, punitive damages can be awarded if there is clear and convincing evidence that the other party acted with malice. The appellate court remanded, holding that the chancellor had the right to award attorneys' fees, but since she had not specified that she was awarding attorneys' fees in lieu of punitive damages, this issue would need to be clarified.[6]

There is yet another way of obtaining attorneys' fees. That is, one can seek to claim slander of title. In certain slander of title cases, special damages may include attorneys' fees.[7]

---

3 Ariz. Rev. Stat. § 12-1103(B).
4 Okla. Stat. Ann. tit. 12, §§ 1141.1 *et seq.*
5 *See* Hernandez v. Reed, 239 P.3d 186, 191–92 (Okla. Civ. App. 2010).
6 Cronier v. ALR Partners L.P., 248 So. 3d 861, 871–72 (Miss. Ct. App. 2017).
7 *See, e.g.*, Paidar v. Hughes, 615 N.W.2d 276 (Minn. 2000); Phelps v. Clinkscales, 247 So. 2d 819, 821 (Miss. 1971); S.D. Codified Laws § 43-30-9.

California defines slander of title as follows: "One who, without a privilege to do so, publishes matter which is untrue and disparaging to another's property in land, chattels or intangible things under such circumstances as would lead a reasonable man to foresee that the conduct of a third person as purchaser or lessee thereof might be determined thereby is liable for pecuniary loss resulting to the other from the impairment of vendibility thus caused."[8] A Maine court described the elements as follows: "To prove slander of title a claimant must prove (1) there was a publication of a slanderous statement disparaging claimant's title; (2) the statement was false; (3) the statement was made with malice or made with reckless disregard of its falsity; and (4) the statement caused actual or special damages."[9]

However, courts are not unanimous on how to apply this law in the context of a party that obtained property by adverse possession. For example, an adverse possessor may obviously own the property, but may not have yet obtained a court order indicating this. (Remember—a party does not need to file an action or obtain formal relief in order to adversely possess and legitimately claim land.) In such a case, if the title holder of record (for instance) claims that the land belongs to himself, even though title holder knows that to be false, and knows that he lost those rights to the adverse possessor, then it is not clear whether that title holder of record could even conceivably be liable for slander of title. There is a split of authority on the issue.[10]

In one Maine case,[11] a party that definitely did not own the property in question was aware of the adverse possessors' potential rights to that property. That non-owning party then filed a quitclaim deed as an attempt to prevent the adverse possessor from fully gaining those rights. That quitclaim deed purportedly conveyed her own alleged interest in the land, that she knew was claimed by the adverse possessors, to "each and every citizen of the United States of America equally."[12]

Ultimately, the adverse possession claimant successfully proved that this deed was frivolous, so the claimant was successful in the slander of title case. The court held that the "majority position," which it adopted, was that "attorney fees incurred in removal of a cloud on a title caused by a spurious and vexatious deed do constitute proof of special damages in a slander of title action . . . ."[13] However, in that case, the court

8 Howard v. Schaniel, 113 Cal. App. 3d 256, 262–63 (Cal. Ct. App. 1980), citing section 624 of the Restatement of Torts.

9 Colquhoun v. Webber, 684 A.2d 405, 409 (Me. 1996).

10 *See id.* at 409–10, comparing 113 Cal. App. 3d 256, with Davis v. Sponhauer, 574 N.E.2d 292 (Ind. Ct. App. 1991).

11 *Colquhoun*, 684 A.2d 405.

12 If this had effect, perhaps we would all get one piece of dirt.

13 *Colquhoun*, 684 A.2d at 411.

noted that the costs of litigation and attorneys' fees that could be recovered in such an action were only for those fees and expenses incurred to remove the cloud on the title, but not those incurred specifically to prosecute the slander of title action.[14] In that case, since the damages were awarded based on the costs of prosecuting the slander of title count and not based on the expense of measures reasonably necessary to counteract the publication of the slander, the matter was remanded.

One must also check one's state law about a lis pendens and whether that filing could potentially lead to a slander of title claim. A lis pendens is a document filed in the context of a case concerning real property, which is notice to the world that ownership of the property is being litigated, and that if a third party, for example, purchases that property from the "wrong" owner, the third party may wind up with nothing. In some states like Rhode Island, the lis pendens could be the basis of a slander of title claim.[15] In at least one state, Wisconsin, there is a specific statute indicating one can be liable for the false or frivolous filing of a lis pendens, even if it is not labeled as a "slander of title."[16]

In other states, like Utah, the recording of the lis pendens is privileged, and gives no right of action for slander of title.[17] But in some states, like New York, there may be a method of obtaining attorneys' fees with respect to the lis pendens. A relevant statute indicates that the court, if it cancels a notice of pendency, "may direct the plaintiff to pay any costs and expenses occasioned by the filing and cancellation, in addition to any costs of the action."[18]

If there is no specific statute allowing your client as title holder to obtain attorneys' fees, one may try to simply claim that the adverse possession argument raised was frivolous. In such a case, that may be sufficient to award attorneys' fees.[19]

If one does seek attorneys' fees, one obtaining such relief should make sure that if the trial court awards attorneys' fees, the court has articulated the grounds on which it is basing its decision. Otherwise, there is a danger of reversal.

Except for Appendix A and Appendix B, and of course the ever popular index, this wraps up this book, even though the nature of the topic makes it impossible to do more than scratch the surface of this area of law in just one book. If you made it to the end, you are one of a kind and I thank you for your patience. Anyone seeking further assistance or advice is welcome to contact me directly.

---

14 *Id.*

15 Carrozza v. Voccola, 90 A.3d 142, 154 (R.I. 2014).

16 Wis. Stat. § 706.13(1).

17 Hansen v. Kohler, 550 P.2d 186, 189 (Utah 1976).

18 N.Y. C.P.L.R. 6514(c).

19 *See* Boveland v. Young Women's Christian Ass'n of Greater Atlanta, Inc., 227 Ga. App. 241 (1997).

Appendix A
Sample Complaints

FIRST SAMPLE

1. Plaintiff, ______________, is a natural person who resides at ______________.
2. Upon information and belief, Defendant ______________, is a natural person who resides at ______________.
3. A dispute has arisen between Plaintiff and Defendant as to who is the fee simple owner of all right, title, and interest in a strip of land that runs near the shared border of their properties (hereinafter "the Strip").
4. The Strip is located at ______________.
5. Both Plaintiff and his predecessor-in-interest, ______________ (hereinafter "Predecessor"), have vigorously asserted their claims of right over the Strip by adverse possession for approximately ______________ years.
6. Plaintiff owns the Strip and continues to use it legally.
7. Defendant has interfered with Plaintiff's lengthy, notorious and uninterrupted possession of the Strip by trespassing on to the Strip and removing Plaintiff's fence, which had largely enclosed the Strip.
8. Defendant's acts have caused damage to the Strip and its installations, as well as challenging the exclusive and unfettered use and ownership of the Strip by Plaintiff.
9. Pursuant to a written deed, dated ______________ (the "Deed"), Plaintiff is the owner in fee simple absolute of certain property described in Schedule "A" to the Deed. Such property is known as ______________ (the "Premises").
10. Upon information and belief, Defendant is the owner of a certain parcel of real property with improvements thereon, known as ______________ (Defendant's property hereinafter being referred to as "Defendant's Property"). The Defendant's Property is directly ______________ of the Premises.
11. The Strip, located at the ______________ly record line of the Premises, borders the Defendant's Property.

12. Plaintiff and Predecessor have always treated the Strip as part of their property and reasonably believed they had a claim of right to the Strip.
13. When Plaintiff purchased the Premises, his Predecessor informed him that he has use of the Strip up to the fence. Mr. ______________ explained that since his purchase of the Premises in ______________, he cleared the Strip of trees and plantings and converted the wooded forest area into a lawn, thereby completely changing the character of the Strip.
14. The Predecessor maintained and installed the ______________, which is a permanent structure on the Strip, and maintained the fence on the Strip, and cultivated trees and plantings on the Strip, until he sold the Premises to Plaintiff.
15. Over the years, Plaintiff continued the open, notorious, exclusive and hostile use of the Strip by (1) improving the Strip by cultivating trees and gardens, (2) maintaining and repairing the permanent structure of a ______________ on the Strip, and (3) and maintaining and repairing a fence at the border of the Strip. Such encroachments were and are substantial in nature.
16. Legal title to the Strip vested to the Predecessor by, at the latest, ______________ and transferred to Plaintiff upon his purchase of the Premises in ______________.
17. Commencing only after the date Plaintiff's rights were vested, which was on or about ______________, Defendant has claimed that the Strip is part of Defendant's Property.
18. Plaintiff's possession of the Strip, which is tacked on to the adverse possession of his Predecessor, has been actual, open, hostile, notorious, continuous and exclusive since ______________.
19. Plaintiff and his Predecessor have maintained clear and exclusive possession of the Strip, which was sufficiently open to put a diligent owner on notice.
20. Defendant's predecessors-in-interest acquiesced to the installation and maintenance of the fence and substantial alterations to the land, and the structural element of a ______________, and therefore acquiesced to Plaintiff's and his Predecessor's adverse possession.
21. Title to the Strip vested in Plaintiff long ago and cannot now be disturbed.
22. Plaintiff and his Predecessor have been in continuous possession during the ______________ year statutory period, adverse to Defendant and all other persons.
23. On information and belief, on or about ______________, Defendant trespassed onto the Strip, when Defendant knew Plaintiff was out of town, tore down the fence and deposited the fence materials on a nearby roadway.

24. Defendant and/or his agents, while trespassing on the Strip, damaged and/or destroyed Plaintiff's property and such actions demonstrate Defendant's willful disregard of Plaintiff's property rights.
25. Defendant's trespass onto the Strip and his actions caused Plaintiff to expend money to rebuild the fence, and the ______________ structural element.
26. At all times relevant hereto, Defendant knew, or should have known, that Defendant and/or his agents had no right to enter upon the Strip or to perform any acts upon the Strip.
27. Upon information and belief, there are no unknown defendants and no defendant hereto is an infant, mentally retarded,[1] mentally ill or an alcohol abuser.
28. Upon information and belief, no judgment hereunder will affect a person or persons not in being or ascertainable at the commencement of the action.
29. Pursuant to RPAPL Article 15, plaintiff is entitled to a judgment declaring that it is the sole owner of the Strip, and that the defendant has no right, title or interest therein.

As and for a First Cause of Action
(Declaratory Judgment)

30. A dispute exists between Plaintiff and Defendant with respect to who holds title to the Strip. Defendant claims an estate or interest in the Strip that is adverse to the Plaintiff. Plaintiff seeks judgment that Plaintiff is the owner of all right, title, and interest in and to the Strip by adverse possession and that Defendant does not have any right, title, or interest in, or lien with regard to the Strip.
31. Plaintiff and his Predecessor have possessed the Strip continuously under claim of right for a period of time not fewer than ______________ consecutive years.
32. The character of the possession of the Strip during that time by the Plaintiff and his Predecessor was hostile in nature, actual, notorious, open and obvious, exclusive and continuous.
33. Plaintiff, by reason of the foregoing, adversely possessed title to the Strip.
34. In view of the foregoing, it is desirable and necessary that a judicial determination be made establishing the identity of the party that has the legal and equitable title to the Strip, free and clear of all claims by any other party.
35. Plaintiff has no other adequate remedy at law.

---

1 A term of art in the state statute.

36. By reason of the foregoing, Plaintiff is entitled to a declaratory judgment declaring the rights of the Plaintiff with respect to the matters set forth in this Complaint, and, in particular, declaring and specifying: (a) that Plaintiff is the sole and exclusive legal and equitable owner of the Strip; (b) that Plaintiff is entitled to sole, exclusive and unfettered use of and access to the Strip; and (c) that Defendant has no legal or equitable claim to the ownership or use of the Strip, whether by claim of legal title, adverse possession, prescriptive easement, or under or pursuant to any other legal or equitable principle.

As and for a Second Cause of Action (Injunction)

37. Plaintiff has suffered and continues to suffer damages and is entitled to injunctive relief enjoining Defendant from making any entry upon the Strip, any further use of the Strip or from destroying any installations on the Strip including the fence.

As and for a Third Cause of Action (Trespass-Damages)

38. Plaintiff is the sole and exclusive legal and equitable owner of the Strip, under a claim of right.
39. At all times relevant hereto, Defendant knew, or should have known, that Defendant and/or their agents had no right to enter upon the Strip or to perform any acts upon the Strip.
40. Defendant intentionally trespassed upon the Strip.
41. Defendant's, and/or his agent's actions in removing the fence, trampling the plantings, fixtures and/or other items on the Strip, damaged Plaintiff.
42. Plaintiff has been damaged in an amount equal to the cost of restoring and rebuilding the Strip to the condition which preceded the Defendant's activities thereon.
43. Plaintiff should be granted a final judgment in an amount to be determined at trial, but in no event less than $____________.

SECOND SAMPLE

1. At all times hereinafter mentioned, Plaintiff EM is a natural person over the age of eighteen years old and resides at ____________ ("Plaintiff's Property," and the building thereat, "Plaintiff's Home").
2. At all times hereinafter mentioned, Defendant AZ is, upon information and belief, a limited liability company organized

pursuant to the laws of the State of New York, with offices in the ______________; and is the titled owner of ______________ ("the AZ Property").

3. Upon information and belief, John Does No. 1–10 are persons whose identities are unknown but who may claim an interest in Plaintiff's Property.
4. Plaintiff's Home is a ______________ story residence, of about ______________ square feet.
5. Plaintiffs' Property lies directly to the ______________ of the AZ Property along ______________ Street.
6. The two lots are separated by a property line running ______________, of roughly ______________ feet in length.
7. On or about ______________, Plaintiff obtained title to Plaintiff's Property.
8. The metes and bounds description in the deed of conveyance of Plaintiff's Property to Plaintiff in ______________ stated that the ______________ boundary of Plaintiff's Property ran through a party wall.
9. Plaintiff has lived in Plaintiff's Home since purchasing it in ______________, as her primary residence and domicile.
10. In 1990, Plaintiff dug a rectangular well into the earth in front of a window on the basement level of Plaintiff's Home, along the ______________ wall of Plaintiff's Home, so as to provide better light and air circulation to the window ("the Window Well").
11. The Window Well is about ______________ feet deep, about ______________ feet long along the length of Plaintiff's Home, and ______________ feet wide.
12. Plaintiff lined and framed the Window Well with an enclosure of bricks, and installed a drainpipe that runs from the bottom of the Window Well to Plaintiff's sewer.
13. The Window Well lies on the AZ Property.
14. On or about ______________, AZ obtained title to the AZ Property.
15. The metes and bounds description in the deed of conveyance of the AZ Property to AZ in ______________ stated that the ______________ boundary of the AZ Property ran through a party wall.
16. On or about ______________, AZ filed an application with DOB to demolish the building on the AZ Property that shared a party wall with Plaintiff's Home.
17. On or about ______________, DOB issued a demolition permit to AZ, and AZ began demolition of that building.
18. AZ completed demolition on or about ______________.

19. The result of the demolition was the total removal of the building that had been on the AZ Property.
20. The wall that had once been a party wall was left standing, and constitutes the ______________ wall of Plaintiff's Home.
21. Beginning on or about ______________, AZ had also begun filing a series of applications with DOB for construction of a new building at the AZ Property.
22. AZ obtained its first permit on or about ______________, for excavation, shoring, and underpinning in conjunction with its new building project.
23. AZ filed for permits to underpin the ______________ wall of Plaintiff's House without asking for or receiving Plaintiff's permission therefor.
24. On ______________, Defendant started excavation. This excavation came very close to the ______________ wall of Plaintiff's Home, and threatens the integrity of the party wall, the Window Well, the foundation, and Plaintiff's Home generally.

As and for a First Cause of Action: Real Property Actions and Proceedings Law Article 15 Quiet Title

25. Possession of the Window Well by Plaintiff has been and is under an adverse possession not under written instrument or judgment, and has been and is adverse, under claim of right, exclusive of any other right, and open and notorious, continuous, exclusive, and actual, for more than ______________ years prior to the commencement of this action, and such possession continues to the present time.
26. Plaintiff has cultivated and improved the Window Well and there have been acts sufficiently open to put a reasonably diligent owner on notice for more than ______________ years prior to the commencement of this action.
27. Defendant AZ claims or may claim to have or it appears by the public records that it may claim some estate or interest in the Window Well which belongs to Plaintiff.
28. Recently, over the objections of Plaintiff, Defendant AZ has threatened to and in fact encroached, trespassed and caused damage to the Window Well and has disturbed and interfered with Plaintiff's quiet enjoyment thereof.
29. All claims which defendants may advance as to the Window Well are invalid, and that all claims have been extinguished and barred by the acts which have continued for a period in excess of that required by statute for the vesting of title through adverse possession and that plaintiff is seized and possessed

of the Window Well free from any and every such claim or demand.

30. Defendant AZ is known and is not an infant, incompetent, mentally ill, mentally retarded, or an alcohol abuser.
31. There are no persons not in being or ascertained at the commencement of this action who by any contingency contained in a devise or grant or otherwise, could afterward become entitled to a beneficial estate or interest in the property involved in this action and any judgment rendered herein adjudging Plaintiff to be vested with an absolute title in fee simple will not and may not affect any such person not in being or not ascertained at the time of the commencement of this action.
32. No personal claim is made against any Defendant other than a Defendant who shall assert a claim adverse to the claim of Plaintiff as set forth in the complaint.
33. Accordingly, Plaintiff seeks a judgment that she owns the Window Well in adverse possession, as set forth in the WHEREFORE clause below.

As and for a Second Cause of Action: Declaratory Judgment

34. Plaintiff has repeatedly communicated to AZ that the ______________ wall of Plaintiff's Home is no longer a party wall, and that AZ has no rights thereto, since Defendant has demolished the building that once incorporated the wall.
35. Defendant continues nevertheless to threaten Plaintiff with intrusive and destructive construction operations to the ______________ wall of Plaintiff's Home.
36. Plaintiff credits Defendant's representation and legitimately believes that Defendant will initiate intrusive and destructive construction operations to the ______________ wall of Defendant's Home.
37. Plaintiff makes no further claim for consequential relief, other than that demanded herein.
38. Plaintiff has no remedy at law.
39. Accordingly, Plaintiff, as set forth in the WHEREFORE clause below, hereby prays for a declaratory judgment that the ______________ wall of Plaintiff's Home is not a party wall, because Defendants have demolished the building on the AZ Property that incorporated that wall, thus extinguishing the AZ's party wall easement over it; and that Defendant cannot perform construction operations on it, touch it in any way, or incorporate it into its construction.

THIRD SAMPLE

1. Plaintiff ______________ ("Plaintiff") is a New York corporation with its principal place of business located at ______________.
2. Defendant ("John Former") is a natural person, residing in the State of New York, County of ______________.
3. There are no unknown defendants in this action and no defendant is or might be an infant, mentally retarded, mentally ill or an alcohol abuser.

Relevant Factual History

4. On or about ______________, John Former acquired title and ownership to the real property and premises located at 111 1st Avenue, ______________, New York, County of ______________, and more fully identified as ______________ (the "Property"), by deed which was recorded with the Office of the City Register of ______________ County on ______________ date at reel ______________, page ______________.
5. In or around December ______________, Plaintiff paid John Former the sum of $______________ as key money for the right to take possession and occupy the Property as a tenant of John Former, in order to operate a business at the Property.
6. Immediately upon the Plaintiff's payment to John Former, Plaintiff took exclusive possession and control of the Property and began to operate a ______________ business at the Property.
7. No written lease was ever entered into between Plaintiff and John Former regarding the Property.
8. After Plaintiff took exclusive possession and control of the Property, Plaintiff never paid to John Former any further monies for rent or compensation for the use and occupancy of the Property.
9. Plaintiff continued with the cultivation, upkeep, management, maintenance, and use of the Property for a ______________ business, and paid all of the taxes, insurance and expenses relating to the Property without paying any monies, rent or consideration to any party claiming to own the Property for a period of ten (10) years after taking exclusive possession and control of the Property.
10. After the passing of such ten (10) year period, Plaintiff openly declared, in a hostile manner, its claim of right and ownership to the Property.
11. As part of Plaintiff's hostile claim to the Property, Plaintiff revised any documents or public records, including the Property's tax

bill, water bill and insurance was recorded with the Office of the City Register of _____________ County on _____________ 20_____________ at _____________.

12. After the passing of the initial ten (10) year period, Plaintiff openly declared, in a hostile manner, its claim of right and ownership to the Property. As part of Plaintiff's hostile claim to the Property, Plaintiff revised any documents or public records, including the Property's tax bill, water bill and insurance coverages, which reflected John Former's ownership of the Property so that all documents or public records reflected that Plaintiff was the owner of the Property.
13. By reason of such hostile acts and conduct of the Plaintiff, John Former was put on notice and was aware of Plaintiff's hostile declaration of ownership of the Property.
14. John Former never took any steps or measures to remove Plaintiff's name from any documents or public records as the owner of the Property and had effectively abandoned the Property.
15. After the initial lapse of ten (10) years from the date Plaintiff took exclusive possession and control of the Property to the present, Plaintiff has operated and continues to operate an auto repair business from the Property and Defendants have had actual knowledge of Plaintiff's exclusive and hostile possession, control, maintenance and claim of right to the Property.
16. Since at least _____________, Plaintiff has continuously, openly, and notoriously and in a hostile manner claimed all the right, title and interest to the Property for itself and continued with the cultivation, upkeep, management, maintenance and payment of all expenses of the Property such that Plaintiff engaged in at least the following actions, including but not limited to:

    a. Satisfied a tax lien on the Property;
    b. Satisfied various complaints by the New York City Department of Buildings that were issued against the Property in Plaintiff's sole name as the Owner of the Property;
    c. Paid all property taxes charged to the Property, which were transferred by Plaintiff into Plaintiff's sole name;
    d. Paid all water and sewer taxes charged to the Property, which were transferred by Plaintiff into Plaintiff's sole name;
    e. Erected a security fence around the perimeter of the Property lot in which Plaintiff operates its used car dealership on the Property, without seeking the consent of anyone claiming to be the owner of the Property;

f. Replaced the roof on the building which sits on the Property without seeking the consent of anyone claiming to be the owner of the Property;
g. Replaced the gates to the Property's entrances without seeking the consent of anyone claiming to be the owner of the Property;
h. Replaced the heating system in the building which sits on the Property without seeking the consent of anyone claiming to be the owner of the Property;
i. Replaced the plumbing service line in the building which sits on the Property without seeking the consent of anyone claiming to be the owner of the Property;
j. Replaced the electrical service in the building which sits on the Property without seeking the consent of anyone claiming to be the owner of the Property;
k. Repaired and replaced the sidewalk which surrounds the Property without seeking the consent of anyone claiming to be the owner of the Property;
l. Repaved the Property's parking lot without seeking the consent of anyone claiming to be the owner of the Property;
m. Painted the interior and exterior of the building which sits on the Property without seeking the consent of anyone claiming to be the owner of the Property;
n. Erected external security and display lighting on the Property without seeking the consent of anyone claiming to be the owner of the Property;
o. Openly, notoriously, and in a hostile manner, declared to all persons in the vicinity and immediate area of the Property, including persons known to John Former, that it was the owner of the Property; and
p. Altered and changed any public records and documentation to reflect that Plaintiff, and not John Former, is the owner of the Property.

17. Such hostile acts and conduct by Plaintiff sufficiently put John Former on notice as to Plaintiff's hostile claim of ownership to, and adverse possession of, the Property.
18. All of the foregoing hostile acts and conduct by Plaintiff, including Plaintiff's nonpayment of any rent to John Former, gave John Former a cause of action against Plaintiff for ejectment from the Property.
19. Since Plaintiff took exclusive possession and control of the Property, no one ever objected to Plaintiff's continuous exclusive possession, use and occupancy of the Property, sought to collect any rent from Plaintiff for Plaintiff's possession and use of the

Property, paid any taxes for the Property, or asserted any ownership interest in the Property or attempted to restore his/her name to any document or public record which reflected that Plaintiff was the owner of the Property.

20. Plaintiff, since at least ____________, that being ten (10) years after Plaintiff's permissive possession of the Property ceased, has reasonably believed and openly declared in a hostile manner that it is the owner of the Property.
21. Plaintiff has adversely possessed the Property since at least the lapse of ten (10) years after Plaintiff took possession and control of the Property for a continuous period of at least an additional ten (10) years.
22. Notwithstanding the foregoing, on ____________, John Former sent Plaintiff a notice of termination ("the Termination Notice"), seeking to terminate Plaintiff's tenancy at the Property on or before ____________.
23. John Former's service of the Termination Notice is void and of no force and effect, as Plaintiff's initial tenancy of the Property terminated and Plaintiff already acquired the right, title and interest to the Property through its adverse possession of the Property as early as ____________, that being the date in which title to the Property vested with Plaintiff by operation of law.

As and for a First Cause of Action for a Judgment of Adverse Possession

24. Pursuant to R.P.A.P.L. § 531, Plaintiff is presumed to have possessed the Property from the landlord, until the expiration of ten (10) years after Plaintiff's $____________ key money payment of rent.
25. The presumption that Plaintiff was deemed to have possessed the Property from the landlord effectively ceased in ____________, ten (10) years after Plaintiff's only payment, at which point Plaintiff commenced its hostile and adverse possession of the Property.
26. Since at least ____________, and for at least ten years after the initial permissive period expired, Plaintiff openly declared, in a hostile manner, its claim of right and ownership to the Property.
27. Since at least ____________, and for a period of at least ten (10) years thereafter, Plaintiff exclusively possessed and controlled the Property without interruption and openly, notoriously and in a hostile manner claimed all the right, title and interest to the Property for itself and continued with the exclusive

possession, use, cultivation, upkeep, management, maintenance and payment of all expenses of the Property.

28. The Defendant may claim to have, or it appears by the public records, may claim some right in, title to, claim or demand against, or lien or encumbrance upon the Property, the exact nature, extent and quality of which is unknown to Plaintiff.
29. Plaintiff alleges that any such claims are unjust and that all such claims which the Defendants may have had upon the Property are wholly and effectually extinguished, cut off and barred by the subsequent adverse possession by Plaintiff.
30. Accordingly, Plaintiff alleges that it is fully seized and possessed of the Property free of and wholly discharged from each and every such claim.
31. No personal claim is made against any defendant other than a defendant who shall assert a claim adverse to the claim of the Plaintiff.
32. Any judgment herein will not affect a person or persons not in being or ascertained at the commencement of this action, who by any contingency contained in a devise or grant or otherwise, could afterward become entitled to a beneficial estate or interest in the Property involved.
33. Based on the adverse possession of the Property by Plaintiff since at least ______________, Plaintiff is the sole and rightful owner of the Property.
34. Plaintiff therefore demands judgment against the Defendants and all persons claiming under them that they be forever barred from all claim or claims to an estate in the Property, or lien or encumbrance thereupon of any kind or nature whatsoever and that it be adjudged and decreed that Plaintiff is the lawful owner of the Property in fee simple and is entitled to the lawful, peaceable and uninterrupted possession thereof as against the Defendants, and all others whomsoever, and for such other and further relief as may be deemed just, together with the costs of this action.

As and for a Second Cause of Action for a Declaratory Judgment to Quiet Title to the Property

35. Since at least December 20______________, Plaintiff has, without interruption, openly, notoriously and in a hostile manner claimed all the right, title and interest to the Property for itself and continued with the exclusive possession, use, cultivation, upkeep, management, maintenance and payment of all expenses of the Property.

36. Plaintiff has adversely possessed the Property for a continuous period of ten (10) years commencing from at least ____________ 20 ____________.
37. Plaintiff has acquired all right, title and ownership interest in the Property by adverse possession since at least ____________, 20 ____________.
38. Plaintiff remains the true and sole owner of the Property by reason of the fact that Plaintiff acquired title and ownership to the Property since at least December 20 ____________.
39. Equity demands that a declaratory judgment be issued by this Court which quiets title and declares that Plaintiff is the sole and rightful owner of the Property free and clear of any encumbrance, lien or mortgage.

FOURTH SAMPLE

As and for a First Cause of Action to Quite Title—Adverse Possession

1. This first cause of action is brought pursuant to Article 15 of the Real Property Actions and Proceedings Law to compel the determination of certain claims to a disputed piece of real property described herein.
2. Plaintiff ____________ is an individual residing at ____________.
3. Upon information and belief, Defendant, ____________, is an individual residing at ____________.
4. That at all times since ____________, the plaintiff was and still is the owner of and in possession of the premises known as ____________.
5. That plaintiff acquired title thereto by deed from the prior owners of record, ____________, dated ____________ and recorded on ____________ in the office of the Clerk of ____________ County in Land Document #____________.
6. Upon information and belief, the construction of the building that currently exists on the lot at ____________ was completed on or about ____________.
7. That since at least ____________ and for some time prior thereto, plaintiff's predecessors in interest and then plaintiff has been in continuous and uninterrupted occupation and possession adversely of the land which neighbors the property he obtained by title (as indicated above), and this adversely occupied property is situated entirely within the County of ____________

and lies in and is a part of Block ______________ Lot ______________ and is bounded and described as follows: ______________.

8. The premises possessed adversely by plaintiff and described above is contiguous and lies immediately to the ______________ of the premises owned of record by the plaintiff and described in paragraph ______________ hereof.
9. That Plaintiff's possession of the premises described in paragraph ______________ hereof, and that of Plaintiff's predecessors in title, through whom they claim has been and is an adverse possession under a claim of title not written, exclusive of any other right, and has been and is hostile, under claim of right, actual, open, notorious, exclusive and has been continuous for more than ten years as such adverse possession has existed continuously since at least ______________ and for a period time prior to ______________.
10. Plaintiff and his predecessors in title through whom they claim cultivated and improved the premises described above as part of their front lawn, walkway, retaining wall and rear yard for more than ten years as such adverse possession has existed continuously since at least ______________ and for a period time prior to ______________.
11. Plaintiff and his predecessors in title through whom they claim continuously protected a vast majority of the premises described above by a substantial enclosure, beginning at ______________ to the ______________ line of the disputed property and running along the ______________ side of the masonry wall which extended past the garage that existed on the premises known as ______________ prior to ______________. Such adverse possession has existed continuously since at least ______________ and for some time prior thereto.
12. The Plaintiff and his predecessors in title through whom they claim, have continuously cultivated, by tending to the lawn by cutting grass and landscaping of that portion of the premises described above that is to the ______________ of the most ______________ fence post of the fence that runs along the above mentioned masonry wall and is to the west of the of the premises owned of record by the Plaintiff as described in above here of, as such adverse possession has existed continuously since at least ______________ and for some time prior thereto
13. Upon information and belief, that at all times since, ______________, the defendant became and is the record owner of the premises known as ______________, Tax Block ______________, Lot ______________.

14. The Plaintiff and his predecessors in interest have exclusively used and maintained their entire property, including the area in dispute and have had exclusive, uninterrupted possession of same—without objection since at least ______________ and for some time prior thereto until in or about ______________ when defendant removed a portion of the retaining wall and erected a new garage which now encroaches on that portion of the property that was owned by Plaintiff by way of adverse possession.
15. That this garage erected by defendant contravenes Plaintiff's rights as adverse possessor of the area in dispute.
16. Plaintiff's possession of the area in dispute has, therefore, been hostile and under claim of right.
17. Plaintiff's possession of the area in dispute has been actual, in that the property has been continuously used and improved.
18. At all times relevant since at least ______________ and for a period time prior to ______________, Plaintiff and his predecessors in title have used their property including the area in dispute in an open, notorious and adverse manner and under a claim of right.
19. That Defendant, ______________ claims, it appears by the public records, and statements made to the plaintiffs, some estate or interest, to wit, an estate in fee, in the property described in Paragraph ______________ above which belongs to the Plaintiff as alleged herein.
20. That recently, over the objection and opposition of Plaintiff, defendant has encroached, trespassed and inflicted damage to said property and has disturbed and interfered with Plaintiff's quiet enjoyment thereof, but Plaintiff allege that all such claims which Defendant may advance as to such premises are invalid and of no legal force and effect and that all such claims have been wholly and effectually extinguished, cut off and barred by the acts and occurrences of a continuing nature which have continued for a period in excess of that required by statute for the vesting of title through the medium of adverse possession and that the Plaintiff is seized and possessed of said premises free and wholly discharged from any and every such claim or demand.
21. That the defendant is known to the Plaintiff and is not an infant, nor under any mental or physical disability.
22. That any judgment granted herein will not affect any person or person not in being or ascertained at the commencement of this action, who by any contingency contained in a devise or grant or otherwise, could afterward become entitle to a beneficial estate

or interest in the aforesaid premises, and that every person in being who would have been entitle to such estate or interest, if such event had happened immediately before the commencement of the action is named as a party hereto.

23. That no personal claim is made against any defendants other than a defendant who shall assert a claim adverse to the claim of the Plaintiff as set forth in the complaint herein.

As and for a Second Cause of Action for a Judgment of Ejectment

24. That defendant be ejected from plaintiff's property and ordered to remove any and all structures (specifically the defendant's garage) built upon the Plaintiff's land, which Plaintiff claims by way of adverse possession as well as any all personal property, and to restore Plaintiff's premises.

As and for a Third Cause of Action for Loss of Use and Quiet Enjoyment

25. On or about ________________ and continuing thereafter the defendant's construction activities have caused damage to the Plaintiff's property in that the defendant has destroyed the fence in the back yard of the plaintiff without his permission.
26. On or about ________________, and continuing thereafter the defendant constructed a structure on a portion of the Plaintiff's property and in doing so took away a portion of the retaining wall and broke steps from the walk to the back yard next to the retaining wall. Defendant also caused damage to a slab of concrete in at the foot of those steps. Such action now allows water onto and over the Plaintiff's yard where it pools and enters into the lower interior section of the building at ________________, when it rains.
27. That on or about ________________, and continuing thereafter, the defendant caused to have a plywood wall constructed on the Plaintiff's premises which kept plaintiffs from accessing the area.
28. Defendant's actions have caused plaintiff's loss of use of the Premises and the inability of the Plaintiff to have quiet enjoyment of the premises.
29. That by reason of the foregoing, Plaintiff has been damaged in the sum of $________________, together with pre-judgment interest from ________________.

As and for a Fourth Cause of Action for Trespass

30. That by virtue of the foregoing, defendant is guilty of trespass on the Plaintiff's premises, all to the Plaintiff's damage in the amount of $______________.

FIFTH SAMPLE

1. At all times hereinafter mentioned, beginning from the year 19__, to the present date, Plaintiff X Corp, a domestic New York corporation, was and still is the sole owner, in fee absolute, of the building and lot designated as Block ______________, Lot ______________, located at ______________ (the "123 Property").
2. At all times hereinafter mentioned, upon information and belief, Defendant Z Corp., is a New York corporation, having an address at ______________.
3. Upon information and belief, Defendant Z Corp. and each of its predecessors in interest, was and still is the sole owner, in fee absolute, of the building and lot designated as Block ______________, Lot ______________, located at ______________ (the "125 Property").
4. Plaintiff acquired title to the 123 Property by a deed dated ______________, recorded in the office of the Clerk of ______________ County, on January ______ 19 at Rec ______________, Page ______________.
5. Since 19 ______ Plaintiff has been in continual uninterrupted occupation and possession of the 123 Property.
6. At the ______________ly side of the 123 Property, the 123 Property abuts the 125 Property on the ______________ property line between the two properties, for a distance of ______________ feet.
7. The "AP Area" shown in ex. A, is located at the ______________ side of the ______________ property line between 123 Property and 125 Property. The AP area's description and boundaries are described as follows: ______________.
8. This "AP Area" is the premises to which Plaintiff claims title by adverse possession.
9. Beginning at some unknown time after ______________ 1990, but at least as early as 19 ______ throughout the applicable prescriptive period required to acquire title by adverse possession and continuing at all relevant times up to the present

date, Plaintiff has exercised dominion and control over and utilized the AP Area.

10. Plaintiff's possession of the AP Area was hostile and under a claim of right, actual, open, and notorious, exclusive, and continuous, throughout the applicable prescriptive period required to acquire title by adverse possession, for a minimum of ten years, and such possession continues to the present time.
11. At all relevant times, throughout the years ______________, to the present date, Plaintiff had knowledge, direct and indirect, and from public documents, that the record owner and apparent holder of title in the AP Area was and is Defendant.
12. At all relevant times, throughout the years ______________, to the present date, Plaintiff's exercise of dominion and control over and utilization of the AP Area was consistent with the type of usual acts of ownership reasonably expected to be done by the owner of the AP Area.
13. At all relevant times, throughout the years ______________, to the present date, such usual acts of ownership evidencing Plaintiff's dominion and control over and utilization of the AP Area, to the exclusion of all other persons, including Defendant and its predecessors in interest, have consisted, among other things, in Plaintiff using the AP Area continuously to store, throughout and within the enclosed confines of the AP Area, the following items: ____.
14. Plaintiff's agents have continually and routinely cleared the AP Area of the following waste: ______________, and cleaned the ______________ in the AP Area.
15. Plaintiff's agents have continually and routinely, made necessary repairs to the AP Area, including the following: ______________
16. This use of the AP Area was done without any interference or objection from defendant, its predecessors in interest, or any of its or their representatives, agents, or employees.
17. Since at least as early as 199 ______ and throughout the applicable prescriptive period required to acquire title by adverse possession, these usual and continued acts of ownership evidencing the dominion and control Plaintiff exercised over and the use it made of the AP Area, to the exclusion of all other persons, including Defendant and its predecessors in interest, were sufficient to place Defendant and its predecessors in interest on notice.
18. If Defendant itself and/or its predecessors in interest exercised reasonably diligent ownership of the AP Area, regarding

Plaintiff's hostile and exclusive exercise of ownership over the AP Area, it would have had notice of Plaintiff's use and occupancy of the AP Area by reason of the open, actual, continuous, exclusive and notorious nature of Plaintiff's dominion and control over the AP Area.

19. At no time throughout the applicable prescriptive period required to acquire title by adverse possession did Defendant, of any of its predecessors in interest, give Plaintiff permission to exercise dominion and control over or to use the AP Area as described herein. To the contrary, representatives of defendant expressly acknowledged plaintiff's use of, dominion, and control over the AP Area and expressly admitted their belief that the AP Area was part of the 123 Property and belonged to Plaintiff.
20. At no time, from 1989 and throughout the applicable prescriptive period required to acquire title by adverse possession, up to ______________, or thereafter, did Defendant, or any of its predecessors in interest, ever demand that Plaintiff pay rent for the use of the AP Area or tender a lease for the AP Area to Plaintiff.
21. At no time, from 1989 and throughout the applicable prescriptive period required to acquire title by adverse possession, up to ______________, or thereafter, did Plaintiff ever pay, or offer to pay, Defendant, or any of its predecessors in interest, rent for the use of the AP Area or offer to enter into a lease for Plaintiff's use of the AP Area.
22. The type of possession, dominion, and control over and utilization of the AP Area that Plaintiff exercised and manifested, from at least as early as 1989 and throughout the applicable prescriptive period required to acquire title by adverse possession, up to ______________, was in fact of the type of possession that gave Defendant, and/or any of its predecessors in interest, a cause of action for ejectment against Plaintiff.
23. At no time, from 1989 and throughout the applicable prescriptive period required to acquire title by adverse possession, up to ______________, nor thereafter, did Defendant, or any of its predecessors in interest, ever threaten to remove Plaintiff from the AP Area.
24. At no time, from 1989 and throughout the applicable prescriptive period required to acquire title by adverse possession, up to ______________, nor thereafter, did Defendant, or any of its predecessors in interest, ever take any action to remove Plaintiff from the AP Area.
25. At no time, from 1989 and throughout the applicable prescriptive period required to acquire title by adverse possession, up to

______________, nor thereafter, did Defendant, or any of its predecessors in interest, ever commence an action of ejectment against Plaintiff, or commence any other action or proceeding to stop, prevent, or preclude Plaintiff's exercise of dominion and control over and use of the AP Area for Plaintiff's exclusive use and purposes.

26. At no time, from 1989 and throughout the applicable prescriptive period required to acquire title by adverse possession, up to ______________, nor thereafter, did Defendant, or any of its predecessors in interest, ever prevent Plaintiff from having free access to the AP Area.
27. At no time, from 1989 and throughout the applicable prescriptive period required to acquire title by adverse possession, up to ______________, nor thereafter, did Defendant, or any of its predecessors in interest, ever serve Plaintiff with a notice of eviction.
28. At no time, from 1989 and throughout the applicable prescriptive period required to acquire title by adverse possession, up to ______________, nor thereafter, did Plaintiff ever cease exercising dominion and control over the AP Area nor at any time ever abandon the AP Area.

First Cause of Action for a Declaratory Judgment That Plaintiff Has Acquired Title to the AP Area through Adverse Possession under the Common Law

29. Plaintiff possessed, occupied, and exercised dominion and control over the AP Area, continually and without interruption, for the minimum prescriptive period of ten years from at least 1989 to 1999 and thereafter continually to ______________, and thereafter continually to the present date, sufficiently thus to acquire title to the AP Area pursuant to the law of adverse possession.
30. Plaintiff possessed the AP Area, from at least as early as 1989, for the applicable ten-year prescriptive period required to acquire title to the AP Area by adverse possession prior to ______________.
31. Plaintiff's possession of the AP Area, from at least as early as 1989 up to ______________, was sufficiently continuous, open, hostile, under a claim of right, and exclusive of Defendant's rights, for the applicable prescriptive period required to acquire title to the AP Area by adverse possession prior to ______________.
32. Plaintiff's possession of the AP Area, from at least as early as 1989 up to ______________, was actual for the applicable prescriptive period required to acquire title to the AP Area by adverse possession prior to ______________.

33. Plaintiff's possession of the AP Area, from at least as early as 1989 up to ______________, was open and notorious for the applicable prescriptive period required to acquire title to the AP Area by adverse possession prior to ______________.
34. Plaintiff's possession of the AP Area, from at least as early as 1989 up to ______________, was continuous for the applicable prescriptive period required to acquire title to the AP Area by adverse possession prior to ______________.
35. Plaintiff's possession of the AP Area, from at least as early as 1989 up to ______________, was exclusive of Defendant's rights, and those of Defendant's predecessors in interest, for the applicable prescriptive period required to acquire title to the AP Area by adverse possession prior to ______________.
36. From at least as early as 1989 and for the applicable prescriptive period required to acquire title to the AP Area by adverse possession prior to ______________, Plaintiff declined to recognize a superior title to the AP Area in Defendant or any of its predecessors in interest.
37. Defendant and its predecessors in interest had grounds to eject Plaintiff from the AP Area, from at least as early as 1989 to ______________, and thereafter to the present date, from the date that defendant, or any of its predecessors, first had, or with the exercise of due diligence should have had, notice of Plaintiff's exercise of dominion and control over and use of the AP Area for Plaintiff's exclusive use and purposes, but neither defendant, nor any of its predecessors in interest, ever sought to eject Plaintiff from the AP Area at any time from 1989 up to ______________, or at any time thereafter.
38. By reason of the foregoing, Plaintiff is entitled to a judgment declaring Plaintiff the legal owner of title to the AP Area by having satisfied all of the common law requirements for acquiring title through adverse possession prior to ______________.

As and for a Second Cause of Action for a Declaratory Judgment That Plaintiff Has Acquired Title to the AP Area through Adverse Possession under RPAPL § 521 and § 522(1)

39. Plaintiff has been in actual continued occupation of the AP Area under a claim of title, but not founded upon a written instrument or a judgment or decree, exclusive of any other rights in the AP Area, including any rights claimed by Defendant for the applicable prescriptive period required to acquire title to the AP Area by adverse possession prior to ______________.
40. During the applicable prescriptive period required to acquire title to the AP Area by adverse possession prior to ______________,

Plaintiff engaged in acts sufficiently open to put a reasonably diligent owner on notice of Plaintiff's use of the AP Area, in accordance with RPAPL § 522(1).

41. Plaintiff's use of the AP Area, to the exclusion of all other persons, including the Defendant, during the applicable prescriptive period required to acquire title to the AP Area by adverse possession prior to _______________, included, but was not limited to using the AP Area to store, throughout and within the enclosed confines of the AP Area, the following items _______________, and other items related to the activities Plaintiff.
44. By reason of the foregoing, Plaintiff is entitled to a judgment declaring Plaintiff the legal owner of title to the AP Area by having satisfied all of the requirements prescribed by RPAPL § 521 and § 522 for acquiring title not founded upon a written instrument or a judgment or decree prior to _______________.

As and for a Third Cause of Action to Quiet Title in the AP Area

45. By reason of the Plaintiff's actual, continuous, open, hostile, and exclusive possession of the AP Area, under claim of right, exclusive of the Defendant's rights therein, for the applicable prescriptive period required to acquire title to the AP Area by adverse possession prior to _______________, the Plaintiff is entitled to a judgment declaring Plaintiff the rightful owner of title to the AP Area.

Appendix B

Sample Questions for Depositions

George Orwell wrote that "restatement of the obvious is the first duty of intelligent men." In the context of depositions, asking obvious questions about obvious issues is the first duty of intelligent attorneys. Do not run before you learn to walk. The following are some basic questions that one may need to ask in a deposition concerning adverse possession claims. Even if an attorney does not use any of these directly, they may trigger other ideas to include in a good deposition outline.

QUESTIONS TO ASK THE ADVERSE POSSESSION CLAIMANT WHEN REPRESENTING THE TITLE OWNER

CLAIM OF RIGHT AND HOSTILITY

What made you believe the property was yours?
Did anyone inform you that it belonged to you?
Why did you believe it?
Why did you occupy the premises in the first place?
When you started occupying it, what was your goal?
Did you ever ask for permission from the title owner to use any portion?
Did you ever ask to purchase or lease the space?
What agreements did you reach with the legal owner during the statutory time period?

COLOR OF TITLE

Is this the document you relied on to claim the property belonged to you?
Tell me about how you obtained it, and who can confirm the details of how it got executed.
Did you have any reason to believe it was properly prepared and executed by the true owner?

Did anyone read it to you? Did you examine it? What did you pay for it? Why?
How much did you pay for the property originally? What evidence do you have?
Why did you think this deed covered your land?

HOLDING ONTO IT FOR THE STATUTORY TIME PERIOD

How long have you occupied the property?
What documents reveal that length?
What was the first date you took possession, and what documents confirm it?
What makes you so sure that ______________ was the first date?
Who else can confirm this?

EXCLUSIVE

Wasn't there a time you actually allowed someone else onto the property, even if both of you were using it at the same time?
If not, how do you know? What did you do to make sure?
Did you exclude anyone from using or accessing the property? If so, who and when, and in what manner?

OPEN AND NOTORIOUS

In what manner did you use the property?
What neighbors, if any, would have seen how you used it?
Identify your neighbors, and anyone else who you believe would confirm they saw your use of the property.
Do you have photographs indicating in what manner you used it?
Did you place signs indicating your claim?
Tell me about your neighbors, including their names, and what interactions you had with them.
What documentation, photographs, or records demonstrate your possession of the property?

CONTINUOUS

What vacations did you take? How often? How long were you gone for each time?
What other property do you own, and how often do you go to that property or live there?
During what periods of time did you not use or occupy the property?

CULTIVATION AND IMPROVEMENTS

What, if anything, did you do to improve or maintain the property during your possession?
What contractors did you use? What receipts or contracts reveal this work was done?
Why didn't you use it more effectively?

TACKING

Did you obtain the rights from someone else who occupied the space? Who?
Tell me their contact information.
What did they tell you about how they obtained ownership?
How long was that prior person occupying it, and how do you know?

PAYING TAXES

Why did you not pay real estate taxes on the property for the years ______________?
If you were a true owner, why not take such a step?
If you did pay those taxes, what evidence do you have on that?

MISCELLANEOUS

What made you ultimately realize you lacked record title?
When did you discover that, and how did you find out?
What did you do when you found out?
Why is it that you did not discover this sooner?
Did you make any attempts to contact or communicate with the legal owner regarding your possession, at any point?
What documentation, photographs, or records demonstrate your use of the property?
Describe the boundaries of the property you adversely claim.
What made you think those are the boundaries? How would an outsider know those are the new boundaries?
Did you conduct any surveys before or after you took possession?
Did you check the deeds to see where the boundaries were?
Did the legal owner say or do anything that let you think he might have known about your possession or use?
Did the legal owner ever grant you permission to use or occupy the property?

What efforts did the legal owner take, in order to reclaim possession of the property?
What was your relationship with the legal owner?
What interactions did you have with the legal owner?

QUESTIONS TO ASK THE TITLE OWNER WHEN REPRESENTING THE ADVERSE POSSESSION CLAIMANT

CLAIM OF RIGHT AND HOSTILITY

What did the claimant ever tell you about why he occupied the premises?
Tell me about all of the conversations you had with the claimant.
Did the claimant make any statements or take any actions that indicated his belief of ownership?

COLOR OF TITLE

Do you have any reason to believe that the claimant did not obtain this deed in good faith?
What do you know about the claimant's deed and how it came to be drafted, if anything?

HOLDING ONTO IT FOR THE STATUTORY TIME PERIOD

The claimant believes he has been there for __ years. Do you agree? If not, why not?
How did you use or possess the property during the statutory time period? What records reveal it?

EXCLUSIVE

Have you ever seen anyone else use or occupy the space?
When was the last time you used it, and in what way?
What efforts, if any, did you take to exclude others from using or accessing the property?
And what efforts, if any, did you see the claimant take, to prevent anyone else from using the property?
When others used it, how did they use it?
Did the claimant prevent you from occupying or using your own property? When? How? And what was your response?

ACTUAL POSSESSION

The claimant claims he did the following things on the property ________________. Do you agree or disagree, and why?

When did you first become aware of the adverse possessor's occupation or use of the property?

Can you describe any specific instances or evidence that led to your awareness of the claimant's possession?

OPEN AND NOTORIOUS

The claimant claims he was well known in the community to be occupying the space. Do you agree or disagree, and why?

Do you know anyone who would claim that he thought you owned the space at issue?

How is it possible that you did not discover he was using the premises for so many years?

Do you think there was something hidden about the way he used the property? How so? In what way?

CONTINUOUS

The claimant claims he never left the property for more than a few days during the time period. Do you agree or disagree, and why?

What photos or documents do you have that show you occupying the property during the statutory time period?

What photos or documents do you have that indicate the claimant did not occupy the property during the time period?

PEACEFUL POSSESSION

What steps, if any, did you take (prior to filing a litigation) to remove the claimant from the land?

CULTIVATION AND IMPROVEMENTS

The claimant claims he put in a garden, took care of the space etc. Do you agree or disagree, and why?

If you disagree, do you believe you took any steps to improve or build upon the property? Like what?

Tell me about your improvements on the property during that time, if any. If you made those improvements, did you not notice the claimant's improvements?

TACKING

Do you know who the previous occupant of the same space was?
What was your relationship to that person?
How long was he on the property? Why?

PAYING TAXES

The claimant claims he paid the taxes on the premises. If that is true, why did you not pay the taxes?

MISCELLANEOUS

Where do you live? What property do you own? How often do you go to each property? What records reveal that?
Who else used it? When? What did you say to them? Why did you allow them to use it?
How did you use it? In what way? Who saw you use it?
What evidence of maintenance of the property at issue do you have?
Where did you live during the various times claimant alleges that he occupied the premises?
How did you acquire the title to the property in question?
Can you provide specific details regarding the history of ownership and transfers of the property?
Do you know of any documentation that contradicts the adverse possession claim?
Did you have any interactions with the adverse possessor during the statutory time period? Tell me about them.
Do you know if anyone else had interactions with the adverse possessor during the statutory time period? Tell me about them.
How, if at all, did you exercise control of the property during the statutory time period?
Did you receive any communications, warnings, or legal documents from the adverse possessor asserting his claim of adverse possession?
Did you take any legal steps or actions to address the potential adverse possession claim during the statutory time period? If not, why not?
Did the claimant do anything that made you think he was not claiming ownership of the premises? Like what?
Did the claimant fail to do something one would expect an owner to do, and that failure made you believe he was not claiming ownership of the premises? Like what?

Did you communicate with the adverse possessor regarding his occupation or claim of adverse possession?

Prior to filing the date this action was filed, can you provide any correspondence, notices, or legal filings related to your efforts to assert ownership?

Did you have any discussions or interactions with the claimant regarding his intentions to claim ownership through adverse possession?

Can you provide any witnesses or evidence that support your understanding of the claimant's intentions?

Tell me about your activities on the property during the statutory time.

When did you first learn the claimant was on your property?

How did you find out?

What did you believe he was doing on your property?

Why didn't you stop him?

Did you lease out your property during any of the time the adverse possessor was using it?

Why did you allow the claimant on the property for such a long time?

Is it possible you could have simply overlooked that he occupied your space?

Tell me about all of your conversations with the claimant—whether they concerned the property or otherwise.

Tell me about all of your conversations with anyone related to the claimant, which concerned the property.

What surveys do you have of the property?

What are the boundaries, as you understand it? What makes you think so?

Does any witness also know the property's boundaries?

Did you ever have conversations with the claimant regarding the true boundary line between the properties? Tell me about them.

Index